Information Security and Privacy Quick Reference

Information Security and Privacy Quick Reference

The Essential Handbook for Every CISO, CSO, and Chief Privacy Officer

MIKE CHAPPLE

JOE SHELLEY

JAMES MICHAEL STEWART

WILEY

Copyright © 2025 by John Wiley & Sons, Inc. All rights reserved, including rights for text and data mining and training of artificial intelligence technologies or similar technologies.

Published by John Wiley & Sons, Inc., Hoboken, New Jersey.
Published simultaneously in Canada and the United Kingdom.

ISBNs: 9781394353316 (paperback), 9781394353330 (ePDF), 9781394353323 (ePub)

No part of this publication may be reproduced, stored in a retrieval system, or transmitted in any form or by any means, electronic, mechanical, photocopying, recording, scanning, or otherwise, except as permitted under Section 107 or 108 of the 1976 United States Copyright Act, without either the prior written permission of the Publisher, or authorization through payment of the appropriate per-copy fee to the Copyright Clearance Center, Inc., 222 Rosewood Drive, Danvers, MA 01923, (978) 750-8400, fax (978) 750-4470, or on the web at **www.copyright.com**. Requests to the Publisher for permission should be addressed to the Permissions Department, John Wiley & Sons, Inc., 111 River Street, Hoboken, NJ 07030, (201) 748-6011, fax (201) 748-6008, or online at **http://www.wiley.com/go/permission**.

The manufacturer's authorized representative according to the EU General Product Safety Regulation is Wiley-VCH GmbH, Boschstr. 12, 69469 Weinheim, Germany, e-mail: **Product_Safety@wiley.com**.

Trademarks: Wiley and the Wiley logo are trademarks or registered trademarks of John Wiley & Sons, Inc. and/or its affiliates in the United States and other countries and may not be used without written permission. All other trademarks are the property of their respective owners. John Wiley & Sons, Inc. is not associated with any product or vendor mentioned in this book.

Limit of Liability/Disclaimer of Warranty: While the publisher and authors have used their best efforts in preparing this book, they make no representations or warranties with respect to the accuracy or completeness of the contents of this book and specifically disclaim any implied warranties of merchantability or fitness for a particular purpose. No warranty may be created or extended by sales representatives or written sales materials. The advice and strategies contained herein may not be suitable for your situation. You should consult with a professional where appropriate. Further, readers should be aware that websites listed in this work may have changed or disappeared between when this work was written and when it is read. Neither the publisher nor authors shall be liable for any loss of profit or any other commercial damages, including but not limited to special, incidental, consequential, or other damages.

For general information on our other products and services or for technical support, please contact our Customer Care Department within the United States at (800) 762-2974, outside the United States at (317) 572-3993 or fax (317) 572-4002. For product technical support, you can find answers to frequently asked questions or reach us via live chat at **https://support.wiley.com**.

If you believe you've found a mistake in this book, please bring it to our attention by emailing our Reader Support team at **wileysupport@wiley.com** with the subject line "Possible Book Errata Submission."

Wiley also publishes its books in a variety of electronic formats. Some content that appears in print may not be available in electronic formats. For more information about Wiley products, visit our web site at **www.wiley.com**.

Library of Congress Control Number: 2025936525

Cover image: © kontekbrothers/Getty Images
Cover design: Wiley
SKY10104005_042225

About the Authors

Mike Chapple, PhD, CISSP, CISM, CIPP/US, Security+, CySA+, PenTest+, CISA, CCSP, is a teaching professor of IT, analytics, and operations at the University of Notre Dame. He is also the academic director of the university's master's program in business analytics.

Mike is a cybersecurity professional with over 25 years of experience in the field. Prior to his current role, Mike served as senior director for IT service delivery at Notre Dame, where he oversaw the university's cybersecurity program, cloud computing efforts, and other areas. Mike also previously served as chief information officer of Brand Institute and as an information security researcher with the National Security Agency and the U.S. Air Force.

Mike is a frequent contributor to several magazines and websites and is the author or coauthor of more than 50 books, including *CISSP Official ISC2 Study Guide* (Wiley, 2024), *CIPP/US Certified Information Privacy Professional Study Guide* (Wiley, 2025), and *CISM Certified Information Security Manager Study Guide* (Wiley, 2022).

Mike offers free study groups for the CISSP, CIPP/US, CISM, and other major certifications at his website, **http://certmike.com**.

Joe Shelley, MA, CIPP/US, is a leader in higher education information technologies. He is currently the vice president for libraries and information technology at Hamilton College in New York. In his role, Joe oversees central IT infrastructure, enterprise systems, information security and privacy programs, IT risk management, business intelligence and analytics, institutional research and assessment, data governance, and overall technology strategy. Joe also directs the library and institutional research program. In addition to supporting the teaching and research mission of the college, the library provides education in information sciences, digital and information literacy, and information management.

Before joining Hamilton College, Joe served as the chief information officer at the University of Washington Bothell in the Seattle area. During his 12 years at UW Bothell, Joe was responsible for learning technologies, data centers, web development, enterprise applications, help desk services, administrative and academic computing, and multimedia production. He implemented the UW Bothell information security program, cloud computing strategy, and IT governance, and he developed new initiatives for supporting teaching and learning, faculty research, and e-learning.

Joe earned his bachelor's degree in interdisciplinary arts and sciences from the University of Washington and his master's degree in educational technology from Michigan State University. Joe holds the CIPP/US, CIPM, and

Security+ certifications and is the coauthor of *CIPP / US Certified Information Privacy Professional Study Guide* (Wiley, 2025).

James Michael Stewart, CISSP, CEH, CHFI, ECSA, CND, ECIH, CySA+, PenTest+, CASP+, Security+, Network+, A+, CTT+, CEI, and CFR, has been writing and training for more than 25 years, with a focus on security. He has been teaching CISSP training courses since 2002, not to mention other courses on internet security and ethical hacking/penetration testing. In addition to being a coauthor of every edition of *CISSP Official ISC2 Study Guide* (Wiley, 2024), he is the author of and contributor to more than 80 books on security certification, Microsoft topics, and network administration. Michael is the author of the official online virtual lab sets for CompTIA's Security+, CASP+, and PenTest+, as well as hundreds of other labs focusing on Microsoft Windows, Linux, internet, and security concepts. More information about Michael can be found at his website, **www.impactonline.com**.

Contents at a Glance

INTRODUCTION xiii

1 Security and Privacy Foundations 1

2 Governance, Risk Management, and Compliance 23

3 Security Architecture and Design 39

4 Identity and Access Management 57

5 Data Protection and Privacy Engineering 77

6 Security and Privacy Incident Management 101

7 Network Security and Privacy Protections 121

8 Security Assessment and Testing 145

9 Endpoint and Device Security 163

10 Application Security 183

11 Cryptography Essentials 205

12 Physical and Environmental Security 227

13 Legal and Ethical Considerations 237

14 Threat Intelligence and Cyber Defense 253

15 Business Continuity and Disaster Recovery 269

INDEX **289**

Contents

INTRODUCTION   xiii

1   Security and Privacy Foundations   1

Security 101   1
Confidentiality, Integrity, and Availability (CIA)   3
Disclosure, Alteration, and Destruction (DAD)   4
Authentication, Authorization, and Accounting (AAA)   5
Privacy in the Modern Era   6
Foundational Privacy Principles   8
Security and Privacy Frameworks   11
Security and Privacy Policies: Creation and Enforcement   14
Establishing Security Awareness Programs   16
Security Strategies   19

2   Governance, Risk Management, and Compliance   23

The Role of Governance in Security and Privacy   23
Key Regulations and Standards   26
Regulatory Compliance   29
Building and Managing a Risk Management Framework   32
Managing Third-Party Risks and Vendor Assessments   35

3   Security Architecture and Design   39

Principles of Secure Design   39
Security Operations Foundations   42
Ensuring Confidentiality, Integrity, and Availability   44
Understanding Security Models   46
Implementing Personnel Security   49
Applying Protection Mechanisms   52
System Resilience and High Availability   54

4   Identity and Access Management   57

IAM Core Concepts and Principles   57
Authentication Methods and Multifactor Authentication   60
Role-Based Access Control Versus Attribute-Based Access Control   62
Identity Federation and Single Sign-On   65
Zero Trust Architecture for IAM   68
Identity Governance Life Cycle   71
Access Control Attacks   73

5 Data Protection and Privacy Engineering 77

Data Classification and Labeling 77
Data Masking, Tokenization, and Encryption 80
Data Loss Prevention Strategies 82
Privacy by Design 85
Developing a Privacy Program 87
Cross-Border Data Transfers and Legal Implications 90
Data Subject Rights and Privacy Request Handling 93
Data Retention, Archiving, and Secure Disposal 96

6 Security and Privacy Incident Management 101

Incident Response Planning 101
Detection and Triage of Security and Privacy Incidents 104
Investigating Incidents 106
Communication Plans for Incident Response 110
Post-Incident Review and Lessons Learned 113
Privacy Breach Notifications and Regulatory Reporting 117

7 Network Security and Privacy Protections 121

Secure Network Components 121
Network Segmentation 125
System Hardening 128
Firewalls and Intrusion Detection/Prevention Systems 130
Virtual Private Networks and Secure Access Service Edge 133
Secure Wireless Network Management 136
Securing the Cloud 139
Network Monitoring 142

8 Security Assessment and Testing 145

Building a Security Assessment and Testing Program 145
Vulnerability Management 147
Understanding Security Vulnerabilities 150
Penetration Testing 153
Testing Software 155
Training and Exercises 158

9 Endpoint and Device Security 163

Endpoint Detection and Response 163
Network Device Security 166
Mobile Device Management 169

Understanding Malware   173
Malware Prevention   176
Patching and Vulnerability Remediation   178

10 Application Security   183

Secure Software Development Life Cycle   183
DevSecOps and DevOps Integration   187
Application Attacks   191
Injection Vulnerabilities   192
Authorization Vulnerabilities   194
Web Application Attacks   196
Application Security Controls   198
Coding Best Practices   201

11 Cryptography Essentials   205

Core Cryptography Concepts   205
Symmetric Cryptography   208
Asymmetric Cryptography   210
Hash Functions   213
Digital Signatures   216
Public Key Infrastructure   218
Key Management Best Practices   220
Cryptographic Attacks   222

12 Physical and Environmental Security   227

Security and Facility Design   227
Physical Access Controls and Monitoring   229
Security in Data Centers and Server Rooms   232
Environmental Controls   234
Implement and Manage Physical Security   235

13 Legal and Ethical Considerations   237

Computer Crime   238
Intellectual Property Laws   241
Software Licensing Laws   243
Import/Export Laws   244
Privacy Laws   246
Compliance   249
Ethical Considerations   250

14 Threat Intelligence and Cyber Defense 253

Threat Actors 253
Threat Vectors 256
Threat Intelligence 258
Threat Feeds 259
Threat Hunting 262
Assessing Threat Intelligence 263
Cyber Kill Chain and the MITRE ATT&CK 265

15 Business Continuity and Disaster Recovery 269

Project Scope and Planning 270
Conducting Business Impact Analysis 273
Business Continuity Planning Essentials 277
Recovery Planning Essentials 279
Disaster Recovery Strategies and Solutions 282
Testing and Simulation Exercises 284

INDEX 289

Introduction

It is a massive understatement to say that information security and privacy are enormous domains. Whether you are early in your career in the field or the most senior and experienced leader in your organization, you know the near impossibility of keeping up with the volume of laws, regulations, guidance, standards, and best practices from national, state, provincial, city, and other levels of government along with international standards bodies, helpful industry organizations, individual companies, and other sources of information security and privacy documentation.

As a manager or leader in information security and privacy, you also face the daunting challenge that much of what you learned when you entered the field has changed. Knowing the best way to protect information and privacy in 2000, 2010, or 2020 may not provide you with the right answers in 2025 or 2030. If you spent considerable time studying for one of the major industry certifications or credentials, there's a good chance you haven't cracked open your *Study Guide* or rewatched those helpful videos since the day you passed the exam. Attending industry events or taking continuing education courses online provides you with focused and specific learning opportunities but on very narrow topics.

If you need one more angle to your information overload, you're certainly aware that whether you're looking at government standards or objectives for a certification exam, they often either say the same thing in different ways or overlap in ways that are hard to untangle. And CISOs, CSOs, chief privacy officers, and anyone else leading or managing information security and privacy need to be able to quickly find answers and guidance across the multiple domains of expertise and share information with a common taxonomy regardless of their specific title or role. If your primary expertise is either information security or privacy, you know that there is critical information in the other domain that is important to your success but not immediately in your personal knowledge base.

This collection of challenges is what *Information Security and Privacy Quick Reference: The Essential Handbook for Every CISO, CSO, and Chief Privacy Officer* aims to address for your day-to-day work. Unlike a certification study guide that may be many hundreds or a thousand pages, and unlike the maze of government and industry documentation, the *Information Security and Privacy Quick Reference* gives you a small, one-source reference to the most common guidance, definitions, and best practices. This is by design *not* an encyclopedia of information security and privacy but instead core information that you might turn to daily or carry with you anywhere.

By gathering the key information that professionals may have learned if they studied for the CISSP, CISM, or CIPP/US, looking for common ground, and exploring a broader body of knowledge that encompasses all three, this book should be a useful reminder on any critical information security or privacy task you face.

Information Security and Privacy Quick Reference

CHAPTER 1

Security and Privacy Foundations

In the ever-evolving landscape of information security and privacy, it is crucial for professionals to have a solid foundation in both domains. This chapter is designed to equip you with essential knowledge and insights that are fundamental to safeguarding information and ensuring privacy in your organization. As security and privacy threats become more sophisticated, understanding the core principles and frameworks that underpin these fields will enable you to develop robust strategies and implement effective controls.

By exploring the foundational concepts of security and privacy, you will gain a comprehensive understanding of key principles such as confidentiality, integrity, availability, authentication, authorization, and accounting. Additionally, you will delve into the intricacies of privacy in the modern era and the foundational principles that guide privacy practices. This chapter also covers critical frameworks and policies that provide structure and guidance for security and privacy initiatives. By the end of this chapter, you will be well-versed in the foundations of creating and enforcing policies, establishing security awareness programs, and developing strategic approaches to security and privacy management. This knowledge is vital for protecting your organization's assets and ensuring compliance with regulatory requirements.

Security 101

We often hear how important security is, but we don't always understand why. Security is essential because it helps to ensure that an organization can continue to exist and operate despite any attempts to steal its data or compromise its physical or logical elements. Security is an element of business management rather than only an information technology (IT) or information systems (IS) concern. Furthermore, IT/IS and security are different. IT/IS comprises the hardware and software that support the operations or functions of a business. Security is the business management tool that ensures the reliable and protected operation of IT/IS. Security exists to support the organization's objectives, mission, and goals.

Generally, a security framework that provides a starting point for implementing security should be adopted. Once security is initiated, fine-tuning that security is accomplished through continuous evaluation and stress testing. There are three common types of security evaluation:

- **Risk assessment** is identifying assets, threats, and vulnerabilities to calculate risk. Once risk is understood, it is used to guide the improvement of the existing security infrastructure.
- **Vulnerability assessment** uses automated tools to locate known security weaknesses, which can be addressed by adding more defenses or adjusting the current protections.
- **Penetration testing** uses trusted teams to stress test the security infrastructure to find issues that may not be discovered by the prior two means and to find those concerns before an adversary takes advantage of them.

Security should be cost-effective. Organizations do not have infinite budgets and, thus, must allocate their funds appropriately. Additionally, an organizational budget includes a percentage of monies dedicated to security, just as most other business tasks and processes require capital, not to mention payments to employees, insurance, retirement, and so on. You should select security controls that provide the most significant protection for the lowest resource cost.

Security should be legally defensible. The laws of your jurisdiction are the backstop of organizational security. When someone intrudes into your environment and breaches security, especially when such activities are illegal, prosecution in court may be the only available response for compensation or closure. Also, many decisions made by an organization will have legal liability issues. If required to defend a security action in the courtroom, legally supported security will go a long way toward protecting your organization from facing significant fines, penalties, or charges of negligence.

Security is a journey, not a finish line. It is not a process that will ever be concluded. It is impossible to fully secure something because security issues are always changing. Our deployed technology is changing with the passage of time, by users' activities, and by adversaries discovering flaws and developing exploits. The defenses that were sufficient yesterday may not be sufficient tomorrow. As new vulnerabilities are discovered, new means of attack are crafted, and new exploits are built, we have to respond by reassessing our security infrastructure and responding appropriately.

Confidentiality, Integrity, and Availability (CIA)

The CIA triad is a fundamental concept in information security, representing the three core principles that guide the protection of data and systems. This section provides an overview of these principles—confidentiality, integrity, and availability—and their importance in maintaining a secure information environment.

Confidentiality

Confidentiality is the concept of ensuring the protection of the secrecy of data, objects, or resources. The goal is to prevent or minimize unauthorized access to data. Confidentiality is maintained through various countermeasures such as encryption, strict access control, rigorous authentication procedures, data classification, and extensive personnel training. Violations of confidentiality can occur through intentional attacks, human error, oversight, or misconfigured security controls. Key concepts related to confidentiality include:

- **Sensitivity:** Determining whether information could cause harm if disclosed.
- **Discretion:** Controlling disclosure to minimize harm.
- **Criticality:** Measuring how vital to the company's mission the information is.
- **Concealment:** Hiding or preventing disclosure of information.
- **Secrecy:** Keeping information secret.
- **Privacy:** Keeping personally identifiable information confidential.
- **Seclusion:** Storing information in a secure location.
- **Isolation:** Keeping information separated from others.

Integrity

Integrity is the concept of protecting the reliability and correctness of data. It ensures that data is not altered in an unauthorized manner. Integrity protection allows for authorized changes while preventing unauthorized modifications, whether they are intentional, malicious, or accidental. Key aspects include:

- **Data integrity:** Ensuring that data remains accurate and consistent over its life cycle.

- **System integrity:** Ensuring that a system performs its intended function in an unimpaired manner.
- **Process integrity:** Ensuring that processes operate correctly without unauthorized modification.

Availability

Availability is the principle that ensures authorized users have timely and uninterrupted access to data and resources. It is crucial for maintaining the functionality of systems and services. Availability can be impacted by hardware failures, software issues, or malicious attacks such as denial of service (DoS). Measures to ensure availability include:

- **Redundancy:** Having backup systems in place.
- **Failover:** Switching automatically to a standby system.
- **Load balancing:** Distributing workloads across multiple systems.
- **Maintenance:** Updating and patching regularly to prevent system failures.

Disclosure, Alteration, and Destruction (DAD)

The DAD triad is a fundamental concept in information security that represents the failures of security protections in the CIA triad. Understanding the DAD triad is essential for identifying and mitigating the risks associated with security breaches. The DAD triad consists of three key elements: disclosure, alteration, and destruction.

- **Disclosure:** Occurs when sensitive or confidential material is accessed by unauthorized entities. This is a direct violation of confidentiality. Disclosure can happen through various means, such as data breaches, unauthorized access, or accidental exposure due to misconfigurations. Attackers who gain access to sensitive information and remove it from the organization are performing *data exfiltration*. Additionally, disclosure can occur accidentally, such as when an administrator misconfigures access controls or an employee loses a device.
- **Alteration:** Refers to the unauthorized modification of information, which violates the principle of integrity. This can happen through malicious activities like injecting fraudulent transactions into financial

records or through accidental means such as typographical errors or system malfunctions. Attackers may seek to alter data for financial gain, reputational damage, or other malicious purposes. Natural activities, such as power surges causing bit flips, can also lead to unintended alterations.
- **Destruction:** Involves the damage or inaccessibility of resources, which violates the principle of availability. This can be the result of intentional actions like distributed denial-of-service (DDoS) attacks or unintentional events such as hardware failures or natural disasters. Destruction can significantly impact an organization's operations by making critical data or services unavailable to authorized users.

The DAD triad is a useful tool for cybersecurity planning and risk analysis. It helps professionals to assess the threats and vulnerabilities associated with their systems and to implement appropriate security controls. For example, when evaluating the security of an organization's website, one might consider the following questions based on the DAD triad:

- Does the website contain sensitive information that would damage the organization if disclosed to unauthorized individuals?
- If an attacker were able to modify information contained on the website, would this unauthorized alteration cause financial, reputational, or operational damage to the organization?
- Does the website perform mission-critical activities that could damage the business significantly if an attacker were able to disrupt the site?

By using the DAD triad, professionals can better understand the potential impacts of security incidents and develop strategies to mitigate these risks.

The DAD triad highlights the critical failures of security mechanisms in protecting confidentiality, integrity, and availability. By recognizing these potential failures, organizations can implement more effective security measures to safeguard their information and systems.

Authentication, Authorization, and Accounting (AAA)

In the realm of information security, AAA services form a foundational mechanism essential for maintaining secure environments. The three As in this abbreviation stand for authentication, authorization, and accounting. These elements are critical in ensuring that only authorized users can access resources and perform actions and that their activities are appropriately logged and monitored.

Authentication

Authentication is the process of verifying the identity of a subject. It ensures that the entity requesting access is, in fact, who they claim to be. This verification can be achieved through various methods such as passwords, smart cards, biometric scans, or other authentication factors. The process of authentication is crucial as it forms the first line of defense against unauthorized access. Without proper authentication, no further security measures can be effectively applied.

Authorization

Once a subject's identity is authenticated, the next step is authorization. Authorization determines what an authenticated subject is allowed to do. It involves defining permissions and access rights, ensuring that users can only perform actions or access resources for which they have been explicitly granted permission. This control is vital in maintaining the principle of *least privilege*, where users have the minimum level of access necessary to perform their job functions.

Accounting

Accounting, sometimes referred to as *auditing*, involves tracking the actions of authenticated and authorized subjects. This process includes recording log entries of user activities, system events, and access to resources. Accounting is essential for maintaining accountability, as it allows organizations to review logs and monitor for compliance with security policies. It also plays a crucial role in detecting and investigating security incidents, ensuring that any unauthorized or suspicious activities can be traced back to specific users or processes.

Privacy in the Modern Era

Privacy concerns are an integral part of our daily lives, as we frequently hear reports of companies misusing personal information and data breaches leading to the exposure of massive quantities of personal data. These issues have led to ongoing legislative debates at both federal and state levels, resulting in new laws aimed at regulating various aspects of privacy. In this complex environment, privacy professionals play a crucial role in guiding organizations through the maze of ethical obligations, laws, regulations, and industry standards.

Introduction to Privacy

Privacy is a fundamental right inherent to every individual, rooted in the principle that people should be able to protect themselves and their information from unwanted intrusions by others or the government. Historically, the concept of privacy in the United States was significantly shaped by Louis D. Brandeis, who in 1890 coauthored an influential article titled "The Right to Privacy." Brandeis emphasized the need for legal remedies to protect individuals from unauthorized intrusions, a sentiment that resonates even more in today's technologically advanced society.

Brandeis's ideas gained further prominence when he became a Supreme Court justice. In his dissenting opinion in the case of *Olmstead v. United States*, he argued for a constitutional right to privacy, asserting that the Fourth Amendment protects individuals from unjustifiable government intrusions. This perspective laid the groundwork for modern privacy rights, emphasizing the importance of safeguarding personal information against both governmental and private sector misuse.

Online Privacy and Privacy Notices

In the digital age, online privacy has become a critical concern. Organizations must navigate the challenges of collecting, using, and protecting personal information in an online environment. Consumers often provide information to companies actively (by filling out forms) or passively (through automated data collection). Therefore, privacy policies must cover both types of data collection and be transparent about how data is used.

Privacy notices are the primary means organizations use to communicate their privacy practices to users. These notices should be posted conspicuously on websites and written in plain language accessible to the general audience. Effective privacy notices strike a balance between satisfying legal and ethical disclosure obligations and remaining readable to laypersons. Layered privacy notices, which provide brief summaries in plain language alongside detailed legal terms, are an excellent approach to achieve this balance.

Managing User Preferences and Accountability

Managing user preferences is another essential aspect of privacy in the modern era. Organizations must provide users with options to control how their data is used, including the ability to opt in or opt out of data collection and sharing practices. This requires implementing procedures and mechanisms that allow users to state their preferences and for the organization to track and honor them. These activities are good privacy practices and may be required by law in some jurisdictions and industries.

Accountability mechanisms are crucial to ensure that organizations adhere to their privacy policies and comply with relevant laws and regulations. This includes regular audits, employee training, and the implementation of robust data protection measures. Organizations must monitor compliance with privacy policies and procedures, maintain a dispute resolution process, and review compliance with privacy laws and regulations annually. Documenting cases of privacy violations and taking corrective actions are also essential components of accountability.

Privacy Program Development

Developing a comprehensive privacy program is vital for organizations to effectively manage and protect personal information. A privacy program should include policies and procedures for data collection, storage, and sharing as well as mechanisms for responding to data breaches and other privacy incidents. The program should be built on strong data governance practices, including creating an inventory of personal information and implementing a data life cycle management process.

Organizations should foster a culture of privacy awareness, ensuring that all employees understand the importance of protecting personal information and their role in maintaining privacy standards. Privacy programs should also include continuous monitoring and enforcement practices to adapt to evolving business needs and information practices. This involves periodic reviews, regular updates to privacy assessments, and dashboard-style monitoring of key metrics such as compliance with data retention standards and the number of privacy incidents.

Privacy in the modern era is a multifaceted issue that requires a careful balance between technological advancements and the protection of individual rights. Historical perspectives, such as those provided by Louis D. Brandeis, continue to influence contemporary privacy practices and legal frameworks. As organizations navigate the complexities of online privacy, managing user preferences, and accountability, the development of robust privacy programs remains essential. Privacy professionals play a key role in guiding organizations through these challenges, ensuring that personal information is safeguarded and ethical standards are upheld.

Foundational Privacy Principles

Privacy is a fundamental right and a critical aspect of information security. Understanding and implementing foundational privacy principles is essential for organizations to protect personal information and comply with legal and ethical standards. This section provides an overview of basic privacy principles, drawing from established frameworks and best practices.

Privacy Principles Overview

Privacy principles serve as guidelines for organizations to manage and protect personal information. These principles ensure that data-handling practices are transparent, accountable, and aligned with the rights of individuals. The generally accepted privacy principles (GAPP) provide a structured approach to privacy management.

Generally Accepted Privacy Principles (GAPP)

The GAPP framework, developed by the American Institute of Certified Public Accountants (AICPA) and the Canadian Institute of Chartered Accountants (CICA), includes 10 key principles that organizations should follow:

- **Management:** Organizations must define, document, communicate, and assign accountability for their privacy policies and procedures. This includes creating written privacy policies, assigning responsibility to a privacy officer, and ensuring policies are consistent with applicable laws. Organizations should also conduct privacy risk assessments regularly and maintain a privacy incident management process.
- **Notice:** Organizations should inform individuals about their privacy practices, including the purposes for which personal information is collected, used, retained, and disclosed. This transparency helps build trust with stakeholders. Notice should be provided at the time of data collection and when there are changes to privacy policies.
- **Choice and consent:** Individuals should have the ability to choose how their personal information is used and shared. Organizations must obtain consent from individuals before collecting or using their data for specified purposes. Consent can be implicit or explicit, depending on the sensitivity of the information and the context of its use.
- **Collection:** Organizations should collect personal information only for legitimate purposes and by lawful and fair means. This minimizes the risk of unnecessary data collection and potential misuse. The collection practices should be clearly stated in the organization's privacy policies, and individuals should be informed about the methods and types of data collected.

- **Use, retention, and disposal:** Personal information should be used only for the purposes for which it was collected. Organizations must retain data only as long as necessary and dispose of it securely when it is no longer needed. This ensures that personal information is not kept longer than required and reduces the risk of unauthorized access or misuse.
- **Access:** Individuals should have the right to access their personal information and request corrections if necessary. This empowers individuals to control their data and ensure its accuracy. Organizations should provide mechanisms for individuals to review and update their information and inform them of the procedures to do so.
- **Disclosure to third parties:** Organizations must disclose personal information to third parties only for legitimate purposes and with appropriate safeguards. This includes ensuring that third parties adhere to the same privacy standards. Organizations should inform individuals about any third-party disclosures and obtain their consent when necessary.
- **Security for privacy:** Organizations must implement appropriate security measures to protect personal information from unauthorized access, use, or disclosure. This includes physical, technical, and administrative controls. Security practices should be included in the organization's privacy policies, and individuals should be informed about the precautions taken to protect their data.
- **Quality:** Organizations should maintain the accuracy and completeness of personal information. This ensures that data is reliable and relevant for its intended use. Individuals should be informed about their responsibility to provide accurate information and to notify the organization of any corrections needed.
- **Monitoring and enforcement:** Organizations must regularly monitor their privacy practices and enforce compliance with privacy policies. This includes conducting privacy risk assessments and audits to identify and address potential issues. Organizations should also have procedures in place to handle privacy-related inquiries, complaints, and disputes and to take corrective actions when necessary.

Foundational privacy principles provide a comprehensive framework for managing and protecting personal information. By adhering to these principles, organizations can ensure that their privacy practices are transparent, accountable, and aligned with the rights of individuals. Implementing the GAPP helps organizations build trust with stakeholders, comply with legal and ethical standards, and effectively safeguard personal information. These principles are essential for maintaining the integrity and security of data in today's information-driven world.

Security and Privacy Frameworks

In today's interconnected world, organizations face a myriad of security and privacy challenges that require comprehensive frameworks to manage risks effectively. Security and privacy frameworks provide structured approaches for identifying, managing, and mitigating risks. These frameworks are essential for establishing consistent security policies, ensuring compliance with regulations, and protecting sensitive information.

Understanding Security Control Frameworks

Security control frameworks are structured collections of best practices, standards, and guidelines that organizations use to manage and mitigate security risks. These frameworks help organizations to implement effective security controls and establish a baseline for security practices. Key components of security control frameworks include:

- **Policies and procedures:** Formalized rules and guidelines that dictate how security measures are to be implemented and maintained.
- **Risk management:** Processes for identifying, assessing, and prioritizing risks, followed by the application of resources to minimize their impact.
- **Control implementation:** Specific security controls that are put in place to protect information assets, including technical, administrative, and physical controls.
- **Monitoring and reporting:** Continuous monitoring of security controls and regular reporting to ensure their effectiveness and compliance with standards.

Common Security Control Frameworks

Several well-known security control frameworks are widely adopted across various industries:

- **International Organization for Standardization (ISO) Standards:** ISO 27001 and ISO 27002 provide guidelines for establishing, implementing, maintaining, and continually improving an information security management system (ISMS).
- **National Institute of Standards and Technology (NIST):** The NIST Cybersecurity Framework (CSF) offers a policy framework of computer

security guidance for how private sector organizations in the United States can assess and improve their ability to prevent, detect, and respond to cyberattacks.
- **Control Objectives for Information and Related Technology (COBIT):** COBIT is a framework for developing, implementing, monitoring, and improving IT governance and management practices.
- **Sherwood Applied Business Security Architecture (SABSA):** SABSA is a framework and methodology for enterprise security architecture and service management.
- **Payment Card Industry Data Security Standard (PCI DSS):** PCI DSS is a set of security standards designed to ensure that all companies that accept, process, store, or transmit credit card information maintain a secure environment.
- **Federal Risk and Authorization Management Program (FedRAMP):** FedRAMP provides a standardized approach to security assessment, authorization, and continuous monitoring for cloud products and services used by U.S. federal agencies.

These frameworks often include maturity models that allow organizations to assess their progress and identify areas for improvement. They also offer certification programs that provide independent assessments of an organization's adherence to the framework.

Adopting Standard Frameworks

Adopting standard frameworks for security and privacy is crucial for organizations aiming to achieve a robust security posture. The process of adopting these frameworks involves several key steps:

- **Legal, regulatory, and contractual requirements:** Ensure that the security framework addresses all relevant legal, regulatory, and contractual obligations, including compliance with data protection laws, industry-specific regulations, and contractual security requirements.
- **Assessment and gap analysis:** Evaluate current security and privacy practices against the chosen framework to identify gaps and areas for improvement. This provides a clear roadmap for implementation.
- **Strategic planning and resource allocation:** Allocate necessary resources, develop budgets, and create business cases to support the implementation and maintenance of the framework. This step aligns the adoption process with the organization's goals and capacity.

- **Information governance and corporate integration:** Implement information governance frameworks to manage information assets effectively and ensure data integrity, confidentiality, and availability. Integrate security frameworks into the broader corporate governance structure to align security initiatives with the organization's overall strategy and objectives.
- **Customization and integration:** Tailor the framework to fit the organization's specific needs and context and integrate it with existing processes and systems for seamless adoption.
- **Development of policies, procedures, and guidelines:** Develop comprehensive policies, procedures, and guidelines that provide the foundation for implementing and maintaining security controls across the organization.
- **Implementation of security controls:** Deploy the necessary controls, policies, and procedures to align with the framework's requirements, ensuring consistent security practices throughout the organization.

Benefits of Security and Privacy Frameworks

Implementing security and privacy frameworks offers several benefits:

- **Enhanced security posture:** Frameworks provide a systematic approach to identifying and mitigating risks, leading to stronger security defenses.
- **Regulatory compliance:** Adhering to recognized frameworks helps organizations meet legal and regulatory requirements, avoiding potential fines and penalties.
- **Operational efficiency:** Standardized processes and controls streamline security operations, reducing redundancies and improving efficiency.
- **Stakeholder confidence:** Demonstrating a commitment to security and privacy through the adoption of frameworks builds trust with customers, partners, and stakeholders.

Security and privacy frameworks are indispensable tools for organizations striving to protect their information assets and maintain compliance with regulatory requirements. By adopting and implementing these frameworks, organizations can establish a strong foundation for managing risks, enhancing security, and safeguarding privacy in an increasingly complex digital landscape.

Security and Privacy Policies: Creation and Enforcement

Creating effective security and privacy policies is essential for safeguarding an organization's information assets. These policies serve as the foundation for maintaining a secure and compliant environment.

Understanding Policy Documents

Policies are high-level documents that outline an organization's security and privacy objectives and the strategies to achieve them. They provide direction and set expectations for behavior and decision-making. Effective policies should be clear, concise, and aligned with the organization's goals and regulatory requirements.

Creation of Security and Privacy Policies

The creation of security and privacy policies starts with a thorough understanding of the organization's objectives, legal and regulatory requirements, and industry standards. Policies should be clear, concise, and enforceable, providing a high-level framework that dictates the organization's approach to security and privacy. This framework is typically supported by detailed standards, procedures, and guidelines that offer specific instructions for implementing policy directives.

Policy Types and Hierarchy

- **Policies:** High-level statements that reflect the organization's values and goals. They provide the overall direction and set the tone for the security and privacy posture.
- **Standards:** Specific, mandatory controls that help enforce and support the policies. They ensure consistency and compliance across the organization.
- **Procedures:** Detailed, step-by-step instructions for performing specific tasks. Procedures ensure that all personnel understand how to implement policies and standards in their daily activities.
- **Guidelines:** Recommended practices that provide flexibility in achieving the objectives outlined in policies and standards. They offer advice on best practices without being mandatory.

Development and Documentation

Developing these documents involves collaboration across various departments to ensure that all perspectives are considered and that the policies are practical and applicable to the entire organization. Documentation should be clear and accessible, with periodic reviews and updates to reflect changes in the threat landscape, business objectives, and regulatory requirements.

The policy creation process usually consists of three steps:

- **Assessment:** Identify the organization's security and privacy needs, considering legal, regulatory, and business requirements.
- **Development:** Draft policies that address identified needs, ensuring they are clear, actionable, and enforceable. Engage stakeholders for input and buy-in.
- **Review and approval:** Policies should be reviewed by legal, compliance, and executive teams to ensure alignment with organizational goals and regulatory requirements. Obtain formal approval from senior management.

Enforcement of Security and Privacy Policies

Effective enforcement of security and privacy policies requires a combination of the following:

- **Awareness and training:** Employees must be educated about the policies, the reasons behind them, and their role in maintaining security and privacy. Regular training sessions and awareness programs help reinforce the importance of adhering to these policies.
- **Monitoring and compliance:** Continuous monitoring of compliance with policies is crucial. This involves regular audits, assessments, and reviews to ensure that the policies are being followed and are effective. Non-compliance should be addressed promptly with corrective actions, which may include additional training, policy revisions, or disciplinary measures.
- **Incident response:** Develop and maintain an incident response plan to address policy violations and security incidents promptly and effectively.
- **Review and update:** Regularly review and update policies to reflect changes in the organization, technology, and regulatory landscape. Continuous improvement is key to maintaining effective security and privacy practices.

Security and privacy policies are essential for establishing a strong security posture within an organization. By creating clear, comprehensive, and enforceable policies, supported by detailed standards, procedures, and guidelines, organizations can ensure that their security and privacy efforts are aligned with their strategic objectives and compliance requirements. Effective enforcement through continuous awareness, training, and monitoring ensures that these policies remain relevant and are adhered to by all members of the organization.

Establishing Security Awareness Programs

Security awareness programs are essential for educating employees about the importance of security and their role in protecting organizational assets. These programs aim to instill a culture of security, ensuring that all personnel understand and adhere to security policies and procedures. Effective security awareness programs are comprehensive, continuously evolving, and tailored to the specific needs and risks of the organization.

Program Development and Implementation

An effective security awareness program begins with a solid foundation built on careful assessment, planning, and implementation. This phase focuses on understanding the organization's needs, defining goals, and creating engaging content to support security education.

Assessment of Needs   Conduct a thorough assessment to identify the specific security awareness needs of the organization. This includes:

- Analyzing the organizational structure to understand how information flows and where vulnerabilities may exist.
- Identifying potential internal and external threats to the organization, such as phishing attempts, data breaches, or social engineering tactics.
- Evaluating the current level of security knowledge among employees through surveys, interviews, and assessments. This helps to identify gaps in knowledge and areas that require targeted awareness efforts.

Clear Objectives Define clear and measurable objectives for the security awareness program, ensuring that they align with the organization's overall security strategy and compliance requirements:

- Objectives should include specific goals, such as reducing the number of phishing incidents or increasing participation in security training.
- Establish milestones and key performance indicators (KPIs) to track progress toward achieving these objectives.

Content Creation Create tailored and relevant content that addresses the organization's security risks and employee roles. Effective content educates employees on common threats and their responsibilities in maintaining security:

- **General content:** Covering topics such as password hygiene, recognizing phishing emails, data protection best practices, and incident reporting.
- **Role-specific content:** Customizing material for specific roles (e.g., IT staff, HR, legal, and executive leadership) to address their unique security responsibilities.
- **Relatable content:** Incorporating real-world examples, case studies, and scenarios to make the content more relatable and impactful.

Delivery Methods Ensure that security awareness content reaches all employees using a variety of delivery formats. This increases engagement and accommodates different learning preferences:

- **In-person training sessions:** Interactive workshops or seminars that allow for hands-on learning and discussion.
- **E-learning modules:** Self-paced online training that employees can complete at their convenience.
- **Newsletters and posters:** Visual reminders placed in high-traffic areas or sent digitally to reinforce key messages.
- **Interactive workshops:** Group exercises that encourage collaboration and problem-solving around security topics, such as handling simulated incidents.

Education and Training

Education and training are at the heart of a security awareness program. This phase ensures that employees not only receive the information they need but also retain and apply it through continuous learning and role-specific exercises.

Continuous Learning   Promote an ongoing learning environment to keep employees up to date with the latest security practices and threats:

- Provide regular updates to employees about the latest security threats, incidents, and best practices.
- Conduct refresher courses periodically to ensure that employees retain critical security knowledge.
- Encourage a culture of curiosity and proactive learning by sharing news, security tips, and threat updates.

Role-Based Training   Tailor training to the specific responsibilities and risks associated with different roles within the organization:

- **IT staff:** Require more technical training on threat detection, incident response, and secure configurations.
- **General employees:** Need to understand basic security practices, such as avoiding phishing links and securing sensitive data.
- **Executive leadership:** Should receive training on high-level risks, decision-making in a security crisis, and regulatory compliance.

Simulations and Exercises   Reinforce learning through real-world simulations and exercises to test employee readiness and assess the program's effectiveness:

- **Phishing simulations:** Send mock phishing emails to employees to test their ability to recognize and report phishing attempts.
- **Incident response drills:** Run drills to simulate security incidents (e.g., ransomware attacks) and assess how well teams follow incident response procedures.
- **Analyses:** Analyze the results of these exercises to identify weaknesses and areas for improvement.

Program Maintenance and Evaluation

A security awareness program must evolve over time to remain effective. This phase involves monitoring the program's impact, collecting feedback, and making continuous improvements based on changing threats and organizational needs.

Monitoring and Metrics Track the effectiveness of the security awareness program using relevant metrics and performance indicators.

- **Participation rates:** Track how many employees have completed training sessions and e-learning modules.
- **Assessment scores:** Evaluate employees' knowledge through quizzes and tests after training sessions.
- **Incident reports:** Monitor the number and type of security incidents reported before and after program implementation to measure improvements in security behavior.

Feedback and Improvement Gather feedback from program participants and use it to improve the program's content and delivery.

- Conduct surveys or focus groups to gather input on the training content, delivery methods, and overall program effectiveness.
- Use the feedback to refine training materials, adjust delivery methods, and incorporate new best practices.
- Regularly review the program to address emerging threats and ensure alignment with industry trends and compliance requirements.

Management Support Secure ongoing support from senior management to promote a strong security culture and allocate necessary resources.

- Gain executive buy-in to set the tone from the top, reinforcing security as a priority across the organization.
- Secure adequate funding for program development, training resources, and ongoing maintenance.
- Encourage leadership to participate in awareness activities and communicate the importance of security in company meetings and messages.

Security Strategies

In today's complex threat landscape, organizations must develop robust security strategies to protect their information assets. Effective security strategies are built on a foundation of strong governance, clear objectives, and a comprehensive understanding of the threat environment. This section provides an overview of the key elements involved in managing the security function and building an information security strategy.

Managing the Security Function

Effective security management is crucial for protecting an organization's assets, ensuring compliance, and maintaining operational integrity. The security function encompasses a variety of responsibilities, including risk management, policy development, and incident response. Key elements include:

- **Risk management:** Identifying, assessing, and prioritizing risks to minimize their impact on organizational objectives. This involves regular risk assessments, implementing controls, and continuous monitoring.
- **Policy development:** Establishing comprehensive security policies that align with business goals and regulatory requirements. Policies should be clear, enforceable, and regularly reviewed and updated.
- **Incident response:** Preparing for and effectively responding to security incidents. This includes having an incident response plan, conducting regular training and simulations, and learning from past incidents to improve future responses.
- **Security awareness:** Promoting a culture of security within the organization. This involves regular training and awareness programs to ensure all employees understand their role in maintaining security.
- **Compliance and governance:** Ensuring adherence to relevant laws, regulations, and standards. This includes regular audits, assessments, and reporting to demonstrate compliance.

Building an Information Security Strategy

Creating a robust information security strategy involves aligning security initiatives with business objectives, ensuring that security measures support the overall mission of the organization. The strategy should be dynamic, adaptable, and comprehensive. Key components include:

- **Alignment with business goals:** Security strategies must support and enhance business objectives. This requires understanding the business environment, identifying critical assets, and aligning security initiatives with business priorities.

- **Risk-based approach:** Prioritizing security efforts based on risk assessments. This involves identifying the most significant threats and vulnerabilities and focusing resources on mitigating those risks.
- **Comprehensive framework:** Developing a holistic security framework that encompasses all aspects of information security, including technical, physical, and administrative controls. This framework should be scalable and adaptable to changing threats and business needs.
- **Continuous improvement:** Regularly reviewing and updating the security strategy to address new threats, technological advancements, and changes in the business environment. This involves continuous monitoring, feedback loops, and incorporating lessons learned from incidents and assessments.
- **Stakeholder engagement:** Involving key stakeholders in the development and implementation of the security strategy. This ensures buy-in, aligns security efforts with business needs, and promotes a shared responsibility for security.

By integrating these principles, organizations can develop a robust and effective security strategy that not only protects assets but also supports and enhances business objectives.

CHAPTER 2

Governance, Risk Management, and Compliance

Policy serves as the foundation for any cybersecurity program, setting out the principles and rules that guide the execution of security efforts throughout the enterprise. Often, organizations base these policies on best practice frameworks developed by industry groups such as the National Institute of Standards and Technology (NIST) or the International Organization for Standardization (ISO). In many cases, organizational policies are also influenced and directed by external compliance obligations that regulators impose on the organization. In this chapter, you will learn about the important elements of the cybersecurity policy framework as well as the compliance obligations imposed on organizations by governments and other regulators.

The Role of Governance in Security and Privacy

Governance is a fundamental component of both security and privacy in any organization. It involves the collection of practices related to supporting, evaluating, defining, and directing an organization's security and privacy efforts. Effective governance ensures that an organization can protect its information assets while complying with relevant laws, regulations, and industry standards. This section explores the role of governance in security and privacy, highlighting key principles, frameworks, and practices that organizations should adopt.

Security Governance Principles

Security governance is the framework through which an organization directs and controls its security activities. It encompasses the policies, procedures, and practices that ensure security measures align with the organization's objectives and risk appetite. Security governance is typically overseen by a board of directors or a governance committee, although in smaller organizations, this responsibility may fall to the chief executive officer (CEO) or chief information security officer (CISO).

The primary goals of security governance are to maintain the confidentiality, integrity, and availability of information, often referred to as the CIA triad (refer to Chapter 1). Confidentiality ensures that sensitive information is accessible only to authorized individuals. Integrity guarantees that information is accurate and has not been tampered with. Availability ensures that information and systems are accessible when needed.

Security governance also involves aligning the security function with the organization's business strategy, goals, mission, and objectives. This alignment ensures that security measures support the overall direction of the organization and contribute to its success. Key elements of security governance include:

- **Organizational processes:** Security governance must be integrated into organizational processes such as acquisitions, divestitures, and governance committees. This integration ensures that security considerations are part of strategic decisions and operations.
- **Roles and responsibilities:** Clear roles and responsibilities are essential for effective security governance. Key roles include senior managers, security professionals, asset owners, custodians, users, and auditors. Each role has specific duties and accountability to ensure the security of information assets.
- **Security control frameworks:** Organizations often adopt security control frameworks to guide their security efforts. Common frameworks include ISO 27001, NIST, COBIT, and PCI DSS. These frameworks provide structured approaches to implementing and managing security controls.
- **Due care and due diligence:** Due care involves taking reasonable steps to protect information assets, while due diligence involves ongoing efforts to identify and mitigate risks. Together, these practices ensure that an organization is proactive in its security efforts.
- **Threat modeling:** Threat modeling is the process of identifying, categorizing, and analyzing potential threats to an organization. It helps in understanding the threat landscape and implementing appropriate security measures.

- **Supply chain risk management (SCRM):** SCRM focuses on ensuring that vendors and partners in the supply chain adhere to security requirements. It includes evaluating risks associated with hardware, software, and services, and implementing measures such as third-party assessments and monitoring.

Data Governance

Data governance programs identify, track, and manage sensitive information within an organization. These programs ensure that data handling practices align with organizational policies and regulatory requirements. Key components of data governance include:

- **Building a data inventory:** Organizations must develop an inventory of the types of sensitive information they maintain and the locations where it is stored, processed, and transmitted. This inventory helps in understanding the data landscape and implementing appropriate controls.
- **Data classification:** Data classification programs categorize information based on its sensitivity and the impact on the organization if disclosed. For example, data may be classified as public, internal, confidential, or restricted. This classification helps in applying appropriate security controls.
- **Data management life cycle:** Managing the data life cycle involves overseeing data from its creation through its use, storage, and eventual destruction. This process ensures that data is protected throughout its life cycle and that obsolete data is securely disposed of.

Information Governance

Information governance is the overarching framework that encompasses data governance and security governance. It ensures that data handling practices are consistent with organizational policies, procedures, and compliance requirements. Information governance involves building a data inventory, classifying sensitive information, mapping data flows, and managing the data life cycle from creation to destruction.

Compliance and Regulatory Requirements

Governance efforts are often driven by compliance and regulatory requirements. Organizations must adhere to various laws and regulations that mandate specific security and privacy practices. For example, the Health Insurance Portability and Accountability Act (HIPAA) requires healthcare organizations to protect patient information, while the General Data Protection Regulation (GDPR) imposes strict data protection requirements on organizations handling the personal data of European Union (EU) citizens.

Compliance with these regulations requires organizations to implement robust governance frameworks that include regular audits and assessments. These audits ensure that security and privacy controls are effective and that the organization remains compliant with applicable laws.

Governance plays a crucial role in ensuring the security and privacy of information within an organization. Effective governance frameworks align security and privacy efforts with organizational objectives, manage risks, and ensure compliance with regulatory requirements. By adopting best practices in security governance, information governance, and data governance, organizations can protect their information assets and maintain the trust of their stakeholders.

Key Regulations and Standards

In the rapidly evolving landscape of information security and privacy, understanding key regulations and standards is crucial for professionals tasked with safeguarding data. These regulations and standards provide a framework for ensuring compliance and protecting sensitive information. This section will provide an overview of some of the most critical regulations and standards, including HIPAA, the European Union GDPR, and other significant laws.

Health Insurance Portability and Accountability Act

HIPAA is a significant regulation in the United States that governs the handling of protected health information (PHI). Enacted in 1996, HIPAA aims to improve the efficiency and effectiveness of the healthcare system by standardizing the electronic exchange of administrative and financial data. HIPAA includes several key provisions:

- **Privacy rule:** Establishes national standards for the protection of PHI, setting limits on the use and disclosure of such information without patient authorization. It grants patients' rights over their health information, including rights to examine and obtain a copy of their health records and request corrections.

- **Security rule:** Specifies a series of administrative, physical, and technical safeguards to ensure the confidentiality, integrity, and availability of electronic protected health information (ePHI). These safeguards include access controls, audit controls, integrity controls, and transmission security.
- **Breach notification rule:** Requires covered entities and their business associates to provide notification following a breach of unsecured PHI. The rule outlines the steps that must be taken to notify affected individuals, the Secretary of Health and Human Services, and, in certain circumstances, the media.
- **Enforcement rule:** Provides guidelines for investigations into HIPAA violations and sets forth the penalties for noncompliance, which can include substantial fines and corrective action plans.

Compliance with HIPAA is mandatory for healthcare providers, health plans, and healthcare clearinghouses as well as their business associates. Ensuring compliance involves implementing robust security measures, conducting regular risk assessments, and maintaining comprehensive documentation of policies and procedures.

European Union General Data Protection Regulation

The GDPR is a comprehensive data protection law that came into effect on May 25, 2018. It applies to all organizations that process the personal data of EU residents, regardless of the organization's location. The GDPR aims to harmonize data protection laws across the EU, enhance individuals' privacy rights, and increase accountability for organizations handling personal data. Key provisions of the GDPR include:

- **Data protection principles:** The GDPR outlines several principles for processing personal data, including lawfulness, fairness, transparency, purpose limitation, data minimization, accuracy, storage limitation, integrity, and confidentiality.
- **Data subject rights:** The regulation grants individuals a range of rights over their personal data, including the right to access, rectify, erase, restrict processing, require data portability, and object to processing. Organizations must have processes in place to respond to data subject requests within specified time frames.
- **Consent:** The GDPR sets strict requirements for obtaining valid consent from data subjects. Consent must be freely given, specific, informed, and unambiguous, with a clear affirmative action indicating agreement.

- **Data protection impact assessments (DPIAs):** Organizations must conduct DPIAs for processing activities that are likely to result in a high risk to individuals' rights and freedoms. DPIAs help identify and mitigate privacy risks.
- **Data breach notification:** The GDPR mandates that organizations report certain types of data breaches to the relevant supervisory authority within 72 hours of becoming aware of the breach. In cases where the breach is likely to result in a high risk to individuals, affected data subjects must also be informed.
- **Accountability and governance:** The regulation emphasizes the importance of accountability, requiring organizations to implement appropriate technical and organizational measures to ensure and demonstrate compliance. This includes maintaining records of processing activities, appointing a data protection officer (DPO) where necessary, and adhering to approved codes of conduct and certification mechanisms.

Noncompliance with the GDPR can result in significant fines, with penalties reaching up to €20 million or 4 percent of the organization's annual global turnover, whichever is higher. Organizations must take proactive steps to ensure compliance, including conducting regular audits, providing staff training, and integrating privacy by design and by default into their operations.

Other Significant Regulations and Standards

In addition to HIPAA and GDPR, several other regulations and standards play a vital role in shaping information security and privacy practices. These include the following:

- **Payment Card Industry Data Security Standard (PCI DSS):** Provides guidelines for securing payment card transactions and protecting cardholder data. It applies to all entities that process, store, or transmit credit card information.
- **Gramm–Leach–Bliley Act (GLBA):** Requires financial institutions to implement measures to protect the security and confidentiality of customer information. It mandates the development of a comprehensive information security program and the designation of an individual responsible for overseeing the program.
- **Sarbanes–Oxley Act (SOX):** Applies to U.S. publicly traded companies and establishes requirements for financial reporting and internal controls. It includes provisions for the security and integrity of financial data and the systems that process this data.

- **Family Educational Rights and Privacy Act (FERPA):** Protects the privacy of student education records and applies to educational institutions receiving federal funding. It grants students and their parents specific rights regarding access to and control over educational records.
- **State data breach notification laws:** Various U.S. states have enacted laws requiring organizations to notify individuals in the event of a data breach. These laws specify the circumstances under which notifications must be made and the information that must be included in the notifications.

Understanding and complying with these regulations and standards is essential for information security and privacy professionals. Organizations must stay informed about the evolving regulatory landscape and implement robust compliance programs to protect sensitive information and mitigate risks.

Regulatory Compliance

Regulatory compliance is a critical aspect of information security and privacy management, ensuring that organizations adhere to the laws, regulations, and standards set by governing bodies. Compliance is not only about avoiding penalties but also about fostering trust with customers and stakeholders by demonstrating a commitment to protecting sensitive information.

Understanding Compliance

Compliance involves conforming to a set of rules, whether they are internal policies or external legal requirements. These rules can be imposed by various entities, including governmental bodies, industry groups, and contractual obligations. The complexity of compliance is amplified by the overlapping and sometimes conflicting requirements of different jurisdictions and regulatory frameworks.

Organizations must navigate a myriad of compliance requirements, such as the GDPR in the European Union, HIPAA in the United States, and the California Consumer Privacy Act (CCPA). Each of these regulations imposes specific obligations on organizations regarding the collection, storage, processing, and sharing of personal data.

Categories of Laws

In the United States, three main categories of laws play a role in the legal system, and each category addresses different types of violations and imposes varying penalties:

- **Criminal law:** Includes laws that prohibit actions such as hacking, fraud, and identity theft. Violations can result in severe penalties, including imprisonment and fines.
- **Civil law:** Deals with disputes between individuals or organizations, such as breaches of contract or negligence. Penalties typically involve monetary compensation.
- **Administrative law:** Governs the activities of administrative agencies, such as the Federal Trade Commission (FTC). Violations can lead to regulatory actions, including fines and sanctions.

Legal and Regulatory Requirements

Organizations must identify and understand the legal and regulatory requirements applicable to their operations. This involves staying informed about changes in laws and regulations and ensuring that internal policies and procedures are updated accordingly. Key areas of focus include:

- **Cybercrimes and data breaches:** Laws addressing cybercrimes and data breaches require organizations to implement measures to prevent unauthorized access and respond appropriately when breaches occur.
- **Licensing and intellectual property:** Compliance with intellectual property laws ensures that organizations respect the rights of creators and avoid legal disputes.
- **Import/export controls:** Regulations governing the transfer of technology and data across borders must be adhered to, especially in the context of international operations.
- **Transborder data flow:** Organizations must comply with laws regulating the transfer of personal data between countries, such as the GDPR's restrictions on data transfers outside the EU.
- **Privacy requirements:** Laws like the GDPR and CCPA impose stringent requirements on how organizations handle personal data, emphasizing transparency, consent, and data subject rights.

Compliance Programs

A robust compliance program is essential for managing regulatory requirements effectively. Such a program typically includes the following components:

- **Policies and procedures:** Clear policies and procedures that outline the organization's approach to compliance and provide guidance to employees.
- **Training and awareness:** Regular training programs to ensure that employees understand their compliance obligations and the importance of adhering to policies.
- **Monitoring and auditing:** Ongoing monitoring and periodic audits to assess compliance with policies and regulations, identify gaps, and implement corrective actions.
- **Reporting and documentation:** Maintaining comprehensive records of compliance activities and incidents to demonstrate adherence to regulatory requirements and facilitate audits.

Compliance Risk

Compliance risk arises when an organization fails to meet its legal or regulatory obligations, potentially resulting in penalties, fines, and reputational damage. Managing compliance risk involves:

- **Risk assessment:** Identifying and assessing the risks associated with noncompliance, including the likelihood and impact of potential violations.
- **Risk mitigation:** Implementing controls and measures to reduce the likelihood of noncompliance and mitigate the impact of any incidents.
- **Continuous improvement:** Regularly reviewing and updating compliance programs to address emerging risks and changes in the regulatory landscape.

Integrating Compliance into Governance

Effective governance integrates compliance into the broader framework of organizational management. This involves aligning compliance efforts with the organization's strategic objectives and ensuring that senior leadership is committed to supporting compliance initiatives. Key steps include:

- **Establishing a governance framework:** Developing a comprehensive framework that outlines the roles, responsibilities, and processes for managing compliance.
- **Engaging stakeholders:** Involving key stakeholders, including senior leadership, in the development and implementation of compliance programs.

- **Monitoring and reporting:** Establishing mechanisms for monitoring compliance activities and reporting on compliance status to senior leadership and other stakeholders.

Regulatory compliance is a multifaceted and dynamic challenge that requires a proactive and integrated approach. By understanding the legal landscape, implementing robust compliance programs, and integrating compliance into governance frameworks, organizations can effectively manage compliance risks and safeguard their operations against legal and regulatory pitfalls.

Building and Managing a Risk Management Framework

A robust risk management framework is essential for any organization aiming to protect its information assets and ensure the confidentiality, integrity, and availability of its data. This section provides an overview of the key concepts and processes involved in building and managing a risk management framework.

Understanding and Applying Risk Management Concepts

Risk management is a comprehensive process that involves identifying potential threats to an organization's assets, evaluating the likelihood and impact of those threats, and implementing measures to mitigate or manage the risks. The primary goal is to reduce risks to an acceptable level, which varies depending on the organization's risk appetite, asset value, and available resources.

Key Components of Risk Management

There are three major components to risk management.

- **Risk assessment (also called risk analysis):** This involves identifying and evaluating risks by examining the environment for potential threats and vulnerabilities. A threat is any event that could negatively impact the confidentiality, integrity, or availability of information, while a vulnerability is a weakness that could be exploited by a threat. Risk exists at the intersection of a threat and a vulnerability.

- **Risk response:** After assessing risks, organizations must decide how to address them. This includes evaluating countermeasures and security controls, performing cost/benefit analyses, and selecting appropriate responses. The goal is to implement measures that effectively reduce risk to an acceptable level.
- **Risk awareness:** Increasing knowledge of risks within the organization is crucial. This involves understanding the value of assets, identifying existing threats, and knowing the implemented responses to those threats. Risk awareness helps in fostering a security-conscious culture.

Analyzing Risk

Risk analysis is a systematic approach to understanding the nature and level of risks faced by an organization. It involves several steps:

- **Identifying risks:** Organizations must first identify potential risks. This includes recognizing threats such as natural disasters, cyberattacks, and human errors, and understanding how these threats could exploit vulnerabilities.
- **Evaluating risks:** Once risks are identified, they must be evaluated in terms of their likelihood and potential impact. This involves estimating the probability of a threat occurring and the severity of its consequences. This step helps prioritize risks based on their criticality.
- **Assessing risks:** Various methods can be used for risk assessment, including qualitative, quantitative, and hybrid approaches. Qualitative methods involve subjective evaluations of risk, while quantitative methods use numerical data and statistical analysis. Hybrid methods combine both approaches for a more comprehensive assessment.

Risk Treatment and Response

After assessing and analyzing risks, organizations must develop strategies to manage them. This involves selecting and implementing appropriate risk treatment options.

- **Avoidance:** Eliminating the risk by discontinuing the activity that generates it.
- **Mitigation:** Reducing the likelihood or impact of the risk through controls and safeguards.
- **Transfer:** Shifting the risk to another party, such as through insurance or outsourcing.

- **Acceptance:** Acknowledging the risk and deciding to accept it without further action, typically when the cost of mitigation exceeds the potential impact.
- **Risk and control ownership:** Assigning responsibility for managing specific risks and implementing controls is crucial. This ensures accountability and effective risk management.
- **Risk monitoring and reporting:** Monitoring risks and controls continuously is necessary to ensure they remain effective. Regular reporting to stakeholders helps in making informed decisions and maintaining transparency.
- **Risk communication:** Communicating risks and risk management effectively is essential for organizational alignment and support. This includes regular updates to senior management and other stakeholders about the status of risks and the effectiveness of controls.

Integrating Risk Management into Business Processes

Successful risk management requires integration into the organization's overall business processes. This involves:

- **Aligning risk management with business objectives:** Risk management activities should support the organization's strategic goals and objectives. This alignment ensures that risk management efforts contribute to the overall success of the organization.
- **Embedding risk management in corporate governance:** Risk management should be a core component of the organization's governance framework. This includes establishing policies, procedures, and guidelines that support risk management activities.
- **Continuous improvement:** Risk management is an ongoing process that requires regular review and improvement. Organizations should continuously assess their risk management practices and make necessary adjustments to address emerging threats and changing business environments.

By understanding and applying these risk management concepts, organizations can build and manage an effective risk management framework that protects their information assets and supports their strategic objectives. This framework not only helps in mitigating risks but also enhances the organization's resilience and ability to respond to potential threats.

Managing Third-Party Risks and Vendor Assessments

In the realm of information security and privacy, managing third-party risks and conducting vendor assessments are critical components of a comprehensive risk management strategy. Organizations today often rely on a complex web of third-party vendors, consultants, and contractors to deliver essential services and products. This interconnectedness introduces significant risks that must be managed effectively to safeguard sensitive information and maintain operational integrity.

Third-Party Governance

Third-party governance involves establishing and maintaining a framework to manage the risks associated with third-party relationships. This governance framework should align with the organization's overall security strategy and business objectives. It typically includes policies, procedures, and standards that define the expectations and requirements for third-party interactions.

Effective third-party governance starts with thorough due diligence during the selection process. Organizations must assess potential vendors' security practices, financial stability, and compliance with relevant regulations. This assessment helps identify any inherent risks associated with the third party and determines their suitability for the organization's needs.

Once a third party is selected, organizations should formalize the relationship through comprehensive contracts and service-level agreements (SLAs). These documents should clearly outline the security requirements, performance expectations, and consequences for noncompliance. SLAs are particularly important as they provide a mechanism for enforcing security standards and ensuring that third parties meet their obligations.

Vendor, Consultant, and Contractor Agreements and Controls

Vendor, consultant, and contractor agreements and controls are essential tools for managing third-party risks. These agreements should specify the levels of performance, compensation, and penalties for noncompliance. They should also include provisions for regular security assessments and audits to ensure ongoing compliance with security requirements.

SLAs play a crucial role in managing third-party risks. SLAs should include specific security metrics and performance indicators that are regularly monitored and reported. For example, an SLA might stipulate that a critical data circuit must have a maximum downtime of 15 minutes, with financial penalties for any breaches of this threshold. By clearly defining these expectations, organizations can mitigate the risks associated with third-party services and ensure that they receive the level of service required to maintain their security posture.

Outsourcing, or the use of external third parties to perform tasks or operations, is a common practice that can introduce additional risks. While outsourcing can be a cost-effective solution, it expands the organization's attack surface and increases the potential for vulnerabilities. Therefore, it is essential to evaluate the security implications of outsourcing arrangements and implement appropriate controls to manage these risks.

Third-Party Relationships

Managing third-party relationships involves continuous monitoring and assessment to ensure that third parties comply with security requirements and do not introduce new risks. This process includes regular security assessments, audits, and reviews of third-party performance against established SLAs and contractual obligations.

Organizations should establish a risk management framework that integrates third-party risk management into the overall enterprise risk management (ERM) program. This framework should include processes for identifying, assessing, and mitigating risks associated with third-party relationships. It should also define the roles and responsibilities of internal stakeholders involved in managing third-party risks.

Effective third-party risk management requires collaboration and communication between the organization and its third parties. Organizations should foster a culture of security awareness and encourage third parties to adopt best practices and continuous improvement in their security posture. This collaborative approach helps ensure that third parties remain aligned with the organization's security objectives and can respond effectively to emerging threats.

Risk Assessment and Monitoring

Risk assessment is a critical component of managing third-party risks. Organizations should conduct thorough risk assessments to identify potential threats and vulnerabilities associated with third-party relationships. These assessments should consider factors such as the sensitivity of the data being shared, the criticality of the services provided, and the third party's security practices and history.

Once risks are identified, organizations must implement appropriate risk mitigation strategies. This may include additional security controls, increased monitoring, or even reconsidering the relationship with the third party. Continuous monitoring is essential to ensure that third parties maintain compliance with security requirements and that any changes in their security posture are promptly addressed.

Regular audits and assessments help organizations verify that third parties adhere to contractual obligations and SLAs. These audits should be conducted by independent third parties to ensure objectivity and thoroughness. The results of these audits should be used to inform risk management decisions and drive continuous improvement in third-party risk management practices.

Managing third-party risks and conducting vendor assessments are vital components of a robust information security and privacy program. By establishing a comprehensive third-party governance framework, formalizing relationships through detailed agreements, and continuously monitoring third-party performance, organizations can effectively mitigate the risks associated with third-party relationships. This proactive approach helps ensure that third parties contribute to, rather than detract from, the organization's overall security posture.

CHAPTER 3

Security Architecture and Design

In today's rapidly evolving digital landscape, the importance of robust security architecture and design cannot be overstated. As cyber threats become increasingly sophisticated, organizations must adopt comprehensive strategies to protect their information systems and sensitive data. This chapter delves into the core principles and practices that form the foundation of secure system design, providing you with the knowledge necessary to build and maintain resilient security infrastructures. By understanding and implementing these essential concepts, you can significantly enhance your organization's defenses against potential breaches and ensure the ongoing integrity, confidentiality, and availability of critical information assets.

This chapter serves as a vital resource for security professionals seeking to deepen their understanding of security architecture and design. It covers a range of topics, from secure design principles and foundational security operations concepts to advanced techniques for ensuring system resilience and high availability. You will gain insights into the fundamental security models, protection mechanisms, and personnel security measures that are crucial for safeguarding modern information systems. By the end of this chapter, you will be equipped with practical knowledge and actionable strategies to effectively design, implement, and manage secure information systems within your organization.

Principles of Secure Design

Security is a critical consideration at every stage of a system's development. From the initial planning phases through to deployment and maintenance, secure design principles must be integrated to ensure robust and resilient systems.

The principles of secure design are foundational to developing robust, resilient, and secure systems. By prioritizing security from the outset and integrating these principles throughout the development process, organizations can reduce the risk of vulnerabilities, protect sensitive data, and ensure compliance with regulatory requirements. Security is not a one-time effort but an ongoing commitment that must be maintained throughout the system's life cycle.

This section provides an overview of essential principles that guide the secure design of systems and applications, ensuring that security is not an afterthought but a fundamental component of the development process.

Secure Defaults

Secure defaults refer to the principle that systems should be secure out of the box. Default configurations should prioritize security, requiring users to explicitly opt in to less secure settings if necessary. This reduces the risk of vulnerabilities being introduced through misconfiguration or oversight.

Fail Securely

Failing securely means that when a system encounters an error or failure, it should do so in a way that maintains security. This principle ensures that even in the event of a malfunction, the system does not expose sensitive data or provide an attack vector for malicious actors. For example, a secure failure might involve shutting down a system or application in a controlled manner or reverting to a known secure state.

Keep It Simple and Small

Complex systems are more challenging to secure due to the increased potential for vulnerabilities and errors. The principle of keeping it simple and small advocates for minimalism in design, reducing complexity to make systems easier to understand, manage, and secure. This approach limits the attack surface and simplifies the identification and mitigation of security issues.

Zero Trust or Trust but Verify

The zero trust model operates on the assumption that threats can exist both inside and outside the network. Therefore, no entity, whether internal or external, is trusted by default. Instead, every request for access must be verified, authenticated, and authorized. This principle contrasts with the traditional "trust but verify" approach, which assumes that internal entities are trustworthy. Zero trust emphasizes continuous monitoring and validation of all interactions.

Privacy by Design

Privacy by design integrates privacy considerations into the development process from the outset. This principle ensures that privacy is a default setting and that personal data is protected throughout the system's life cycle. By embedding privacy into the design, developers can prevent data breaches and ensure compliance with privacy regulations.

Secure Access Service Edge (SASE)

Secure Access Service Edge (SASE) is a framework that combines network security functions with wide area network (WAN) capabilities to support the dynamic secure access needs of organizations. SASE principles advocate for the convergence of security and networking services into a single, cloud-delivered solution, enhancing security while simplifying management.

Shared Responsibility

Shared responsibility recognizes that security is a collective effort involving multiple stakeholders, including developers, administrators, users, and third-party providers. Each party has a role to play in maintaining security, and responsibilities must be clearly defined and communicated. This principle ensures that security is not siloed but is a shared objective across the organization.

Engineering Processes Using Secure Design Principles

Incorporating secure design principles into engineering processes involves a structured approach to integrating security at every stage of development. This includes threat modeling, defense in depth, and adhering to best practices for secure coding and system configuration. By embedding security into the engineering process, organizations can proactively address potential vulnerabilities and build more resilient systems.

Security Operations Foundations

Security operations are fundamental to safeguarding an organization's assets, including information, systems, devices, facilities, and applications. These practices help identify threats and vulnerabilities and implement controls to mitigate risks to these assets. The concept of due care and due diligence is central to security operations, emphasizing the responsibility of senior management to protect the organization's assets continuously. Implementing common security operations practices and conducting periodic security audits and reviews demonstrate due care and due diligence, reducing liability when losses occur.

Security operations are the backbone of an organization's security posture, encompassing a wide range of practices and principles designed to protect assets and reduce risks. By implementing foundational security operations concepts such as need-to-know, least privilege, segregation of duties, privileged account management, job rotation, SLAs, media management, patch and vulnerability management, change management, and personnel safety, organizations can create a robust security framework that safeguards their assets and maintains operational integrity. The next few sections discuss these and other security operations foundations.

Need-to-Know and Least Privilege

Two critical principles in any secure IT environment are need-to-know and least privilege. These principles limit access to valuable assets, ensuring that individuals only have access to the information necessary for their roles. While often used interchangeably, they are distinct concepts. Need-to-know restricts access to information based on the necessity for performing specific tasks, while least privilege ensures individuals have the minimum level of access required to perform their job functions.

Segregation of Duties

Segregation of duties (SoD) is a crucial control to prevent fraud and errors by dividing responsibilities among different individuals or groups. This principle ensures that no single person has control over all aspects of any critical process, reducing the risk of unauthorized actions. Implementing SoD involves separating tasks such as authorization, custody, and record-keeping to create checks and balances within the organization.

Privileged Account Management

Managing privileged accounts is essential to prevent misuse of elevated access rights. Privileged accounts, such as those belonging to system administrators, have significant control over IT systems and data. Effective privileged account management involves monitoring and controlling the use of these accounts, ensuring that they are only used when necessary and that their activities are logged and reviewed regularly.

Job Rotation

Job rotation is a strategy to reduce the risk of fraud and enhance security by periodically moving employees between different roles. This practice helps prevent individuals from becoming too comfortable in a single position, where they might exploit their knowledge for malicious purposes. Job rotation also promotes cross-training, ensuring that multiple employees are familiar with various roles and responsibilities, which can be beneficial in case of staff absences or turnover.

Service-Level Agreements

SLAs are contracts between service providers and clients that define the expected level of service, including security requirements. SLAs should include specific metrics for performance, availability, and security, ensuring that service providers meet the organization's security standards. Regularly reviewing and updating SLAs helps maintain the desired level of security and performance.

Media Management and Protection

Proper management and protection of media, such as storage devices and backup tapes, are critical to prevent unauthorized access and data breaches. Media management involves tracking and controlling the movement of media, while media protection techniques include encryption, secure storage, and secure disposal. Ensuring that data at rest and data in transit are protected is essential for maintaining the confidentiality, integrity, and availability of information.

Patch and Vulnerability Management

Effective patch and vulnerability management is vital to protect systems from known vulnerabilities and exploits. This process involves regularly scanning for vulnerabilities, applying patches and updates promptly, and verifying that the patches are effective. A robust patch management process helps minimize the risk of security breaches and ensures that systems remain secure and up to date.

Change Management

Change management processes are essential to prevent outages and security incidents caused by unauthorized or poorly executed changes. A formal change management process involves documenting, reviewing, and approving changes before implementation. This process ensures that changes are tested and evaluated for potential security impacts, reducing the risk of disruptions and vulnerabilities.

Personnel Safety and Security

Addressing personnel safety and security concerns is a critical aspect of security operations. This includes ensuring the safety of employees during travel, providing security training and awareness programs, and preparing for emergency situations. Security training should cover topics such as insider threats, social media impacts, and two-factor authentication (2FA) fatigue. Additionally, organizations should have emergency management plans in place to handle crises and ensure the safety of their personnel.

Ensuring Confidentiality, Integrity, and Availability

Ensuring the CIA of information is a core objective in the field of information security. These three principles are often referred to as the CIA triad and form the foundation upon which security policies and practices are built. By implementing the appropriate techniques and following established security models, organizations can protect their data from unauthorized access or alteration and ensure it is available when needed. Understanding and applying these principles is fundamental for any information security professional. The following sections delve into each of these principles and the techniques used to ensure them.

Confidentiality

Confidentiality is about ensuring that information is accessible only to those authorized to have access. It is the principle that protects data from unauthorized disclosure. Techniques for ensuring confidentiality include:

- **Encryption:** Converting information into a code to prevent unauthorized access. Encryption can be applied to data at rest, in transit, and in use.

- **Access controls:** Implementing strict access control mechanisms ensures that only authorized users can access specific data. This includes the use of authentication methods like passwords, biometrics, and multifactor authentication.
- **Data classification:** Classifying data based on its sensitivity and implementing appropriate handling procedures helps in protecting confidential information.
- **Training and awareness:** Educating employees about the importance of confidentiality and the measures they need to take to protect sensitive information is crucial.

Integrity

Integrity refers to the accuracy and completeness of data. It ensures that information is not altered in an unauthorized manner. Techniques for ensuring integrity include:

- **Hashing:** Generates a fixed-size numerical representation—called a *hash value*—from data, which can be used to verify the data's integrity. If the data is altered, the hash value will change.
- **Digital signature:** Provides a way to verify the authenticity and integrity of a message, software, or digital document.
- **Checksums and error-detection codes:** Help in detecting accidental changes to raw data.
- **Version control:** Keeps track of changes to data and maintains a history of modifications, which helps in ensuring integrity.

Availability

Availability ensures that information and resources are accessible to authorized users when needed. Techniques for ensuring availability include:

- **Redundant systems:** Implementing redundant systems and components ensures that there is no single point of failure. This includes using backup power supplies, redundant network connections, and failover systems.
- **Regular backups:** Backing up data regularly ensures that it can be restored in the event of data loss or corruption.
- **Disaster recovery plans:** Having a comprehensive disaster recovery plan helps in quickly restoring operations after a disruption.
- **Maintenance and updates:** Maintaining and updating systems regularly helps in preventing failures and ensuring smooth operation.

CIA Triad in Practice

In practice, ensuring the CIA of information requires a combination of these techniques. For example, an organization might use encryption to protect the confidentiality of data, hashing to ensure its integrity, and redundant systems to maintain its availability. Additionally, security policies and procedures must be in place to guide the implementation and management of these techniques.

Security Models

Several security models provide frameworks for implementing the CIA principles. Consider these examples:

- **Bell–LaPadula model:** Focuses on maintaining the confidentiality of data by enforcing access controls.
- **Biba model:** Emphasizes data integrity by preventing unauthorized data modification.
- **Clark–Wilson model:** Ensures both integrity and confidentiality through well-formed transactions and separation of duties.

The next section provides more information on these and other security models.

Understanding Security Models

Security models provide structured frameworks to implement and enforce security policies within an organization. These models help manage, enforce, and maintain security across various systems and environments, ensuring robust protection against threats and vulnerabilities.

Understanding these fundamental security models is crucial for designing and implementing effective security policies and controls. Each model offers unique principles and rules that address different aspects of security, such as confidentiality, integrity, and access control. By leveraging these models, security professionals can create robust and comprehensive security architectures that protect against a wide range of threats and vulnerabilities.

Bell–LaPadula Model

The Bell–LaPadula (BLP) model focuses on maintaining the confidentiality of data. It is based on three primary rules:

- **Simple security property (no read up):** Subjects (users or processes) at a given security level cannot read data at a higher security level.
- **Star (*) security property (no write down):** Subjects at a given security level cannot write data to a lower security level.
- **Discretionary security property:** The system uses an access matrix to enforce discretionary access control, allowing users to control access to their own data based on a need-to-know basis.

The BLP model is widely used in military and government systems where the protection of classified information is paramount.

Biba Model

The Biba model is designed to maintain data integrity. It operates on the principle that data should not be corrupted by unauthorized modifications. The model includes three main rules:

- **Simple integrity property (no write up):** Subjects cannot write data to a higher integrity level.
- **Star (*) integrity property (no read down):** Subjects cannot read data from a lower integrity level.
- **Invocation property:** Subjects at a lower integrity level cannot invoke (request) services from subjects at a higher integrity level.

The Biba model is useful in environments where data integrity is more critical than confidentiality, such as financial systems and healthcare applications.

Clark–Wilson Model

The Clark–Wilson model emphasizes both data integrity and well-formed transactions. It uses a set of rules and certification processes to ensure that data is manipulated in a consistent and controlled manner. The key components of the Clark–Wilson model include:

- **Well-formed transactions:** Ensuring that data transformations follow predefined rules.

- **Separation of duties:** Dividing tasks and privileges among multiple users to prevent fraud and errors.
- **Access control triplet:** A subject (user), a program (or transformation procedure), and an object (data item). Access is mediated through the program, ensuring that only authorized operations are performed on the data.

This model is particularly effective in commercial applications where integrity and consistency of transactions are crucial.

Brewer–Nash Model

The Brewer–Nash model is designed to prevent conflicts of interest. It ensures that users cannot access conflicting sets of data, which could lead to unethical behavior or misuse of information. The model is commonly used in financial and consulting firms where maintaining client confidentiality and avoiding conflicts of interest are essential.

Harrison–Ruzzo–Ullman (HRU) Model

The HRU model focuses on access control and the management of privileges. It defines a set of rules for creating, deleting, and managing access rights to objects. The HRU model provides a framework for understanding how permissions can be granted and revoked in a system, making it useful for designing robust access control mechanisms.

Graham–Denning Model

The Graham–Denning model outlines a set of eight primitive operations for managing subjects, objects, and access rights. These operations include creating and deleting subjects and objects, and granting and revoking access rights. The model provides a comprehensive approach to access control and is useful for understanding the dynamics of permissions and privileges in a system.

Take–Grant Model

The take–grant model is a simplified approach to understanding how permissions can be transferred between subjects. It defines two primary operations:

- **Take:** Allows a subject to take permissions from another subject.
- **Grant:** Allows a subject to grant permissions to another subject.

This model helps in analyzing the flow of permissions and understanding potential security risks associated with the transfer of access rights.

Lattice-Based Model

The lattice-based model uses a mathematical framework to define security levels and the relationships between them. It is based on the concept of a lattice, where each point represents a security level, and the paths between points define the allowed access relationships. This model is useful for implementing complex security policies that require fine-grained control over access rights.

Common Criteria

The Common Criteria (CC) is an international standard for evaluating and certifying the security of IT products and systems. It provides a framework for specifying security requirements and assessing the security features of products. The CC helps organizations ensure that their systems meet defined security standards and provides a basis for trust in the security of evaluated products.

Implementing Personnel Security

Personnel security is a critical aspect of any organization's overall security strategy. It encompasses a range of policies, procedures, and practices designed to protect the organization from threats posed by its own employees, contractors, and other insiders. This section discusses the importance of personnel security, the key components of an effective personnel security program, and the role of social engineering in compromising personnel security.

Importance of Personnel Security

Humans are often considered the weakest link in any security solution. Regardless of the physical or logical controls in place, individuals can find ways to bypass, subvert, or disable them. Therefore, it is essential to consider the human element when designing and deploying security solutions. Properly trained and motivated personnel can become key security assets, protecting both themselves and the organization.

Personnel security is crucial at all stages of a security solution's development, deployment, and ongoing management. It is important to evaluate the impact that users, designers, programmers, developers, managers, vendors, consultants, and implementers have on the security process. By addressing the human factor, organizations can mitigate risks and enhance their overall security posture.

Key Components of Personnel Security

Implementing effective personnel security measures is essential for protecting an organization from internal and external threats. By addressing the human factor, providing comprehensive training, and fostering a security-conscious culture, organizations can significantly enhance their overall security posture. Here are the key components of an effective personnel security program:

- **Candidate screening and hiring:** The first step in personnel security is thorough candidate screening and hiring processes. This includes background checks, reference checks, and verifying qualifications and experience. By ensuring that only trustworthy individuals are hired, organizations can reduce the risk of insider threats.
- **Employment agreements and policy-driven requirements:** Employment agreements should clearly outline the organization's security policies and expectations. Employees should be required to sign agreements that acknowledge their understanding and acceptance of these policies. This helps to ensure that employees are aware of their responsibilities and the consequences of noncompliance.
- **Onboarding, transfers, and termination processes:** Effective onboarding processes help to integrate new employees into the organization and familiarize them with security policies and procedures. Similarly, transfers and terminations should be managed carefully to ensure that access to sensitive information is appropriately granted or revoked. This includes deactivating accounts, retrieving company assets, and conducting exit interviews to identify any potential security concerns.
- **Vendor, consultant, and contractor agreements and controls:** Organizations must also consider the security of third-party vendors, consultants, and contractors. Agreements with these external parties should include security requirements and expectations. Regular assessments and audits can help ensure that third-party partners comply with the organization's security policies.
- **Security awareness, education, and training programs:** Continuous education and training are essential to maintaining a security-aware workforce. Training programs should cover a range of topics, including social engineering, phishing, and emerging technologies. By keeping employees informed about the latest threats and best practices, organizations can reduce the risk of security breaches.

- **Continuous monitoring and improvement:** Regular monitoring and assessment of personnel security policies and procedures are crucial for identifying areas of improvement. Organizations should implement continuous improvement processes to ensure that their security measures remain effective and up to date.

Social Engineering

Social engineering is a significant threat to personnel security. It involves manipulating individuals into divulging confidential information or performing actions that compromise security. Social engineers exploit human psychology to gain unauthorized access to systems, data, or facilities.

Types of Social Engineering Attacks There are many types of social engineering exploits, but the following dozen are the most common:

- **Phishing:** Attackers send fraudulent emails or messages that appear to come from legitimate sources, tricking recipients into revealing sensitive information or clicking on malicious links.
- **Spear phishing:** A more targeted form of phishing where the message is crafted and directed specifically to a group of individuals, often using information from stolen customer databases to make the communication appear legitimate.
- **Whaling:** A form of spear phishing that targets high-value individuals, such as CEOs or other C-level executives, requiring more research and planning to fool the victim.
- **Spam:** Unsolicited and undesired email that can carry malicious content or social engineering attacks, or simply waste time and resources.
- **Shoulder surfing:** Observing someone's screen or keyboard to gain information, often prevented by positioning screens away from public view and using screen filters.
- **Invoice scams:** Presenting false invoices to steal funds, often accompanied by urgent requests for payment to pressure the victim.
- **Hoax:** A false warning or alert designed to cause unnecessary panic or prompt users to take harmful actions.
- **Impersonation and masquerading:** Pretending to be someone else to gain unauthorized access to information or systems, often using stolen credentials.
- **Tailgating:** Gaining physical access to restricted areas by following an authorized person without their knowledge or permission.

- **Piggybacking:** A form of tailgating where an unauthorized entity gains access to a facility under the authorization of a valid worker by tricking the victim into providing consent.
- **Dumpster diving:** Searching through trash to find sensitive information that has not been properly disposed of, highlighting the importance of secure disposal practices.
- **Typosquatting:** Registering domain names that are similar to legitimate ones, hoping that users will mistype the URL and be directed to a malicious site.

Recognizing and Preventing Social Engineering Attacks

To help recognize and prevent social engineering attacks, your organization should implement the following:

- **Awareness training:** Educate employees about the various types of social engineering attacks and how to recognize them. Training should include real-world examples and practical exercises to reinforce learning.
- **Verification procedures:** Implement procedures for verifying the identity of individuals requesting sensitive information or access. This may include requiring multiple forms of identification or using secure communication channels.
- **Reporting mechanisms:** Encourage employees to report suspicious activities or potential social engineering attempts. Establish clear reporting procedures and ensure that employees feel comfortable coming forward with concerns.
- **Regular testing:** Conduct regular social engineering tests, such as simulated phishing attacks, to assess employee awareness and response. Use the results to identify areas for improvement and provide additional training as needed.

Applying Protection Mechanisms

In the realm of information security, applying protection mechanisms is fundamental to safeguarding systems and data from a myriad of threats. Protection mechanisms are the tools and strategies used to defend against vulnerabilities and attacks, ensuring the integrity, confidentiality, and availability of information. These mechanisms provide a layered approach to security, addressing both software and hardware aspects to protect against a wide range of threats. By integrating these protection mechanisms into the design and operation of systems, security professionals can enhance the overall security posture and resilience of their organizations.

This section provides an overview of essential security protection mechanisms that are critical for professionals in the field of security architecture and design. Specifically, this section will cover process isolation, hardware segmentation, root of trust, and system security policy.

Process Isolation

Process isolation is a fundamental security mechanism that ensures individual processes operate in separate memory spaces, preventing them from interfering with each other. This isolation is crucial for maintaining system stability and security. By confining each process to its own allocated memory, the system can prevent a malfunctioning or malicious process from affecting others, thereby reducing the risk of system-wide failures or breaches.

Process isolation is typically implemented through the operating system, which enforces boundaries around each process. This isolation allows processes to run independently, ensuring that any behavior, whether normal or malicious, will only impact the isolated process. Modern operating systems often use virtual machines to achieve process isolation, presenting each process with a virtual environment that mimics having sole access to the system's resources. This approach not only simplifies programming but also enhances security by protecting processes from each other.

Hardware Segmentation

Hardware segmentation is similar to process isolation but relies on physical hardware controls rather than software-based mechanisms. This method is used to enforce security requirements by physically separating resources and processes at the hardware level. Hardware segmentation is particularly valuable in high-security environments, such as national security applications, where the sensitivity of the information justifies the additional cost and complexity.

By using dedicated hardware components to enforce segmentation, systems can achieve a higher level of security. These hardware controls prevent unauthorized access to information belonging to different processes or security levels, ensuring that sensitive data remains protected. Although hardware segmentation is less common in commercial environments due to its expense, it provides an extra layer of security for critical applications.

Root of Trust

The root of trust (RoT) is a foundational concept in cybersecurity and cryptographic systems. It represents the starting point or anchor of a security chain, providing a secure and trustworthy foundation for various security functions. The RoT is critical for establishing and verifying the integrity, authenticity, and confidentiality of digital information within a system.

A trust anchor is a specific entity or component within a system that is inherently trusted. It serves as a reference point for establishing trust in other entities or components within the system. Typically, the trust anchor is a well-protected and tamper-resistant element, and the overall system's trustworthiness is derived from this anchor.

Hardware-based RoT implementations often involve secure hardware modules, such as trusted platform modules (TPMs) or hardware security modules (HSMs). These modules provide a secure environment for cryptographic operations and key management, isolating critical security functions from the general-purpose computing environment. This isolation enhances security by making the RoT more resistant to various forms of attacks, ensuring the integrity and trustworthiness of digital interactions.

System Security Policy

A system security policy is an essential protection mechanism that guides the design, development, implementation, testing, and maintenance of a particular system. This policy provides a framework for ensuring that security measures are consistently applied throughout the system's life cycle, from initial design to eventual decommissioning.

The role of a system security policy is to inform and direct the security requirements and controls necessary to protect the system. It outlines the rules and procedures for managing access, protecting data, and responding to security incidents. By establishing clear guidelines, a system security policy helps ensure that all aspects of the system are designed and operated with security in mind.

A robust system security policy addresses various aspects of security, including access controls, data protection, incident response, and compliance with relevant regulations. It also defines the responsibilities of different stakeholders, ensuring that everyone involved in the system's operation understands their role in maintaining security. Regular reviews and updates to the policy are necessary to adapt to evolving threats and technological changes, ensuring that the system remains secure over time.

System Resilience and High Availability

In the realm of information security, system resilience and high availability are critical components ensuring that IT systems can withstand and recover from adverse events while maintaining their operational capabilities. These concepts are essential for achieving the availability aspect of the CIA triad, which is fundamental to any robust security architecture.

Incorporating system resilience and high availability into the design of IT systems is essential for maintaining continuous operations and minimizing downtime. By employing fault tolerance, eliminating single points of failure, and using redundant components, organizations can ensure that their systems are robust and capable of withstanding and quickly recovering from various disruptions. This proactive approach to system design not only supports business continuity but also enhances overall security posture.

System Resilience

System resilience refers to the ability of a system to maintain acceptable levels of service during adverse events, whether those events are hardware faults, cyberattacks, or other disruptions. Resilient systems are designed to handle faults gracefully and can return to their normal state after the fault is resolved. This includes the ability to fail over to backup systems or components and then fail back to the original state once the issue is fixed.

Fault Tolerance

Fault tolerance is a specific aspect of system resilience that focuses on the system's ability to continue operating despite faults or failures. This is typically achieved through redundancy—having multiple instances of critical components such as disks, servers, or network paths. For instance, a redundant array of independent disks (RAID) configuration can provide fault tolerance by ensuring that data remains accessible even if one disk fails. Similarly, failover clustering allows a secondary server to take over if the primary server fails.

High Availability

High availability aims to minimize downtime and ensure that systems are accessible and operational as close to 100 percent of the time as possible. This is often measured by the percentage of uptime, with common targets being "three nines" (99.9 percent uptime) or "five nines" (99.999 percent uptime). Achieving high availability typically involves using load balancing, failover systems, and other redundancy measures to quickly recover from failures with minimal disruption.

Eliminating Single Points of Failure

A single point of failure (SPOF) is any component whose failure would cause the entire system to fail. If a computer has data on a single disk, failure of the disk can cause the computer to fail, so the disk is an SPOF. If a database-dependent website includes multiple web servers all served by a single database server, the database server is an SPOF.

Identifying and eliminating SPOFs is crucial for enhancing system resilience and high availability. This can involve adding redundancy at various levels, such as having multiple power supplies, network paths, or storage arrays.

Measuring Availability

The effectiveness of system resilience and high availability measures is often quantified by the amount of uptime a system achieves. For example, a system with 99.9 percent availability can afford only 44 minutes of downtime per month, while a system with 99.999 percent availability is permitted just 26 seconds of downtime per month. Meeting these stringent availability targets requires a combination of fault-tolerant design, redundant components, and effective monitoring and maintenance practices.

Technical Controls for Resilience and Availability

Several technical controls can enhance system resilience and high availability, including:

- **RAID array:** Protects data by distributing it across multiple disks, ensuring that data remains accessible even if one disk fails.
- **Failover clustering:** Allows secondary systems to take over automatically if the primary system fails.
- **Load balancing:** Distributes workloads across multiple servers to ensure no single server becomes a bottleneck or single point of failure.
- **Intrusion prevention system (IPS):** Detects and prevents attacks that could disrupt system operations.
- **Backup and recovery solution:** Ensures that data can be restored quickly in the event of a failure or data loss.

CHAPTER 4

Identity and Access Management

In today's digital landscape, the management of identities and access is a cornerstone of robust information security and privacy. As a security and privacy professional, understanding identity and access management (IAM) is crucial for safeguarding your organization's assets, ensuring compliance, and mitigating risks associated with unauthorized access. This chapter delves into the essential concepts and practices of IAM, providing you with a comprehensive understanding of how to effectively control and monitor access to critical resources. By mastering these principles, you will be better equipped to design and implement secure access controls that align with your organization's security policies and objectives. By the end of this chapter, you will have a solid foundation in IAM, enabling you to enhance your organization's security posture and protect sensitive information from potential threats.

IAM Core Concepts and Principles

IAM is a critical component of any organization's security strategy. It encompasses the policies, processes, and technologies used to manage digital identities and control access to resources. Effective IAM ensures that the right individuals have access to the right resources at the right times for the right reasons. This section provides a comprehensive overview of the core concepts and principles of IAM, focusing on key areas such as identification, authentication, authorization, and the management of the identity life cycle. The rest of this chapter delves deeper into many of the following concepts.

Identification and Authentication

Identification is the process by which a subject (such as a user or a device) claims an identity, typically by providing a unique identifier like a username or an ID number. This is the first step in establishing the authenticity of a subject and is crucial for subsequent access control processes.

Authentication follows identification and involves verifying the claimed identity by comparing one or more authentication factors against a database of valid identities.

Multifactor authentication (MFA) enhances security by requiring two or more of these factors, significantly reducing the likelihood of unauthorized access.

Authorization and Access Control Models

Authorization determines what an authenticated subject is allowed to do. This process involves granting or denying specific permissions to access resources based on predefined policies. Several access control models are used to implement authorization, including:

- **Role-based access control (RBAC):** Access rights are assigned based on the roles a user holds within an organization. This simplifies management by grouping permissions into roles rather than assigning them individually.
- **Rule-based access control:** Access is granted or denied based on a set of rules defined by the organization. These rules can be dynamic and context sensitive.
- **Mandatory access control (MAC):** Access is determined by a central authority based on the classification of information and the clearance level of the users. This model is often used in environments requiring high security, such as military or government institutions.
- **Discretionary access control (DAC):** Resource owners have the discretion to grant or deny access to their resources. This model is flexible but can be less secure if not managed properly.
- **Attribute-based access control (ABAC):** Access decisions are based on attributes of the user, resource, and environment. This model allows for more granular and flexible access control policies.
- **Risk-based access control:** Access decisions are influenced by the risk level associated with the access request, considering factors such as the user's location, the sensitivity of the resource, and the current threat landscape.

Identity Life Cycle Management

Managing the identity life cycle is essential to maintaining secure and efficient IAM processes. The identity life cycle includes the following stages:

- **Provisioning:** Creating and configuring user accounts with appropriate access rights. This includes assigning roles and issuing credentials.
- **Maintenance:** Regularly updating and managing user accounts to ensure that access rights remain appropriate as roles and responsibilities change. This includes password resets, role changes, and access reviews.
- **Deprovisioning:** Disabling or deleting user accounts when they are no longer needed, such as when an employee leaves the organization. This step is crucial to prevent unauthorized access by former employees or contractors.

Single Sign-On and Federated Identity Management

Single sign-on (SSO) allows users to authenticate once and gain access to multiple systems without needing to log in separately to each one. This improves user experience and reduces the burden of managing multiple credentials. However, it also requires robust security measures to protect the single point of authentication.

Federated identity management (FIM) extends SSO capabilities across different organizations or domains. It allows users to use their credentials from one domain to access resources in another, facilitating collaboration and access management in multiorganizational environments. FIM relies on trust relationships between identity providers and service providers, often using standards such as Security Assertion Markup Language (SAML) or OpenID Connect (OIDC).

Credential Management Systems

Effective credential management is vital for maintaining the security of authentication processes. Credential management systems (CMSs) help organizations securely store, manage, and distribute credentials. Features of a robust CMS include:

- **Password vaults:** Implementing secure storage for passwords, enabling users to manage and retrieve complex passwords without needing to remember them.
- **Just-in-time (JIT) access:** Provisioning temporary access to resources only when needed, reducing the risk of long-term exposure of sensitive credentials.

- **Passwordless authentication:** Utilizing methods such as biometrics, security tokens, or other factors that do not rely on traditional passwords, enhancing security and user convenience.

Access Review and Auditing

Regular access reviews and audits are essential to ensure that IAM policies and practices remain effective and compliant with regulatory requirements. This involves:

- **Account access review:** Periodically reviewing user accounts and their access rights to ensure they are still appropriate.
- **Auditing:** Monitoring and logging access activities to detect and respond to unauthorized access attempts or policy violations.

Authentication Methods and Multifactor Authentication

In the realm of information security, ensuring that only authorized individuals can access sensitive data and systems is paramount. Authentication is the process of verifying the identity of a user, device, or entity before granting access. This section delves into various authentication methods and the concept of multifactor authentication (MFA), which enhances security by requiring multiple forms of verification.

The AAA Model

The AAA model is a foundational framework in information security. It encompasses three critical components: authentication, authorization, and accounting. Each component plays a vital role in securing access to systems and data.

Authentication Authentication is the process of verifying the identity of a user or device. It ensures that the entity attempting to access a system is who they claim to be. Authentication methods can be categorized into three primary factors:

- **Something you know:** Includes passwords, PINs, and security questions. These are the most common forms of authentication but are also the weakest due to the risk of being guessed or stolen.

- **Something you have:** Involves physical devices such as smart cards, USB tokens, or mobile devices. These methods require the user to possess a specific item to gain access.
- **Something you are:** Refers to biometric authentication methods such as fingerprint scans, facial recognition, and retinal scans. These methods are based on unique physical characteristics of the user.

Authorization Once authentication is successful, authorization determines what resources the authenticated entity can access and what actions they can perform. This is typically managed through access control lists (ACLs) and RBAC mechanisms.

Accounting This component involves tracking and logging user activities to provide an audit trail. Accounting helps in monitoring usage patterns, detecting anomalies, and ensuring compliance with security policies.

Identification, Authentication, and Authorization

Identification, authentication, and authorization are sequential processes that work together to secure access to systems and data:

- **Identification:** The first step in the access control process is identification, where a user or device presents an identifier, such as a username or ID card, to claim an identity. This step does not verify the identity but merely asserts it.
- **Authentication:** Following identification, authentication verifies the claimed identity by comparing the provided credentials against a database of valid identities. This step ensures that the entity is who they claim to be. Various authentication methods, as mentioned earlier, fall under this category.
- **Authorization:** After successful authentication, the system determines the level of access granted to the user or device. Authorization policies define what resources can be accessed and what actions can be performed based on the authenticated identity.

Multifactor Authentication

MFA enhances security by requiring multiple forms of verification from different categories of authentication factors. MFA significantly reduces the risk of unauthorized access by ensuring that even if one factor is compromised, additional factors provide a layer of protection.

For example, a common implementation of MFA combines two or more of the standard authentication factors: something you know (such as a password), something you have (such as a mobile device that receives a one-time password), and something you are (such as a fingerprint that can be scanned).

By combining these factors, MFA provides robust security against various attack vectors, including phishing, keylogging, and brute-force attacks.

Authentication Techniques

Various authentication techniques can be employed to verify user identities. Let's explore some common methods:

- **Password-based authentication:** The most widely used method, where users provide a password to authenticate. Strong password policies, including complexity and expiration requirements, help enhance security.
- **Biometric authentication:** This method uses unique physical characteristics of users, such as fingerprint scans, facial recognition, or retinal scans. Biometric authentication is highly secure but requires specialized hardware.
- **Token-based authentication:** Users possess a physical device, such as a smart card or USB token, which generates a unique code for authentication. This method is secure but can be inconvenient if the token is lost or damaged.
- **One-time passwords (OTPs):** OTPs are temporary codes generated for a single login session. They can be delivered via SMS, email, or dedicated apps. OTPs provide an additional layer of security over static passwords.
- **Federated identity management (FIM):** FIM allows users to authenticate once and gain access to multiple systems within a trusted network. This is commonly used in SSO implementations, where users log in once to access various applications and services.

Role-Based Access Control Versus Attribute-Based Access Control

In the realm of identity and access management, two prominent access control models are RBAC and ABAC. Both models serve to regulate user permissions and access to resources, but they operate on different principles and offer distinct advantages depending on the context of their application.

Role-Based Access Control

RBAC is a widely used access control model that assigns permissions to users based on their roles within an organization. Each role is associated with a set of permissions that dictate what actions users in that role can perform and what resources they can access. This model is particularly effective in environments where job functions are clearly defined and stable.

Key features of RBAC include:

- **Role assignment:** Users are assigned to roles based on their job responsibilities. For instance, an employee in the finance department may be assigned a role that allows access to financial records and systems.
- **Role authorization:** Permissions are granted to roles, not individual users. This simplifies the management of access rights, as administrators only need to manage roles rather than individual user permissions.
- **Role hierarchy:** RBAC supports hierarchical roles, where higher-level roles inherit permissions from lower-level roles. For example, a manager role might inherit all the permissions of an employee role plus additional managerial permissions.
- **Enforcing least privilege:** RBAC helps enforce the principle of least privilege by ensuring that users only have access to the resources necessary for their job functions. This minimizes the risk of unauthorized access and potential data breaches.

RBAC is beneficial for its simplicity and ease of administration, especially in large organizations with well-defined job roles. However, it can be inflexible in dynamic environments where user responsibilities frequently change. For example, if an employee's job duties change frequently, updating their role assignments can become cumbersome.

Attribute-Based Access Control

ABAC is a granular and flexible access control model that uses attributes to determine access rights. Attributes can be related to the user (e.g., job title, department), the resource (e.g., classification level, owner), the environment (e.g., time of day, location), and more.

Key features of ABAC include:

- **Policy-based access:** Access decisions are made based on policies that evaluate multiple attributes. For example, a policy might allow access to a document only if the user is in the HR department, the document is classified as "internal," and it is within working hours.

- **Dynamic authorization:** ABAC allows for real-time access decisions based on current attributes. This is particularly useful in environments where access needs to be adjusted dynamically based on changing conditions.
- **Fine-grained control:** ABAC provides more precise control over access permissions compared to RBAC. It can accommodate complex scenarios where access rights need to consider multiple factors.
- **Context-aware access:** ABAC can incorporate context-aware attributes such as the user's location, device type, and time of access. This allows for more sophisticated access control policies that can adapt to varying conditions and enhance security.

ABAC is advantageous for its flexibility and adaptability, making it suitable for environments with complex and dynamic access control requirements. However, it can be more complex to implement and manage due to the need for comprehensive policies and attribute management. For instance, developing and maintaining detailed access policies that evaluate multiple attributes can be resource intensive.

Comparison and Use Cases

To help you get a better feel for the difference between RBAC and ABAC, here are some key comparisons:

- **Simplicity versus flexibility:** RBAC is simpler to implement and manage, making it ideal for organizations with stable, well-defined roles. ABAC offers greater flexibility and precision, suitable for dynamic and complex environments.
- **Scalability:** RBAC scales well in organizations with a clear hierarchy and defined roles. ABAC scales better in environments where access decisions need to consider a wide range of attributes and conditions.
- **Policy management:** RBAC requires managing roles and their associated permissions. ABAC requires developing and maintaining detailed access policies that evaluate multiple attributes.
- **Security and compliance:** ABAC can provide enhanced security by allowing for more granular access control policies that can adapt to changing conditions. This can be particularly important in industries with strict regulatory compliance requirements, where access to sensitive data must be tightly controlled.

Practical Examples

Both RBAC and ABAC have their strengths and are suited to different scenarios. Organizations may choose RBAC for its straightforward approach and ease of administration, while ABAC may be preferred for its flexibility and fine-grained control in complex environments. Understanding the specific needs and context of the organization is crucial in selecting the appropriate access control model.

Here are a couple of practical scenarios to consider:

- **A hospital:** A hospital might use RBAC to manage access to patient records. Doctors, nurses, and administrative staff are assigned roles that grant them specific permissions based on their job functions. Doctors might have full access to patient records, nurses might have read-only access, and administrative staff might have access only to billing information.
- **A financial institution:** A financial institution might use ABAC to manage access to sensitive financial data. Access policies could be defined to allow employees to access financial data only if they are in the finance department, using a company-issued device, and within the company's premises. Additionally, access might be restricted to working hours to prevent unauthorized access outside of business hours.

Identity Federation and Single Sign-On

In the landscape of identity and access management, identity federation and SSO are critical concepts that enhance user experience and security. These mechanisms streamline access to multiple systems and applications, reducing the need for multiple credentials and improving security management.

Identity federation and SSO are powerful tools in the IAM toolkit, offering streamlined access, improved user experience, and enhanced security. By understanding and addressing the challenges associated with these mechanisms, organizations can effectively manage user identities and access in today's complex and interconnected digital landscape.

Identity Federation

Identity federation is a system that allows multiple organizations to share and manage user identities across different domains. It enables users to authenticate once and access resources across federated systems without reauthenticating. The key components and benefits of identity federation include:

- **FIM:** This system links user identities in one domain with identities in another, enabling seamless access across different organizations. FIM can be implemented on-premises, in the cloud, or as a hybrid solution.
- **Single identity:** Users maintain a single identity across multiple systems, simplifying identity management and reducing administrative overhead.
- **Trust relationships:** Federations are built on trust relationships between organizations, where each entity agrees to share and accept identity information.
- **Standards and protocols:** Common standards such as SAML, OAuth, and OIDC facilitate interoperability and secure identity sharing between different systems.
- **Use cases:** Federated identity is commonly used in scenarios such as corporate mergers, partnerships, and access to third-party services, where users need to access resources across multiple domains.

For example, a university federation might allow students and faculty to access resources from different universities within the federation using their home institution's credentials. This approach simplifies access while maintaining security and trust between institutions.

Single Sign-On

SSO is a user authentication process that permits a user to enter one set of credentials to access multiple applications or systems. SSO enhances user convenience and security by reducing the number of times users need to log in and the number of passwords they need to remember.

The key aspects of SSO include:

- **Centralized authentication:** SSO centralizes the authentication process, allowing users to authenticate once and gain access to multiple systems without reentering credentials.
- **User experience:** SSO improves the user experience by reducing the frequency of logins and the need to remember multiple passwords. This convenience can lead to increased productivity and user satisfaction.
- **Security benefits:** By reducing the number of credentials users must manage, SSO can lower the risk of password fatigue and related security issues, such as password reuse and weak passwords. Additionally, centralized authentication allows for more robust security measures, such as multifactor authentication.

- **Implementation:** SSO can be implemented using various technologies and protocols, including Kerberos, SAML, OAuth, and OIDC. These technologies ensure secure and efficient authentication and authorization across different systems.

An example of SSO in action is a corporate environment where employees can log in to their workstation and gain access to email, intranet, and other business applications without needing to log in separately to each service.

Integration of Identity Federation and SSO

Combining identity federation and SSO provides a comprehensive solution for managing user identities and access across multiple domains and applications. This integration offers several advantages:

- **Seamless access:** Users can authenticate once and access resources across federated systems and applications without multiple logins, enhancing the user experience.
- **Centralized management:** IT administrators can manage user identities, access rights, and security policies centrally, reducing administrative complexity and improving security oversight.
- **Enhanced security:** The combination of federated identity and SSO supports the implementation of advanced security measures, such as MFA and context-aware access controls, across all federated systems and applications.
- **Scalability:** This integrated approach scales well for organizations of all sizes, from small businesses to large enterprises, and can accommodate growth and changes in the organizational structure.

For instance, a multinational corporation might use federated identity and SSO to provide employees with seamless access to global resources, including internal applications, partner systems, and cloud services. This setup ensures that employees can work efficiently while maintaining robust security controls.

Challenges and Considerations

While identity federation and SSO offer significant benefits, they also present challenges that organizations must address:

- **Complexity:** Implementing and managing federated identity and SSO can be complex, requiring careful planning, coordination, and ongoing maintenance.

- **Trust and interoperability:** Establishing and maintaining trust relationships between federated entities and ensuring interoperability between different systems and protocols can be challenging.
- **Security risks:** Centralized authentication systems can become attractive targets for attackers. Organizations must implement strong security measures, such as MFA, encryption, and regular security assessments, to mitigate these risks.

Zero Trust Architecture for IAM

Zero trust architecture (ZTA) is a security model that operates on the principle "never trust, always verify." Unlike traditional security models that assume everything inside an organization's network can be trusted, zero trust assumes that threats can exist both inside and outside the network. Therefore, it requires strict verification for every user and device attempting to access resources, regardless of their location or whether they are within the organization's perimeter.

Key Principles of Zero Trust Architecture

ZTA represents a paradigm shift in how organizations approach security. By adopting a "never trust, always verify" mindset and implementing robust access policy enforcement mechanisms, organizations can significantly enhance their security posture and protect against evolving threats.

To achieve these goals, ZTA implements the following key principles:

- **Verify explicitly:** Always authenticate and authorize based on all available data points, including user identity, location, device health, service or workload, data classification, and anomalies. This ensures that every access request is thoroughly vetted before granting access.
- **Use least privilege access:** Limit user access with just-in-time and just-enough-access (JIT/JEA), risk-based adaptive policies, and data protection to minimize exposure to sensitive data and resources. This principle reduces the risk of overprivileged access and potential misuse of resources.
- **Assume breach:** Minimize the blast radius and segment access. Verify end-to-end encryption and use analytics to get visibility, drive threat detection, and improve defenses. By assuming that a breach has already occurred, organizations can better prepare and respond to potential threats.

Implementing Zero Trust in IAM

Careful planning and execution are essential to overcome the challenges associated with implementing ZTA. Implementing ZTA for IAM involves the following tasks:

- **Identity verification:** Every access request is verified, and identity is authenticated using multifactor authentication. This ensures that only legitimate users gain access. MFA adds an extra layer of security by requiring users to provide multiple forms of verification.
- **Device compliance:** Devices are continuously monitored and assessed for compliance with security policies. Noncompliant devices are denied access or given limited access. This helps to ensure that only secure and trusted devices can connect to the network.
- **Least privilege access:** Access controls are dynamically adjusted based on the user's role, context, and the sensitivity of the data or application being accessed. This reduces the risk of overprivileged access. By granting the minimum necessary access, organizations can limit the potential damage from compromised accounts.
- **Microsegmentation:** Network segments are divided into smaller zones to maintain separate access controls for different parts of the network. This limits lateral movement within the network in case of a breach. Microsegmentation helps to contain breaches and prevent them from spreading across the network.
- **Continuous monitoring and analytics:** Real-time monitoring and analytics are employed to detect and respond to anomalies and potential threats. This involves logging and analyzing user activities, network traffic, and system behaviors. Continuous monitoring helps to identify suspicious activities and respond to them promptly.

Zero Trust Access Policy Enforcement

To enforce zero trust policies effectively, organizations must implement robust access policy enforcement mechanisms. These mechanisms ensure that access decisions are made in real time and are based on the most current security posture of users and devices:

- **Policy decision point (PDP):** Responsible for making access decisions based on predefined security policies. It evaluates the context of each access request and determines whether to grant or deny access. The PDP uses a combination of rules, threat intelligence, and analytics to make informed decisions.

- **Policy enforcement point (PEP):** Enforces the access decisions made by the PDP. It acts as a gatekeeper, ensuring that only authorized users and devices can access the requested resources. The PEP can be deployed at various points in the network, including endpoints, gateways, and cloud services.

Benefits of Zero Trust Architecture

Here are the main benefits that most organizations can expect when using ZTA:

- **Reduced risk:** By continuously verifying identities and monitoring devices, ZTA reduces the risk of unauthorized access and data breaches. The principle of least privilege further minimizes the potential impact of compromised accounts.
- **Improved compliance:** ZTA helps organizations meet regulatory requirements by enforcing strict access controls and maintaining detailed logs of access activities. This can simplify audits and demonstrate adherence to security standards.
- **Enhanced visibility:** Continuous monitoring and analytics provide better visibility into user activities and network traffic, enabling faster detection and response to threats. This visibility helps organizations to proactively identify and address security issues.

Challenges of Zero Trust Architecture

ZTA is not without its challenges:

- **Complexity:** Implementing ZTA can be complex and requires significant changes to existing IT infrastructure and processes. Organizations may need to invest in new technologies and reconfigure their networks to support zero trust principles.
- **Cost:** The cost of deploying and maintaining ZTA solutions can be high, especially for organizations with large and diverse IT environments. However, the investment can be justified by the potential reduction in security incidents and breaches.
- **User experience:** Strict access controls and continuous verification can impact user experience and productivity if not implemented carefully. Organizations need to balance security with usability to ensure that users can perform their tasks efficiently.

Identity Governance Life Cycle

Identity governance is a critical component of IAM that ensures the right individuals have the appropriate access to technology resources. It encompasses the full life cycle of user identities, from creation to deactivation, and includes processes for managing, auditing, and reviewing access rights. Effective identity governance helps organizations mitigate risks, maintain compliance, and enhance operational efficiency.

The identity governance life cycle encompasses a comprehensive set of processes and practices for managing user identities and access rights throughout their life cycle. By implementing effective provisioning and deprovisioning processes, managing roles and transitions, and conducting regular access reviews and audits, organizations can enhance security, maintain compliance, and improve operational efficiency.

Account Provisioning and Deprovisioning

The identity life cycle begins with provisioning, which involves creating user accounts and granting appropriate access rights based on the user's role within the organization. Effective provisioning ensures that new employees, contractors, and other users can quickly access the resources they need to perform their duties.

This process typically includes:

- **Account creation:** Setting up new user accounts in various systems, applications, and services. This involves assigning a unique identifier or username to each user, ensuring that the account is created according to organizational policies and standards.
- **Access assignment:** Granting access rights and permissions based on the user's role, department, and job function. This step ensures that users have the necessary privileges to perform their tasks without having excessive access that could pose a security risk.
- **Hardware issuance:** Providing necessary hardware, such as laptops, smartphones, and security tokens, to new users. Accurate records must be maintained to track the issuance and return of hardware to prevent loss or misuse.
- **Onboarding:** Educating new users about organizational policies, procedures, and security best practices. Onboarding processes often include training on acceptable use policies, mobile device policies, and how to avoid common security threats like phishing attacks.

Deprovisioning is the process of disabling or deleting user accounts when they are no longer needed, such as when an employee leaves the organization or a contractor's engagement ends. Effective deprovisioning is crucial for maintaining security and compliance, as it ensures that former users no longer have access to sensitive information and systems.

Essential steps in the deprovisioning process include:

- **Account deactivation:** Disabling user accounts in various systems, applications, and services. This step ensures that the user can no longer access organizational resources, reducing the risk of unauthorized access.
- **Access revocation:** Removing access rights and permissions associated with the user's role. This involves updating access control lists and removing the user from relevant groups and roles.
- **Hardware recovery:** Collecting issued hardware, such as laptops, smartphones, and security tokens, from departing users. Ensuring that all hardware is returned helps protect organizational assets and sensitive information stored on these devices.
- **Offboarding:** Ensuring that departing users return all organizational assets and are informed of any post-employment obligations, such as nondisclosure agreements. This step helps protect the organization's intellectual property and sensitive information.

Role Definition and Transition

Roles play a crucial role in identity governance by defining the access rights and permissions associated with specific job functions. Effective role management helps organizations maintain a clear and consistent approach to access control, reducing the risk of unauthorized access and ensuring compliance with regulatory requirements.

Important aspects of role management include:

- **Role definition:** Establishing clear and consistent roles based on job functions, departments, and organizational hierarchy. This involves identifying the specific tasks and responsibilities associated with each role and determining the necessary access rights for each role.
- **Role assignment:** Assigning users to appropriate roles based on their job responsibilities and organizational position. This ensures that users have the necessary access to perform their tasks while minimizing the risk of excessive access.
- **Role transition:** Managing changes in user roles, such as promotions, transfers, or changes in job functions, to ensure that access rights and permissions are updated accordingly. This involves updating user accounts

to reflect new roles and responsibilities and ensuring that access rights are adjusted to match the new role.
- **Role review:** Periodically reviewing and updating roles to ensure they remain aligned with organizational needs and regulatory requirements. This helps ensure that roles continue to accurately reflect job functions and that access rights are appropriate for each role.

Access Reviews and Audits

Regular access reviews and audits are essential components of identity governance, ensuring that user access rights and permissions remain appropriate and aligned with organizational policies. These reviews help identify and remediate potential security risks, maintain compliance with regulatory requirements, and improve overall access management processes.

Key aspects of access reviews and audits include:

- **User access review:** Periodically reviewing user access rights and permissions to ensure they remain appropriate based on the user's current role and job responsibilities. This helps identify any excessive or outdated access rights that could pose a security risk.
- **System access review:** Assessing access rights and permissions for critical systems, applications, and services to identify and remediate potential security risks. This involves evaluating access control lists, group memberships, and role assignments to ensure that access is appropriate and secure.
- **Service account management:** Regularly reviewing and managing service accounts to ensure they are used appropriately and do not pose security risks. Service accounts often have elevated privileges and can be targeted by attackers, so it is important to monitor and manage these accounts carefully.
- **Audit trails and logs:** Maintaining detailed records of user access and activity to support audits, investigations, and regulatory compliance efforts. These logs provide a valuable source of information for identifying potential security incidents and ensuring accountability for user actions.

Access Control Attacks

Access control attacks are attempts by unauthorized individuals to bypass security mechanisms and gain access to systems, data, or other resources.

These attacks can lead to significant losses, including unauthorized disclosure of data, unauthorized alteration of assets, and disruption of service availability. Understanding and mitigating these attacks is crucial for maintaining the security and integrity of information systems.

Password Attacks

Password attacks involve attempts to obtain or guess a user's password to gain unauthorized access to a system. Common methods include:

- **Brute force attacks:** Attackers use automated tools to try every possible combination of characters until the correct password is found.
- **Dictionary attacks:** Attackers use a predefined list of common passwords and phrases to guess the password.
- **Phishing:** Attackers trick users into revealing their passwords through deceptive emails or websites that appear legitimate. Once attackers have a valid password, they can impersonate the user and access their resources, leading to potential data breaches and unauthorized actions.

Pass-the-Hash Attacks

In pass-the-hash attacks, the attacker captures a hashed version of a password and uses it to authenticate without needing to know the actual password. This is particularly effective against systems that use new technology LAN manager (NTLM) authentication. By exploiting vulnerabilities in the authentication process, attackers can gain access to the system with the same privileges as the user whose hash was captured.

Kerberos Exploitation

Kerberos exploitation involves attackers taking advantage of vulnerabilities in the Kerberos authentication protocol. Techniques include:

- **Ticket-granting ticket (TGT) theft:** Attackers steal the TGT, which allows them to request service tickets for accessing resources.
- **Forging Kerberos tickets:** Attackers create fake tickets, such as golden tickets, which grant them unrestricted access to network resources. These attacks can lead to widespread unauthorized access within an organization, as Kerberos is often used for SSO in enterprise environments.

Privilege Escalation

Privilege escalation involves exploiting a system vulnerability to gain higher-level access than initially granted. Attackers may use various methods, such as:

- **Rootkits:** Malicious software designed to hide the presence of an attacker and provide elevated privileges.
- **Fileless malware:** Malware that resides in memory and does not leave traces on the disk, making it harder to detect.
- **Malicious scripts:** Scripts that exploit vulnerabilities to execute commands with elevated privileges.

By gaining administrative or root access, attackers can perform unauthorized actions and access sensitive data.

Man-in-the-Middle (MitM) Attacks

In man-in-the-middle (MitM) attacks, the attacker intercepts and possibly alters communication between two parties without their knowledge. This can lead to unauthorized access to sensitive information, such as login credentials, financial data, and personal information. Attackers can also inject malicious content into the communication stream, leading to further exploitation.

Session Hijacking

Session hijacking occurs when attackers take over an active session by stealing session tokens or cookies. This allows them to impersonate the user and access their resources without needing to authenticate again. Session hijacking can lead to unauthorized actions, data breaches, and potential financial loss.

Replay Attacks

In replay attacks, valid data transmission is maliciously or fraudulently repeated or delayed. Attackers capture legitimate authentication messages and retransmit them to gain unauthorized access. This type of attack can be particularly effective against systems that do not use time-sensitive or one-time authentication tokens.

Preventive Measures

To protect against access control attacks, organizations should implement a variety of security measures:

- **Strong password policies:** Enforce the use of complex passwords that combine letters, numbers, and special characters. Regularly require password changes and prohibit the reuse of old passwords. Implement multifactor authentication to add an extra layer of security, making it more difficult for attackers to gain access with just a password.
- **Regular patch management:** Keep systems and applications up to date with the latest security patches to mitigate known vulnerabilities. Regular patching helps protect against exploits that attackers use to gain unauthorized access or escalate privileges.
- **Intrusion detection and prevention systems (IDPSs):** Use IDPSs to monitor network traffic for suspicious activity and respond to potential threats. These systems can detect and block malicious attempts to bypass access controls, providing an additional layer of defense.
- **User education and awareness:** Train users to recognize phishing attempts and other social engineering tactics that attackers use to steal credentials. Educate users on the importance of strong passwords, the risks of sharing passwords, and how to report suspicious activities.
- **Secure authentication protocols:** Use secure authentication protocols, such as Kerberos, and ensure they are properly configured to prevent exploitation. Implement measures like time synchronization and ticket expiration to enhance security.
- **Session management:** Implement secure session management practices, including the use of secure cookies, session timeouts, and mechanisms to invalidate sessions after logout or inactivity. These measures help prevent session hijacking and replay attacks.
- **Access control reviews:** Regularly review and audit access controls to ensure that only authorized users have access to sensitive resources. Implement the principle of least privilege, granting users the minimum access necessary to perform their job functions.

CHAPTER 5

Data Protection and Privacy Engineering

Data protection and privacy engineering are critical components of any organization's security strategy. As a security and privacy professional, you are responsible for ensuring that sensitive information is adequately protected from unauthorized access, misuse, and breaches. This chapter provides you with a concise overview of the essential concepts and practices that underpin effective data protection and privacy engineering. By delving into these topics, you will be better equipped to implement robust security measures and privacy-preserving technologies within your organization.

This chapter covers a wide range of topics, from data classification and encryption to privacy by design and cross-border data transfers. Each section is designed to provide you with practical insights and actionable strategies to help you navigate the complex landscape of data protection and privacy. By the end of this chapter, you will have a deeper understanding of how to develop and maintain a privacy program, handle data subject rights, and ensure the secure retention and disposal of data. This knowledge will empower you to make informed decisions and implement best practices that safeguard your organization's information assets and uphold the privacy rights of individuals.

Data Classification and Labeling

Data classification and labeling are fundamental practices in data protection and privacy engineering. These processes help organizations manage and safeguard sensitive information by categorizing data based on its sensitivity and importance. Proper classification and labeling enable the implementation of appropriate security controls, ensuring that data is protected throughout its life cycle.

By systematically classifying and labeling data, organizations can better protect sensitive information and comply with regulatory requirements. Proper data governance ensures that data handling practices are consistent with organizational policies, reducing the risk of data breaches and enhancing overall security posture. Effective data classification and labeling not only protect the organization's assets but also build trust with customers and stakeholders by demonstrating a commitment to data privacy and security.

Identifying and Classifying Information and Assets

The first step in data classification is identifying the types of information and assets an organization handles. This includes sensitive data, the hardware used to process it, and the media used to store it. Organizations often define classification categories within their security policies, guiding personnel to label assets accordingly. Sensitive data encompasses any information that isn't public or unclassified, such as confidential, proprietary, or protected data, which must be secured due to its value or regulatory requirements.

Two types of sensitive data are particularly critical:

- **Personally identifiable information (PII):** Includes any information that can identify an individual, such as names, social security numbers, dates of birth, and biometric records. Organizations have a responsibility to protect PII, as many laws mandate notification of individuals if a data breach compromises their PII. Protecting PII involves implementing security measures such as encryption, access controls, and regular audits to ensure compliance with regulations.
- **Protected health information (PHI):** Includes medical records that must be safeguarded to ensure privacy and compliance with legal standards. PHI encompasses a wide range of information, including medical histories, test results, insurance information, and any other data that can be linked to an individual's health status. Organizations handling PHI must implement stringent controls to prevent unauthorized access and ensure data integrity. PHI is governed by regulations like HIPAA in the United States.

Data Governance

Effective data governance is essential for managing sensitive information. It involves building an inventory of the types of data maintained by the organization and mapping data flows to understand how data is stored, processed, and transmitted. This inventory is the foundation for a robust data classification program that organizes data into categories based on its sensitivity and the potential impact of disclosure.

Organizations typically use classification labels such as highly sensitive, sensitive, internal, and public. These labels help specify the security controls required to protect information with varying levels of sensitivity. For example, highly sensitive data may require encryption both at rest and in transit, while public data may only need integrity protection. The classification labels serve as a guide for employees, helping them understand the importance of the data they handle and the necessary precautions to take.

Data roles and responsibilities play a crucial role in data governance. Clear ownership policies designate senior executives as data owners for different types of data. Data owners are responsible for defining classification requirements and ensuring data is properly tagged and protected. Other roles include data controllers, data stewards, data custodians, and data processors, each with specific responsibilities for managing and safeguarding data. Data controllers determine the purposes and means of processing personal data, while data stewards ensure the accuracy and integrity of the data. Data custodians are responsible for the safe storage and protection of the data, and data processors handle data processing tasks on behalf of the data controller.

Implementing Data Classification

Implementing a data classification program involves several key steps:

- **Building a data inventory:** Identify and document the types of sensitive information used by the organization and where the information is stored, processed, and transmitted. This step is crucial for understanding the scope of the data and ensuring that all sensitive information is accounted for.
- **Developing classification categories:** Define classification labels based on the sensitivity of the information and the potential impact of disclosure. Common categories include confidential, private, sensitive, and public. These categories help prioritize data protection efforts and allocate resources effectively.
- **Mapping data flows:** Understand how data moves within the organization and with third parties to ensure appropriate security controls are in place. Data flow diagrams can help visualize the movement of data and identify potential vulnerabilities in the process.
- **Assigning data roles:** Designate data owners and other key roles to ensure clear responsibility for data protection. Clear role definitions help establish accountability and streamline decision-making processes related to data security.
- **Applying security controls:** Implement security measures based on the classification of the data, such as encryption, access controls, and data loss prevention. These controls should be tailored to the specific needs of the organization and the sensitivity of the data.

- **Training and awareness:** Educate employees on the importance of data classification and how to apply labels and security controls correctly. Regular training sessions and awareness programs can help reinforce best practices and reduce the risk of human error.

Data Masking, Tokenization, and Encryption

In today's digital landscape, protecting sensitive information is paramount for organizations aiming to maintain privacy and security. Data masking, tokenization, and encryption are key techniques used to safeguard data from unauthorized access and breaches. By implementing these methods, organizations can safeguard data from unauthorized access, reduce the risk of data breaches, and ensure compliance with privacy regulations. Additionally, leveraging privacy-enhancing technologies can further enhance data protection and privacy, providing a robust framework for managing sensitive information. This section provides an overview of these methods and their applications in data protection and privacy engineering.

Data Masking

Data masking is a technique used to hide sensitive information by replacing it with fictional but realistic data. This method ensures that the original data remains confidential while allowing the use of the masked data for testing, development, or training purposes. Data masking is particularly useful in scenarios where data needs to be shared with third parties or used in nonproduction environments without exposing sensitive information.

There are two approaches to data masking:

- **Static data masking:** Creates a masked copy of the database, which can be used for nonproduction purposes. The original data remains unchanged in the production environment.
- **Dynamic data masking:** Masks data in real time as it is accessed by users, ensuring that sensitive information is never exposed to unauthorized individuals.

Data masking can be applied to various types of data, including PII, PHI, and financial data. By implementing data masking, organizations can reduce the risk of data breaches and ensure compliance with privacy regulations.

Tokenization

Tokenization is a process that replaces sensitive data elements with nonsensitive equivalents, known as *tokens*. These tokens can be used in place of the original data without exposing the actual information. The original data is stored securely in a token vault, which is a protected database that maps tokens to their corresponding sensitive data.

Tokenization is commonly used in payment processing systems to protect credit card information. By replacing credit card numbers with tokens, organizations can reduce the risk of data breaches and minimize the impact of potential security incidents.

Key benefits of tokenization include:

- **Enhanced security:** Tokens are meaningless outside the tokenization system, making it difficult for attackers to use them if intercepted.
- **Regulatory compliance:** Tokenization helps organizations comply with data protection regulations, such as the PCI DSS, by reducing the scope of sensitive data storage and processing.

Encryption

Encryption is a method of converting plaintext data into ciphertext, which can only be deciphered by authorized parties with the correct decryption key. Encryption provides confidentiality, integrity, authentication, and nonrepudiation for sensitive information, ensuring that data remains secure while at rest, in transit, and in use.

There are two main types of encryption:

- **Symmetric encryption:** Uses a single shared key for both encryption and decryption. Symmetric encryption algorithms, such as Advanced Encryption Standard (AES), are efficient and suitable for encrypting large volumes of data.
- **Asymmetric encryption:** Uses a pair of keys: a *public key* for encryption and a *private key* for decryption. Asymmetric encryption algorithms, such as Rivest–Shamir–Adleman (RSA), provide enhanced security for key exchange and digital signatures but are less efficient for encrypting large amounts of data.

Encryption can be applied to various data states:

- **Data at rest:** Encrypting stored data ensures that it remains secure even if physical storage devices are compromised.

- **Data in transit:** Encrypting data as it travels across networks protects it from interception and eavesdropping.
- **Data in use:** Encrypting data while it is being processed in memory can protect it from unauthorized access by malicious software or insiders.

Organizations should implement strong encryption practices, including key management and regular updates to encryption algorithms, to maintain the security of their sensitive data.

Privacy-Enhancing Technologies

Privacy-enhancing technologies (PETs) are tools and techniques designed to protect personal information and ensure compliance with privacy regulations. PETs help organizations minimize data collection, storage, and processing, thereby reducing the risk of data breaches and enhancing user privacy.

Some common PETs include:

- **Differential privacy:** This technique adds noise to data sets to prevent the identification of individuals while preserving the overall utility of the data.
- **Homomorphic encryption:** This advanced encryption method allows computations to be performed on encrypted data without decrypting it, ensuring data privacy throughout the processing life cycle.
- **Zero-knowledge proofs**: These cryptographic protocols enable one party to prove to another that a statement is true without revealing any additional information.

By incorporating PETs into their data protection strategies, organizations can enhance privacy and security while maintaining compliance with regulatory requirements.

Data Loss Prevention Strategies

Data loss prevention (DLP) is a critical aspect of data protection and privacy engineering. It involves implementing measures to prevent unauthorized access, use, disclosure, disruption, modification, or destruction of sensitive information. Effective DLP strategies protect data throughout its life cycle, from creation to destruction, ensuring the confidentiality, integrity, and availability of data.

Establishing Information and Asset Handling Requirements

Managing sensitive data effectively is paramount to preventing data breaches. A data breach occurs when an unauthorized entity gains access to sensitive data. Organizations must adopt a comprehensive approach to data protection, which includes establishing robust information and asset handling requirements. Here are the key steps in this process:

- **Identify and classify information and assets:** The first step in protecting data is to identify and classify it based on its sensitivity and value to the organization. Data classification helps determine the level of protection required for different types of data. For instance, highly classified data necessitates stringent security controls, while unclassified data requires fewer controls.
- **Establish handling requirements:** Once data is classified, organizations must establish handling requirements that dictate how data should be managed, stored, transmitted, and disposed of. These requirements should align with the organization's security policy and legal and regulatory obligations.
- **Implement data lifecycle management:** Data lifecycle management involves protecting data from creation to destruction. This includes defining roles and responsibilities for data owners, controllers, custodians, processors, and users. Organizations should also establish policies for data collection, location, maintenance, retention, remanence, and destruction.
- **Ensure appropriate asset retention:** Organizations must ensure that data and assets are retained appropriately, considering factors such as end of life (EOL) and end of support. This helps prevent unauthorized access to outdated or unsupported systems that may contain sensitive information.
- **Determine data security controls and compliance requirements:** Data security controls should be tailored to the specific needs of the organization. This includes selecting appropriate standards and implementing data protection methods such as encryption, access controls, and monitoring. Compliance with relevant laws and regulations is also crucial to avoid legal repercussions and maintain trust with stakeholders.

Data Protection Methods

Data protection methods are essential for safeguarding sensitive information from unauthorized access and ensuring compliance with legal and regulatory requirements. These methods include data masking, tokenization, and encryption covered in the previous section, as well as the following:

- **Data loss prevention systems:** DLP systems help enforce information handling policies and prevent data loss and theft. They monitor systems for sensitive information and network traffic for potential data breaches. DLP systems can be host-based or network-based:
    - **Host-based DLP:** Software agents installed on systems search for sensitive information and monitor user actions. They can block undesirable actions, such as accessing USB devices or transmitting sensitive data without encryption.
    - **Network-based DLP:** Dedicated devices monitor outbound network traffic for unencrypted sensitive information. They can block transmissions that violate the organization's policy or automatically apply encryption to the content.
- **Digital rights management (DRM):** DRM technologies control access to digital content and prevent unauthorized use, copying, and distribution. DRM is commonly used to protect intellectual property, such as software, music, and videos.
- **Cloud access security broker (CASB):** CASBs provide security controls for data stored and processed in cloud environments. They enforce policies for data access, encryption, and monitoring, ensuring that cloud-based data is protected from unauthorized access and breaches.

Implementing DLP Strategies

To implement effective DLP strategies, organizations should follow these steps:

- **Build a data inventory:** Develop an inventory of the types of sensitive information maintained by the organization, including where it is stored, processed, and transmitted. This helps identify potential risks and areas that require protection.
- **Develop a data classification program:** Organize data into categories based on sensitivity and the impact of disclosure. This helps prioritize protection efforts and allocate resources effectively.
- **Map data flows:** Understand how data moves through the organization, including data entry points, storage locations, and transmission paths. This helps identify vulnerabilities and implement appropriate security controls.
- **Implement and monitor DLP systems:** Deploy host-based and network-based DLP systems to monitor and protect sensitive information. Regularly review and update DLP policies to address emerging threats and ensure compliance with legal and regulatory requirements.

- **Train the workforce:** Educate employees about the importance of data protection and their role in preventing data breaches. Provide training on data handling policies, recognizing potential threats, and reporting incidents.
- **Establish an incident response program:** Develop a plan for responding to data breaches and other security incidents. This should include procedures for identifying, containing, and mitigating the impact of incidents, as well as notifying affected individuals and authorities.

By combining these strategies, organizations can create a robust data protection framework that safeguards sensitive information and ensures compliance with privacy regulations.

Privacy by Design

Privacy by design (PbD) is a foundational principle for integrating privacy and data protection into the development and operation of systems, processes, and business practices. It emphasizes proactive measures, ensuring that privacy is embedded into the design and architecture of IT systems and business practices from the outset, rather than as an afterthought. This approach is crucial in today's environment, where data breaches and privacy concerns are increasingly prevalent.

Key Principles of Privacy by Design

By adhering to the principles of privacy by design and implementing best practices, organizations can enhance trust, comply with regulations, improve data security, and achieve operational efficiency. This approach ensures that privacy is a fundamental component of the organization's operations and a core value that guides its actions and decisions.

Here are the key principles of PbD:

- **Proactive, not reactive; preventive, not remedial:** Systems should be designed to prevent privacy risks from occurring in the first place rather than responding to privacy lapses that do occur.
- **Privacy as the default setting:** Systems should protect the privacy of individuals by default, even if they do not take any action. The default approach of any system should be to protect privacy unless the user specifically chooses to take actions that reduce the level of privacy.
- **Privacy embedded into design:** Privacy should be a primary design consideration, not a "bolted-on" afterthought. Privacy is a core requirement of the system, integrated into the architecture of IT systems and business processes.

- **Full functionality—positive-sum, not zero-sum:** Privacy should not be treated as requiring trade-offs with business, security, or other objectives. PbD seeks win-win situations where privacy objectives may be achieved alongside other objectives.
- **End-to-end security—full lifecycle protection:** Security practices should persist throughout the entire information life cycle. Information should be securely collected, retained, and disposed of to preserve individual privacy.
- **Visibility and transparency—keep it open:** The component parts of systems preserving PbD should be open for inspection by users and providers alike. This transparency ensures accountability and trust.
- **Respect for user privacy—keep it user-centric:** Privacy is about protecting personal information, and personal information belongs to individuals. Therefore, PbD practices maintain a focus on the individual, empowering data subjects with user-friendly privacy practices.

The principles of PbD offer an outstanding starting point for integrating privacy thinking into a systems engineering practice. They ensure that privacy is considered from the initial stages of system development and throughout the entire life cycle of data.

Implementing Privacy by Design

Implementing PbD requires a comprehensive approach that includes several key steps:

- **Conduct privacy impact assessments (PIAs):** These assessments help identify potential privacy risks and the impact of data processing activities on individual privacy. PIAs should be conducted at the early stages of project development and revisited regularly.
- **Integrate privacy into system architecture:** Privacy considerations should be embedded into the design and architecture of IT systems and business processes. This includes incorporating privacy-enhancing technologies and ensuring that privacy controls are integrated into the system's core functionalities.
- **Develop privacy policies and procedures:** Organizations should establish and maintain privacy policies and procedures that align with the principles of PbD. These policies should be communicated to all employees and stakeholders to ensure a consistent approach to privacy protection.
- **Train employees on privacy best practices:** Regular training and awareness programs should be conducted to ensure that employees

understand their roles and responsibilities in protecting privacy. This includes training on data handling practices, privacy policies, and the use of privacy-enhancing technologies.
- **Monitor and audit privacy practices:** Regular monitoring and auditing of privacy practices help ensure that privacy controls are effective and that any potential issues are identified and addressed promptly. This includes conducting regular privacy audits and assessments to evaluate compliance with privacy policies and regulations.
- **Engage with stakeholders:** Engaging with stakeholders, including customers, employees, and regulators, is essential for building trust and ensuring that privacy practices align with their expectations and requirements. This includes seeking feedback on privacy practices and addressing any concerns or issues that arise.

Benefits of Privacy by Design

Implementing PbD offers several benefits, including:

- **Enhanced trust and reputation:** By demonstrating a commitment to privacy, organizations can build trust with customers, employees, and other stakeholders. This can enhance the organization's reputation and competitive advantage.
- **Compliance with regulations:** PbD helps organizations comply with privacy regulations and standards, such as the General Data Protection Regulation and the California Consumer Privacy Act. This can reduce the risk of regulatory penalties and legal liabilities.
- **Improved data security:** By integrating privacy into the design and architecture of systems, organizations can enhance their overall data security posture. This can reduce the risk of data breaches and other security incidents.
- **Operational efficiency:** Implementing PbD can lead to more efficient and effective data management practices. This can improve operational efficiency and reduce the costs associated with data breaches and privacy incidents.

Developing a Privacy Program

Developing a robust privacy program is a critical step for organizations to safeguard personal information and ensure compliance with various privacy laws and regulations. A well-designed privacy program not only addresses legal requirements but also instills trust among customers and stakeholders by demonstrating a commitment to protecting their personal data.

Developing a privacy program requires a comprehensive and proactive approach to managing personal information. By crafting clear strategies, appointing responsible officials, defining privacy roles, building data inventories, conducting assessments, implementing controls, and ensuring ongoing monitoring, organizations can create a robust privacy program.

Crafting Strategy, Goals, and Objectives

At the outset of a privacy initiative, senior leadership should outline the purpose, strategy, and goals of the privacy program. These provide the high-level direction needed to guide implementation efforts. For example, the U.S. Department of Commerce (DOC) has a mission statement committed to safeguarding personal privacy. This high-level statement is complemented by specific goals, such as fostering a culture of privacy, providing education and training, ensuring compliance with laws, and developing privacy professionals. Under each goal, specific objectives detail the actions to achieve these goals, such as reviewing programs for compliance and promoting privacy best practices. These objectives ensure that the privacy program remains aligned with the organization's strategic vision and adapts to changing needs over time.

Appointing a Privacy Official

Organizations should appoint a senior leader, often referred to as the chief privacy officer (CPO), to oversee the privacy program. This role involves developing and implementing privacy policies, ensuring compliance with laws, managing privacy risks, and advocating for privacy-preserving strategies. The CPO is responsible for communicating the privacy vision both internally and externally, ensuring that employees and contractors receive appropriate privacy training, and facilitating relationships with senior leaders and external stakeholders. In large organizations, additional privacy officials or liaisons may be designated within different units to ensure thorough program implementation and oversight. This hierarchical approach ensures that privacy considerations are integrated into all levels of the organization.

Privacy Roles

Depending on their involvement in data collection and processing, individuals and organizations may take on roles such as data subjects, data controllers, and data processors. Data subjects are individuals whose personal information is collected. Data controllers determine the purposes and means of data collection. Data processors handle data on behalf of controllers. Understanding these roles is crucial for compliance with regulations like the GDPR, which has specific definitions and requirements for each role. For example, data controllers are responsible for ensuring that data processors adhere to privacy standards and may be held accountable for any breaches. Clearly defining these roles helps organizations navigate legal obligations and maintain accountability throughout the data life cycle.

Building Inventories

Creating a comprehensive inventory of personal information is essential for developing a privacy program. This inventory should detail the types of personal data collected, processed, and maintained, along with storage locations and processes involved. A well-maintained inventory helps organizations understand their data landscape and serves as a basis for conducting privacy assessments and implementing controls. Collaboration between privacy and information security programs can streamline this process by tagging personal information within a broader sensitive data inventory. This integrated approach reduces redundancy and ensures that all sensitive information is appropriately managed and protected.

Conducting a Privacy Assessment

With a data inventory in place, organizations can assess the current state of their privacy program using standard privacy practices from industry frameworks or regulatory requirements. For example, the ISO 27701 framework provides guidelines for privacy information management. Regular assessments help identify gaps and areas for improvement, ensuring that privacy practices evolve with changing business needs and regulatory landscapes. These assessments involve evaluating the effectiveness of existing controls, identifying potential vulnerabilities, and developing remediation plans to address any deficiencies. Conducting thorough privacy assessments is a proactive measure that helps organizations stay ahead of potential privacy risks.

Implementing Privacy Controls

Privacy controls are measures put in place to protect personal information and ensure compliance with privacy policies and regulations. These controls may include technical solutions, such as encryption and access controls, as well as administrative measures, like privacy policies and training programs.

Implementing robust privacy controls helps mitigate risks and demonstrates the organization's commitment to protecting personal data. For instance, access controls ensure that only authorized personnel can access sensitive information, while encryption protects data in transit and at rest. Regularly updating and reviewing these controls ensures that they remain effective in the face of evolving threats and regulatory requirements.

Ongoing Operation and Monitoring

Privacy programs require continuous operation and monitoring to remain effective. This involves periodic reviews, updates to privacy assessments, and monitoring key metrics such as compliance with data retention standards and the handling of privacy incidents. Organizations may also undergo privacy audits conducted by independent auditors to ensure compliance with external standards. Ongoing monitoring and enforcement practices help maintain the integrity of the privacy program and address any issues that arise. This continuous improvement process involves tracking the effectiveness of privacy controls, responding to new privacy challenges, and ensuring that the organization remains compliant with evolving legal and regulatory requirements.

Cross-Border Data Transfers and Legal Implications

As businesses expand globally, managing the flow of data across international borders becomes increasingly critical. The transfer of data internationally is essential for multinational corporations to function efficiently, yet it presents significant privacy and legal challenges. This section will explore the complexities and legal implications of cross-border data transfers and the enforcement issues that arise from differing international privacy regulations.

International Data Transfers

The transfer of data across borders is a fundamental aspect of modern business operations. Multinational corporations need to transfer data globally to manage logistics, sales, product development, and other critical business functions. However, privacy implications arise when data moves from one jurisdiction to another, especially if the receiving country has less stringent privacy protections.

When personal data flows from a country with robust privacy laws to one with weaker protections, the originating country's privacy rights may become meaningless. Conversely, prohibiting international data transfers could cripple multinational business operations and have severe economic consequences. Unlike the United States, where preemption allows for a clear legal standard across states, there is no such concept internationally. Conflicting privacy laws between countries can create situations where compliance with one law means violating another, making it impossible for companies to adhere to both simultaneously.

To address these challenges, several strategies have been developed to facilitate international data transfers while ensuring compliance with privacy regulations. Key mechanisms include:

- **Standard contractual clauses (SCCs):** These are preapproved clauses by the European Commission that can be incorporated into contracts to ensure data protection standards are met when transferring data outside the EU.
- **Binding corporate rules (BCRs):** These are internal policies adopted by multinational companies to ensure data transferred within the organization across borders meets EU data protection standards.
- **Safe harbor programs:** These agreements between countries or regions establish a framework for data protection that companies can adhere to when transferring data internationally.

The European Union's General Data Protection Regulation is a prime example of stringent international privacy legislation that significantly impacts U.S. companies. The GDPR applies across all sectors for all EU member states and offers a sweeping definition of personal information. To comply with the GDPR, U.S. companies must adopt one of the mechanisms mentioned previously to ensure they meet the EU's data protection standards. The GDPR also confers a series of data subject rights, such as the right to erasure, or the right to be forgotten, which enables EU data subjects to order any controller or processor to delete all their personal information. Violations of the GDPR bring steep penalties, making compliance crucial for international business operations.

Cross-Border Enforcement Issues

Enforcing privacy regulations across national boundaries presents additional challenges. Residents of countries with strict privacy laws expect their data to be protected according to their local regulations, even when their data is transferred abroad. However, once data crosses into a jurisdiction with looser privacy laws, it may be compromised despite any safe harbor agreements in place.

The Organisation for Economic Co-operation and Development (OECD) developed the Global Privacy Enforcement Network (GPEN) in 2007 to improve international cooperation in enforcing privacy regulations among member nations. GPEN helps domestic regulatory agencies collaborate on cross-border privacy enforcement issues through a five-point mission that includes:

- Facilitating the sharing of information and best practices.
- Providing training for regulatory agencies.
- Promoting communication between member nations.
- Developing methods for international cooperation.
- Supporting existing internationally recognized privacy standards.

While GPEN does not provide a privacy framework, it plays a crucial role in coordinating enforcement efforts and helping regulators understand the multinational privacy landscape.

Resolving Multinational Compliance Conflicts

Conflicts often arise when transferring data between countries with differing privacy laws. For example, the GDPR provides more robust protections for personal information than U.S. law. A U.S. company managing the personal information of EU citizens might be legally required to disclose information to the U.S. government, a disclosure that could be illegal under the GDPR.

Frameworks such as the Asia-Pacific Economic Cooperation (APEC) Cross-Border Privacy Rules system and other safe harbor programs attempt to resolve these conflicts by aligning privacy standards. However, domestic laws may still override these agreements. The challenge of reconciling conflicting privacy laws remains, and companies must implement strong data management programs to track international data transfers and seek legal advice when facing contradictory compliance obligations.

Cross-border data transfers are essential for multinational business operations but come with significant legal and privacy challenges. Mechanisms like SCCs, BCRs, and safe harbor programs help facilitate these transfers while ensuring compliance with varying international privacy regulations. Organizations must stay informed and proactive in managing these complexities to navigate the global data protection landscape effectively. By understanding and leveraging these mechanisms, companies can better protect personal data and maintain compliance with international privacy laws, thus fostering trust and ensuring smooth business operations across borders.

Data Subject Rights and Privacy Request Handling

Data subject rights are a crucial aspect of data protection and privacy engineering. These rights empower individuals to exercise control over their personal information and ensure that organizations handle this data responsibly. The primary data subject rights include access, deletion/correction, portability, opt-out, and opt-in rights. Each of these rights plays a significant role in maintaining privacy and fostering trust between individuals and organizations.

Privacy request handling is another fundamental component of data protection and privacy engineering. By respecting these rights and implementing robust privacy practices, organizations can build trust with individuals, comply with legal requirements, and protect personal information effectively.

Access Rights

Data subjects have the right to request access to their personal information held by an organization. This right typically includes the ability to know what data is being collected, how it is being used, and with whom it is being shared. Organizations must respond to access requests within a specified time frame and provide the requested information in a clear and understandable format. Access rights help individuals stay informed about their data and verify its accuracy.

Deletion/Correction Rights

Data subjects can request the deletion or correction of their personal information. Deletion rights, often referred to as the right to be forgotten, allow individuals to request the removal of their data when it is no longer necessary for the purposes for which it was collected. Correction rights enable individuals to request updates or corrections to their data to ensure accuracy. Organizations must comply with these requests within a specified time frame unless there are legitimate grounds for retaining the data.

Portability Rights

Portability rights grant data subjects the ability to obtain a copy of their personal information in a structured, commonly used, and machine-readable format. This allows individuals to transfer their data to another organization or use it for their own purposes. Portability rights promote data interoperability and empower individuals to switch service providers without losing their data.

Opt-Out Rights

Opt-out rights provide data subjects with the option to refuse the collection, processing, or sharing of their personal information under certain conditions. For example, individuals may opt out of having their data used for marketing purposes or shared with third parties. Organizations must provide clear and easy-to-use mechanisms for individuals to exercise their opt-out rights and must honor these requests promptly.

Opt-In Rights

Opt-in rights require organizations to obtain explicit consent from data subjects before collecting, processing, or sharing their personal information. This is a more stringent standard than opt-out rights and provides greater control to individuals over their data. Opt-in rights are often required for processing sensitive information or for activities that have a significant impact on privacy.

Selling and Sharing of Personal Information

Many state privacy laws provide data subjects with rights related to the selling and sharing of their personal information. These rights can take various forms, such as the right to opt-in or opt-out, the right to know if their information is being shared or sold, or even the prohibition of sharing and selling personal information entirely. These rights aim to protect individuals from unauthorized or unwanted data transactions.

Automated Decision-Making and Artificial Intelligence (AI)

Rights related to automated decision-making and AI address the use of technology to make decisions that may affect individuals. Automated decision-making often involves the use of algorithms and machine learning to process data and make determinations, such as selecting job applicants or approving loans. State laws may grant individuals the right to know if automated decision-making is being used, regulate its use, or prohibit it altogether. These rights ensure transparency and fairness in decisions that impact individuals.

Privacy Notice Requirements

Many state privacy laws mandate organizations to disclose their privacy practices through written privacy notices. These notices provide transparency about how personal information is collected, used, shared, and protected. Privacy notices must be clear, accessible, and regularly updated to reflect current practices. They help individuals make informed decisions about their data and ensure compliance with legal requirements.

Data Security Requirements

State privacy laws often include requirements for securing personal information. Organizations must implement appropriate technical and organizational measures to protect data from unauthorized access, disclosure, alteration, and destruction. These measures may include encryption, access controls, and regular security assessments. Data security requirements help safeguard personal information and prevent data breaches.

Managing Data Shared with Third Parties

Organizations must carefully manage data shared with third parties to ensure continued protection of personal information. This includes conducting due diligence on third-party partners, establishing data protection agreements, and monitoring compliance with privacy requirements. Effective third-party management helps mitigate risks and maintain trust with data subjects.

Data Retention and Destruction

State privacy laws may specify requirements for data retention and destruction. Organizations must retain personal information only for as long as necessary to fulfill the purposes for which it was collected. Once the data is no longer needed, it must be securely destroyed to prevent unauthorized access. Proper data retention and destruction practices help minimize privacy risks and ensure compliance with legal obligations.

Privacy Request Handling

Handling privacy requests efficiently and effectively is a vital component of respecting data subject rights. Organizations must establish and maintain processes to manage requests related to access, deletion, correction, portability, and consent preferences. These processes should include:

- **Receipt and acknowledgment:** Organizations should have clear channels for receiving privacy requests, such as dedicated email addresses or web forms. Upon receiving a request, the organization should promptly acknowledge receipt and provide an estimated timeline for response.
- **Verification of identity:** To protect against unauthorized access, organizations must verify the identity of the individual making the request. This step ensures that personal information is only disclosed or modified at the request of the legitimate data subject.
- **Assessment and action:** Once a request is verified, the organization should assess the request's validity and determine the appropriate action. This may involve retrieving data from various systems, correcting inaccuracies, or deleting information as requested.
- **Communication:** Throughout the process, organizations should maintain clear communication with the data subject. This includes providing updates on the status of the request and informing the individual of the outcome.
- **Documentation:** Organizations should document all privacy requests and their responses. This documentation helps demonstrate compliance with legal requirements and provides a record for future reference.
- **Training and awareness:** Employees involved in handling privacy requests should receive regular training on the organization's processes and legal obligations. This ensures that requests are managed consistently and in accordance with applicable laws.

Data Retention, Archiving, and Secure Disposal

In the realm of information security and privacy, the management of data retention, archiving, and secure disposal is critical. Organizations must establish clear policies and practices to ensure that data is retained for the appropriate period, archived securely, and disposed of in a manner that prevents unauthorized access and protects sensitive information.

Effective data retention, archiving, and secure disposal practices are essential components of an organization's information security and privacy program.

By implementing clear policies and procedures, organizations can ensure that data is retained for the appropriate period, archived securely, and disposed of in a manner that protects sensitive information and complies with legal and regulatory requirements. These practices not only help prevent data breaches and unauthorized access but also support efficient data management and reduce storage costs.

This section provides an overview of best practices for data retention, archiving, and secure disposal.

Data Retention

Data retention policies determine how long an organization should keep different types of data. These policies are influenced by legal, regulatory, and business requirements. Effective data retention practices help organizations manage data efficiently, reduce storage costs, and comply with legal obligations.

Key elements of data retention policies include:

- **Legal and regulatory requirements:** Organizations must comply with laws and regulations that mandate specific retention periods for certain types of data. For example, financial records may need to be retained for a specific number of years to comply with tax regulations.
- **Business needs:** Beyond legal requirements, organizations must consider their operational needs. Data that supports business processes, decision-making, and historical analysis may need to be retained for longer periods.
- **Data classification:** Different types of data may have different retention requirements. Sensitive data, such as personally identifiable information and protected health information, may require stricter controls and shorter retention periods.
- **Retention schedules:** Organizations should develop and implement retention schedules that specify the retention period for each category of data. These schedules should be regularly reviewed and updated to reflect changes in legal requirements and business needs.

Data Archiving

Data archiving involves the secure storage of data that is no longer actively used but must be retained for legal, regulatory, or business reasons. Proper archiving practices ensure that data is preserved in a secure and accessible manner.

Best practices for data archiving include:

- **Secure storage:** Archived data should be stored in a secure environment that protects it from unauthorized access, tampering, and environmental hazards. This may involve using encryption, access controls, and physical security measures.
- **Data integrity:** Measures should be taken to ensure the integrity of archived data. This includes regular integrity checks, error detection, and correction mechanisms to prevent data corruption.
- **Access controls:** Access to archived data should be restricted to authorized personnel only. Role-based access controls and audit trails can help monitor and enforce access restrictions.
- **Retention management:** Archived data should be managed according to the organization's retention schedules. Data that has reached the end of its retention period should be securely disposed of.

Secure Disposal

Secure disposal of data is essential to prevent unauthorized access and protect sensitive information. When data is no longer needed, it must be disposed of in a manner that ensures it cannot be recovered or misused.

Methods for secure data disposal include:

- **Physical destruction:** Physical destruction methods, such as shredding, incineration, disintegration, pulverizing, and melting, can be used to destroy physical media, such as paper documents and optical discs.
- **Degaussing:** Degaussing involves using a strong magnetic field to erase data from magnetic storage media, such as hard drives and tapes. This method is effective for magnetic media but does not work for solid-state drives (SSDs) or optical media.
- **Overwriting:** Overwriting involves writing random data over the existing data on a storage medium multiple times to prevent data recovery. This method can be used for both magnetic and solid-state storage media.
- **Cryptographic erasure:** Cryptographic erasure involves encrypting data and then securely deleting the encryption keys. Without the keys, the encrypted data is rendered unreadable and effectively destroyed.
- **Certified destruction services:** Organizations may use certified destruction services to ensure that data is securely disposed of in compliance with legal and regulatory requirements. These services provide documentation and certification of the destruction process.

Data Remanence

Data remanence refers to the residual data that remains on storage media after it has been deleted or erased. Advanced tools and techniques can sometimes recover this residual data, posing a security risk.

To mitigate the risk of data remanence:

- **Use secure deletion tools:** Secure deletion tools can overwrite data multiple times to reduce the likelihood of data recovery.
- **Employ encryption:** Encrypting data before storing it can protect it from unauthorized access, even if residual data remains on the media.
- **Regularly update disposal practices:** Organizations should stay informed about new data recovery techniques and update their disposal practices accordingly to ensure ongoing protection against data remanence.

CHAPTER 6

Security and Privacy Incident Management

Security and privacy incident management has become a critical aspect of safeguarding organizational assets and maintaining trust. As a security or privacy professional, you are at the forefront of protecting sensitive information from an ever-growing array of threats. This chapter is designed to provide you with a comprehensive understanding of the essential components of incident management, equipping you with the knowledge and skills needed to effectively respond to and mitigate the impact of security and privacy incidents.

By the end of this chapter, you will be well-equipped to manage security and privacy incidents with confidence and precision. You will be able to create and execute incident response plans, conduct efficient investigations, communicate effectively during a crisis, and ensure compliance with relevant regulations. This knowledge will not only help you protect your organization but also enhance your professional expertise in the field of security and privacy incident management.

Incident Response Planning

Incident response planning is a critical aspect of an organization's security and privacy management strategy. The objective is to ensure that the organization is prepared to handle security incidents effectively, minimize damage, and recover quickly. A well-structured incident response plan (IRP) and a competent computer security incident response team (CSIRT) are essential components of this strategy.

Building the Incident Response Plan

The incident response plan serves as the foundation for the CSIRT's activities. It should include the following key elements:

- **Policy:** The incident response policy provides high-level guidance and authority for the incident response program. It should be approved by top management and include statements of management commitment, purpose and objectives, scope, definitions of incidents, roles and responsibilities, prioritization of incidents, performance measures, and reporting procedures.
- **Procedures and playbooks:** Detailed procedures and playbooks are essential for guiding the CSIRT's response to specific types of incidents. These documents should be developed during periods of calm and be ready for use during an incident. Playbooks should cover common incident scenarios, such as breaches of personal financial information, web server defacement, phishing attacks, and loss of laptops.

Creating an Incident Response Team

A CSIRT is responsible for managing and responding to security incidents. The effectiveness of the CSIRT depends on careful preparation, appropriate training, and a clear understanding of roles and responsibilities.

- **Preparation:** Preparation is crucial for an effective incident response. The organization should ensure that the CSIRT has the necessary resources, including digital forensic workstations, backup devices, laptops, spare server and networking equipment, forensic software, and evidence collection materials. Regular training and exercises, such as tabletop exercises and simulation testing, help ensure that the team is ready to respond when an incident occurs.
- **Roles and responsibilities:** The CSIRT should include members with diverse expertise to handle various aspects of incident response. Core team members typically include cybersecurity professionals with specific incident response skills. Additional roles may be filled by subject matter experts as needed, depending on the nature of the incident.

Plan Training, Testing, and Evaluation

As organizations build out their incident response programs, they must ensure that everyone understands their role in incident response. Training programs should touch every team member and be tailored to each individual's role in incident response efforts. For example, a receptionist might simply need to understand that they must report security incidents to the security operations center (SOC). Incident response team members, on the other hand, will need detailed technical training on their responsibilities. Other employees may fit somewhere in between those two extremes and should receive role-specific training.

Organizations should regularly test their incident response plans to ensure that they continue to meet the organization's security objectives. The results of these tests may identify potential revisions to the plan that will improve future incident response efforts. Common incident response test types include the following:

- **Checklist reviews:** Provide each team member with a copy of their incident response checklists and ask them to walk through their expected actions to ensure that they understand their role and that the steps on the checklist remain relevant.
- **Tabletop exercises:** Gather the team in a central location and lead them through a discussion of how they would respond to a given incident scenario.
- **Incident simulations:** Move beyond tabletop exercises and actually ask the team to carry out some or all portions of the incident response effort in response to a provided scenario.

Testing cybersecurity incident response plans is a critical component of any organization's incident response strategy. Testing reassures the organization that the plan will function properly in the event of an actual incident and provides a critical training exercise for the team members who would respond to a real-world cybersecurity crisis.

In addition to conducting tests, organizations should collect key indicators and metrics to measure the health of their incident response program. NIST suggests monitoring the following key metrics for each incident:

- Number of incidents handled
- Total amount of labor spent working on each incident
- Elapsed time from the beginning of the incident to discovery
- Elapsed time from discovery to an initial impact assessment
- Elapsed time for each stage of the containment, eradication, and recovery process
- How long it took the CSIRT to respond to the initial report of the incident
- How long it took to escalate the incident to management and/or external authorities
- Compliance with established policies and procedures
- Determining whether the cause of the incident was identified successfully

Documenting the Incident Response Plan

When developing the incident response plan documentation, organizations should pay particular attention to creating tools that may be useful during an incident response. These tools should provide clear guidance to response teams that may be quickly read and interpreted during a crisis situation. For example, the incident response checklist provides a high-level overview of the incident response process in checklist form. The CSIRT leader may use this checklist to ensure that the team doesn't miss an important step in the heat of the crisis environment.

Detection and Triage of Security and Privacy Incidents

In the realm of information security and privacy, the ability to detect and appropriately triage incidents is crucial for maintaining the integrity, confidentiality, and availability of information systems. This section provides a comprehensive overview of the processes involved in detecting and triaging security and privacy incidents, drawing on established frameworks and best practices. By following these structured phases and processes, organizations can effectively detect, classify, and triage security and privacy incidents, minimizing their impact and ensuring a swift and coordinated response.

Phases of Incident Response

The incident response life cycle is typically divided into several phases that guide organizations in managing and mitigating the impact of security and privacy incidents. These phases include preparation, detection and analysis, containment, eradication, recovery, and post-incident activities:

- **Preparation:** This phase involves establishing and maintaining an incident response capability. Key activities include developing incident response policies, procedures, and plans; creating communication strategies; and training the incident response team. Organizations should also ensure that they have the necessary tools and resources, such as intrusion detection systems (IDSs), intrusion prevention systems, and security information and event management (SIEM) systems, to effectively detect and respond to incidents.

- **Detection and analysis:** The detection phase is critical for identifying potential incidents. Organizations use various methods and tools to detect incidents, including IDS/IPS, SIEM systems, antimalware software, and log management systems. Detection can be triggered by alerts from these systems, reports from users, or public information about new vulnerabilities and exploits. Once an incident is detected, it must be analyzed to determine its scope, impact, and potential damage. This involves validating the incident, assessing its severity, and identifying the affected systems and data.
- **Containment, eradication, and recovery:** After an incident is detected and analyzed, the next step is to contain it to prevent further damage. Containment strategies vary depending on the type and severity of the incident and may include isolating affected systems, blocking malicious traffic, or disabling compromised accounts. Eradication involves removing the cause of the incident, such as deleting malware or closing vulnerabilities. Recovery focuses on restoring normal operations and ensuring that affected systems are clean and secure. This may involve restoring data from backups, rebuilding systems, and applying patches and updates.
- **Post-incident activity:** The final phase involves reviewing and analyzing the incident to identify lessons learned and improve future incident response efforts. This includes conducting a post-incident review, documenting the incident and response actions, and updating incident response plans and procedures based on the findings. Organizations should also consider conducting root cause analysis to prevent similar incidents in the future.

Classifying Incidents

Effective incident management requires a clear and consistent process for classifying incidents. This helps organizations prioritize their response efforts and allocate resources appropriately. Incident classification typically involves categorizing incidents based on their type, severity, and impact.

- **Incident type:** Incidents can be classified into various types, such as malware infections, unauthorized access, data breaches, denial-of-service attacks, and insider threats. Each type of incident may require different response strategies and resources.
- **Severity:** The severity of an incident is determined by its potential impact on the organization. Factors to consider include the sensitivity of the affected data, the criticality of the affected systems, and the potential for financial, reputational, or legal damage. Severity levels can range from low (minor incidents with limited impact) to high (major incidents with significant impact).

- **Impact:** The impact of an incident refers to the actual damage caused to the organization. This can include data loss, system downtime, financial losses, regulatory penalties, and damage to the organization's reputation. Assessing the impact helps organizations understand the full extent of the incident and prioritize their response efforts.

Detection and Triage Process

The detection and triage process involves several key steps to ensure that incidents are identified, classified, and addressed in a timely and effective manner.

- **Monitoring and detection:** Continuous monitoring of systems, networks, and applications is essential for early detection of incidents. Organizations should use a combination of automated tools (such as IDS, IPS, and SIEM) and manual methods (such as log reviews and user reports) to identify potential incidents.
- **Initial triage:** Once a potential incident is detected, it must be triaged to determine its validity and severity. This involves gathering and analyzing relevant data, such as logs, alerts, and network traffic, to confirm the incident and assess its impact. The initial triage helps prioritize incidents and allocate resources for further investigation and response.
- **Incident classification:** Based on the initial triage, the incident is classified according to its type, severity, and impact. This classification helps guide the response efforts and ensures that the most critical incidents receive immediate attention.
- **Notification and escalation:** Depending on the severity and impact of the incident, it may be necessary to notify and escalate the issue to relevant stakeholders, such as senior management, legal and compliance teams, and external partners. Clear communication channels and protocols should be established to ensure timely and effective notification and escalation.
- **Response coordination:** Once an incident is classified and prioritized, the incident response team coordinates the response efforts. This includes implementing containment measures, conducting further analysis and investigation, and taking steps to eradicate the cause of the incident and recover normal operations.

Investigating Incidents

The investigation of incidents is a critical process that ensures the integrity of an organization's response to security breaches. Effective incident investigation is not only about understanding what happened but also about learning from the incident to prevent future occurrences. This section delves into the essential components of conducting investigations and the containment, eradication, and recovery stages of incident management.

Conducting Investigations

Investigations are a fundamental aspect of incident management. They help ascertain the nature, cause, and impact of an incident. Security professionals must be adept at handling various types of investigations, including administrative, criminal, civil, regulatory, and those involving industry standards. Each investigation type has specific standards of evidence and forensic procedures that must be followed to ensure the investigation's integrity and legality.

Types of Investigations Security professionals must be skilled in conducting various types of investigations, each with its own standards and procedures. These investigations can range from internal administrative probes to complex criminal inquiries involving law enforcement. Understanding the different types of investigations and their specific requirements is crucial for effectively managing and resolving security incidents.

The primary types of investigations include:

- **Administrative investigations:** These are internal probes that examine operational issues or policy violations within an organization. They often support technical troubleshooting or human resources disciplinary procedures. For example, an IT team may conduct an operational investigation to determine the cause of performance issues on web servers. Administrative investigations can quickly transition to another type of investigation if more severe issues, such as a system intrusion, are uncovered.
- **Criminal investigations:** These involve law enforcement and must adhere to rigorous standards to produce admissible evidence in court. They typically address severe incidents such as data breaches involving theft or fraud. Criminal investigations require careful handling of evidence to maintain its integrity for legal proceedings.
- **Civil investigations:** These are often related to lawsuits where one party seeks compensation or remedy for damages caused by another party's actions. Civil investigations focus on gathering evidence that supports the claims of either the plaintiff or the defendant in a legal dispute.
- **Regulatory investigations:** These ensure compliance with laws and regulations, often involving government agencies. Regulatory investigations may be triggered by incidents that violate specific legal requirements, such as data protection laws.

- **Industry standards investigations:** These focus on adherence to industry-specific standards and best practices. Organizations may conduct these investigations to ensure they meet the requirements set by industry bodies or certification organizations.

Investigation Process The investigation process is a structured approach designed to uncover the details of a security incident, determine its root cause, and gather evidence in a manner that is both thorough and legally sound. This process ensures that investigations are conducted systematically, maintaining the integrity of the evidence and adhering to legal and regulatory requirements. A well-defined investigation process helps organizations respond effectively to incidents, mitigate damage, and prevent future occurrences.

Key components of the investigation process include:

- **Evidence collection and handling:** Proper collection and handling of evidence are crucial. This includes documenting the scene, preserving evidence integrity, and following chain-of-custody procedures to prevent tampering or contamination. Evidence might include digital logs, emails, physical documents, and more.
- **Reporting and documentation:** Detailed documentation of the investigation process, findings, and actions taken is essential for legal and regulatory compliance. This includes incident reports, logs, and communication records. Accurate documentation ensures that all steps taken during the investigation are recorded and can be reviewed if necessary.
- **Investigative techniques:** Various techniques, such as interviews, log analysis, and forensic imaging, are used to gather information and analyze the incident. These techniques help investigators piece together the sequence of events and identify the root cause of the incident.
- **Digital forensics:** This involves using specialized tools and procedures to examine digital evidence, such as data from computers, networks, and mobile devices. The goal is to uncover the root cause of the incident and understand the extent of the breach. Digital forensics can reveal how the incident occurred, what data was affected, and who was responsible.

Containment, Eradication, and Recovery

Once an incident is detected and investigated, the next steps involve containing the threat, eradicating its cause, and recovering affected systems and data. These stages are crucial to minimize damage and restore normal operations.

Containment Containment is a critical phase in incident response aimed at limiting the damage caused by a security incident and preventing its further spread. Swift and effective containment measures are essential to protect organizational assets and maintain operational stability. This phase requires a careful balance between halting the incident and minimizing disruption to normal business activities. By implementing both immediate and longer-term containment strategies, organizations can control the situation and prepare for subsequent eradication and recovery efforts.

The key aspects of containment include:

- **Immediate actions:** The primary goal of containment is to limit the damage and prevent further spread of the incident. This may involve isolating affected systems, disabling compromised accounts, or blocking malicious IP addresses. Quick action is essential to prevent the incident from escalating.
- **Short-term containment:** Quick, temporary measures are taken to halt the incident's progression—for example, disconnecting an infected system from the network to stop malware spread. Short-term containment provides immediate relief while longer-term strategies are developed.
- **Long-term containment:** More permanent solutions are implemented to ensure the threat is fully contained. This might include applying patches, reconfiguring firewalls, or enhancing monitoring systems. Long-term containment ensures that the incident does not recur and that the organization is better protected against similar threats in the future.

Eradication The eradication phase of incident response focuses on completely removing the underlying cause of a security incident from the organization's environment. This step is crucial to ensure that the threat is fully neutralized and that there are no lingering vulnerabilities or malicious elements that could lead to a recurrence. Eradication efforts involve identifying and eliminating all traces of the incident, verifying the integrity of affected systems, and addressing any weaknesses that were exploited. By thoroughly eradicating the threat, organizations can restore confidence in their systems and move forward with recovery efforts.

The essential components of eradication include:

- **Removing the threat:** Eradication involves identifying and eliminating the root cause of the incident. This could mean deleting malware, closing vulnerabilities, or removing unauthorized access points. The goal is to ensure that the threat is completely removed from the environment.
- **Verification:** After eradication, systems are thoroughly checked to ensure the threat has been completely removed and no residual issues remain. Verification may involve running security scans, reviewing logs, and conducting penetration tests.

Recovery The recovery phase of incident response is dedicated to restoring affected systems and operations to their normal state following a security incident. This phase is vital for ensuring that business functions can resume smoothly and securely, minimizing downtime and disruption. Recovery involves a series of steps to rebuild and verify the integrity of compromised systems, restore data from backups, and test the environment to confirm that it is free from vulnerabilities. By carefully managing the recovery process, organizations can ensure a seamless transition back to regular operations while maintaining a heightened state of vigilance.

The key steps in the recovery phase include:

- **Restoring systems:** The recovery phase focuses on returning systems to normal operation. This includes restoring data from backups, rebuilding systems, and verifying their integrity. Recovery efforts aim to bring the organization back to full functionality as quickly and securely as possible.
- **Testing and validation:** Systems are tested to confirm they are functioning correctly and securely. This may involve running security scans, performing functional tests, and validating configurations. Testing ensures that the recovered systems are free from vulnerabilities and ready for use.
- **Monitoring:** Enhanced monitoring is often implemented post-recovery to detect any signs of recurring issues or new threats. Continuous monitoring helps ensure that any new incidents are quickly identified and addressed.

Communication Plans for Incident Response

Effective communication is a critical component of incident response. When a security or privacy incident occurs, organizations must ensure that information flows seamlessly among all relevant parties to facilitate a coordinated and efficient response. This section outlines the key elements of communication plans for incident response, emphasizing the importance of clear policies, procedures, and automated tools to support these efforts.

By incorporating these elements into their incident response communication plans, organizations can ensure that they are well-prepared to handle security and privacy incidents effectively. Clear policies, detailed procedures, automated tools, and well-defined communication channels are essential for a coordinated and efficient response that minimizes the impact of incidents on the organization and its stakeholders.

Policy and Authority

The foundation of any incident response communication plan is a well-defined policy that provides the authority for incident response activities. This policy should be approved at the highest level within the organization, ideally by the chief executive officer, to ensure it carries the necessary weight and authority. The policy should include:

- **Statement of management commitment:** This demonstrates the organization's dedication to effective incident response.
- **Purpose and objectives:** Clearly outline the goals of the incident response communication plan.
- **Scope:** Define to whom the policy applies and under what circumstances.
- **Definitions:** Provide clear definitions of cybersecurity incidents and related terms.
- **Roles and responsibilities:** Detail the organizational structure, roles, responsibilities, and levels of authority.
- **Prioritization and severity rating:** Establish a scheme for prioritizing incidents based on their severity.
- **Performance measures:** Set metrics for evaluating the effectiveness of the communication plan.
- **Reporting and contact forms:** Include templates for reporting incidents and contact information for key personnel.

Procedures and Playbooks

Procedures and playbooks provide the tactical information needed to respond to incidents effectively. They represent the collective wisdom of team members and subject matter experts, collected during periods of calm and ready to be applied during an incident. Playbooks should cover specific types of incidents, such as breaches of personal financial information, web server defacements, phishing attacks, and general security incidents. These playbooks should be step-by-step guides that outline the following:

- **Detection and analysis:** How to identify and analyze potential incidents.
- **Containment, eradication, and recovery:** Steps to contain the incident, remove the threat, and restore normal operations.
- **Post-incident activity:** Procedures for conducting post-incident reviews and lessons learned.

Playbooks are not a substitute for professional judgment; responders should have the expertise and authority to deviate from the playbook when necessary.

Automating Incident Response

Automation can significantly enhance the efficiency and effectiveness of incident response communication plans. Automated tools can help detect incidents, alert relevant personnel, and facilitate information sharing. Key elements of automation in incident response include:

- **Intrusion detection and prevention systems:** IDPSs monitor network traffic for signs of malicious activity and can automatically alert administrators when potential incidents are detected.
- **Security information and event management systems:** SIEM systems collect and analyze log data from various sources to identify patterns indicative of security incidents.
- **Continuous monitoring and tuning:** Ongoing monitoring of network activity and tuning of detection systems help to improve their accuracy and effectiveness.
- **Egress monitoring:** Monitor outbound traffic to detect and prevent data exfiltration.
- **Log management:** Collect, store, and analyze log data to support incident detection and investigation.
- **Threat intelligence:** Leverage threat feeds and threat hunting activities to stay informed about emerging threats and vulnerabilities.

Notification and Escalation Procedures

Effective incident response requires clear notification and escalation procedures to ensure that the right people are informed at the right time. These procedures should include:

- **Initial reporting:** Guidelines for how first responders report potential incidents to the incident response team.
- **Team activation:** Processes for notifying team members of an incident and activating the incident response plan.
- **Escalation criteria:** Criteria for escalating incidents to higher levels of management based on their severity and potential impact.
- **Internal communication:** Methods for keeping all relevant internal stakeholders informed throughout the incident response process.
- **External communication:** Procedures for communicating with external parties, such as customers, partners, regulators, and the media.

Post-Incident Review and Lessons Learned

After an incident has been resolved, it is essential to conduct a thorough review and communicate the findings to relevant stakeholders. This post-incident communication is critical for understanding the incident, improving future response efforts, and demonstrating accountability to internal and external parties. The post-incident communication process should be comprehensive and systematic, ensuring that all relevant information is captured, analyzed, and disseminated appropriately. This section outlines the key components of effective post-incident communication.

Chronology of Events

One of the first steps in post-incident communication is to create a detailed timeline of the incident. This chronology should include:

- **Initial detection:** The exact time and method by which the incident was first detected.
- **Notification:** When and how the incident was reported to the incident response team.
- **Containment actions:** A timeline of the steps taken to contain the incident, including any decisions made and their rationale.
- **Eradication efforts:** The actions taken to remove the threat from the environment, along with their timing and effectiveness.
- **Recovery process:** The steps taken to restore normal operations, including system restorations, data recovery, and validation checks.
- **Incident resolution:** The time and method by which the incident was declared resolved.

This detailed timeline helps stakeholders understand the progression of the incident and the response efforts, providing a clear picture of what transpired.

Root Cause Analysis

Identifying the root cause of the incident is crucial for preventing future occurrences. The root cause analysis should include:

- **Incident origin:** Determination of how and where the incident originated.

- **Vulnerabilities exploited:** Identification of the specific vulnerabilities that were exploited by the attackers.
- **Attack vectors:** Analysis of the methods and techniques used by the attackers to gain access and escalate privileges.
- **Contributing factors:** Examination of any additional factors that may have contributed to the incident, such as misconfigurations, human error, or outdated software.

A thorough root cause analysis helps the organization understand the underlying issues that led to the incident and develop strategies to address them.

Evidence Collection

During the incident response process, a significant amount of evidence is typically collected. The post-incident communication should document:

- **Types of evidence:** A description of the evidence collected, such as log files, network traffic captures, and system images.
- **Evidence handling:** Details on how the evidence was collected, preserved, and analyzed to maintain its integrity.
- **Location of evidence:** Information on where the evidence is stored and how it can be accessed for future reference or legal proceedings.

Proper documentation of evidence is essential for supporting any legal actions and for conducting thorough post-incident reviews.

Response Actions

The post-incident communication should provide a detailed account of the actions taken during the response, including:

- **Containment strategies:** The specific measures implemented to contain the incident and prevent further damage.
- **Eradication techniques:** The methods used to remove the threat from the environment, such as patching vulnerabilities, removing malicious code, or isolating affected systems.
- **Recovery steps:** The actions taken to restore normal operations, including system restorations, data recovery, and validation checks.
- **Decision rationale:** The reasoning behind key decisions made during the response, including any trade-offs or risks considered.

This detailed account helps stakeholders understand the effectiveness of the response efforts and provides a basis for evaluating and improving future responses.

Impact Assessment

Assessing the impact of the incident is critical for understanding its consequences and communicating them to stakeholders. The impact assessment should include:

- **Operational impact:** An evaluation of how the incident affected the organization's operations, such as system downtime, service disruptions, and productivity losses.
- **Financial impact:** An estimate of the financial costs associated with the incident, including direct costs (e.g., remediation expenses, legal fees) and indirect costs (e.g., lost revenue, reputational damage).
- **Customer impact:** An analysis of how the incident affected customers, including any data breaches, service interruptions, or trust issues.
- **Regulatory impact:** Identification of any regulatory requirements triggered by the incident, such as mandatory breach notifications or compliance audits.

A comprehensive impact assessment helps the organization understand the full scope of the incident's consequences and informs future risk management efforts.

Post-Recovery Validation

Once the incident has been resolved, it is essential to validate that affected systems are functioning normally and that any additional monitoring measures are in place. Post-recovery validation should include:

- **System checks:** Verification that all affected systems have been restored to their normal operating state and are free from any residual threats.
- **Data integrity:** Confirmation that data has been accurately restored and that no data loss or corruption has occurred.
- **Security controls:** Assessment of the effectiveness of any new or enhanced security controls implemented as part of the recovery process.
- **Continuous monitoring:** Implementation of ongoing monitoring measures to detect any signs of recurring issues or new threats.

Post-recovery validation ensures that the organization has fully recovered from the incident and is better prepared to prevent future occurrences.

Lessons Learned

Conducting a lessons learned review is a critical component of post-incident communication. This review should be facilitated by an independent facilitator and involve all relevant stakeholders. The lessons learned review should address the following questions:

- **What happened and at what times?** A detailed analysis of the incident timeline and key events.
- **How well did staff and management perform?** An evaluation of the effectiveness of the response efforts and the performance of individual team members.
- **Were documented procedures followed?** An assessment of whether existing procedures were followed and if they were adequate.
- **What information was needed sooner?** Identification of any information gaps or delays that hindered the response efforts.
- **Were any steps taken that inhibited recovery?** Analysis of any actions or decisions that may have negatively impacted the recovery process.
- **What would be done differently next time?** Recommendations for improving future incident response efforts.
- **How could information sharing be improved?** Suggestions for enhancing communication and collaboration with internal and external partners.
- **What corrective actions can prevent similar incidents?** Identification of specific measures to address the root causes and contributing factors of the incident.
- **What additional tools or resources are needed?** Recommendations for acquiring new tools, technologies, or resources to improve incident detection, analysis, and response.

The lessons learned review should result in a set of actionable recommendations that are documented and tracked to ensure they are implemented.

Communication with Stakeholders

Effective post-incident communication involves keeping all relevant stakeholders informed about the incident and the response efforts. This includes:

- **Internal stakeholders:** Regular updates to senior management, the incident response team, and other relevant departments to ensure everyone is aware of the incident's status and any ongoing actions.

- **External stakeholders:** Communication with customers, partners, regulators, and the media as appropriate. This may include issuing public statements, providing breach notifications, and cooperating with regulatory investigations.
- **Transparency and accountability:** Providing clear and honest information about the incident, its impact, and the steps taken to address it. This helps build trust and demonstrates the organization's commitment to security and privacy.

By incorporating these elements into their post-incident communication plans, organizations can ensure that they effectively manage the aftermath of an incident, learn from the experience, and continuously improve their incident response capabilities.

Privacy Breach Notifications and Regulatory Reporting

In today's digital landscape, organizations must be prepared to handle privacy breaches effectively. When personal information is compromised, it is not only a matter of managing the technical aspects of the breach but also complying with regulatory requirements. This section provides an overview of privacy breach notifications and regulatory reporting, emphasizing the importance of timely and accurate communication with affected parties and regulatory bodies.

Effective privacy breach management requires a proactive approach that includes understanding regulatory requirements, preparing a robust response plan, and ensuring timely and transparent communication with affected individuals and regulatory bodies. By adhering to these principles, organizations can mitigate the impact of privacy breaches and maintain trust with their stakeholders.

Understanding Privacy Breaches

A privacy breach occurs when there is unauthorized access to or disclosure of personal information. This can happen through various means, such as cyberattacks, inadvertent data leaks, or internal misuse. The impact of a privacy breach can be significant, affecting individuals' privacy and an organization's reputation and financial standing.

Regulatory Landscape

The regulatory landscape for privacy breach notifications varies by jurisdiction, but the overarching goal is to protect individuals' personal information and ensure transparency. Organizations must navigate a complex web of laws and regulations, including state and federal laws in the United States, such as the California Consumer Privacy Act and the Health Insurance Portability and Accountability Act, as well as international regulations like the General Data Protection Regulation.

Key Elements of Data Breach Notification Laws

Most data breach notification laws share common elements, though specifics may vary:

- **Definition of a breach:** A breach is typically defined as unauthorized access to or acquisition of personal information. Some laws may not consider encrypted data as breached if the encryption key remains secure.
- **Personal information:** This usually includes a person's name combined with other identifying information, such as Social Security numbers, driver's license numbers, financial account numbers, or health information.
- **Notification requirements:** Laws specify when and how organizations must notify affected individuals and regulatory bodies. This often includes specific time frames, the format of notifications, and the content that must be included.

Notification Process

When a breach occurs, organizations must follow a structured process to ensure compliance with notification requirements:

- **Detection and assessment:** Identify the breach and assess its scope and impact. Determine the types of personal information involved and the potential risks to affected individuals.
- **Containment and eradication:** Take immediate steps to contain the breach and prevent further unauthorized access. Eradicate the root cause of the breach to prevent recurrence.
- **Notification:** Notify affected individuals and relevant regulatory bodies within the required time frames. Notifications should include:
    - A description of the breach and the types of personal information involved.

- Steps individuals can take to protect themselves from potential harm.
- Contact information for the organization and any support services offered, such as credit monitoring.

- **Reporting:** In addition to notifying individuals, organizations must report the breach to regulatory authorities. This may involve submitting detailed reports on the breach, the organization's response, and measures taken to prevent future incidents.

Compliance and Best Practices

To ensure compliance with data breach notification laws, organizations should implement the following best practices:

- **Develop a breach response plan:** Establish a comprehensive breach response plan that outlines the steps to take when a breach occurs. This plan should include roles and responsibilities, communication protocols, and procedures for notifying affected parties and regulatory bodies.
- **Conduct regular training:** Train employees on data protection practices and the organization's breach response plan. Ensure they understand their roles in preventing and responding to breaches.
- **Monitor and review:** Continuously monitor for potential breaches and regularly review and update the breach response plan to reflect changes in laws and best practices.
- **Engage legal and privacy experts:** Work with legal and privacy experts to navigate the regulatory landscape and ensure compliance with all applicable laws.

CHAPTER 7

Network Security and Privacy Protections

In the rapidly evolving landscape of information security and privacy, understanding and implementing robust network security measures is paramount. As a security or privacy professional, you are tasked with the formidable responsibility of ensuring that your network remains resilient against a myriad of threats while maintaining the confidentiality, integrity, and availability of sensitive information. This chapter delves into critical aspects of network security and privacy protections, providing you with the foundational knowledge and practical strategies necessary to safeguard your organization's digital infrastructure.

Throughout this chapter, you will explore essential components and principles that form the backbone of a secure network architecture. From the intricacies of network segmentation and system hardening to the deployment of advanced firewalls and intrusion detection/prevention systems, each topic is designed to enhance your understanding of how to create and maintain a secure network environment. Additionally, you will gain insights into modern security paradigms such as zero trust networking and secure access service edge, which are crucial for adapting to contemporary security challenges. By the end of this chapter, you should be well-equipped with the knowledge to implement effective network security measures and privacy protections, ensuring your organization's network is both secure and compliant with relevant standards and regulations.

Secure Network Components

In the realm of network security, understanding and implementing secure network components is crucial for maintaining the integrity, confidentiality, and availability of information. Network components, including various devices and protocols, form the backbone of secure communication and data exchange.

Securing network components involves a comprehensive approach that includes robust infrastructure operations, secure transmission media, effective access controls, endpoint security, and the use of secure protocols. By implementing these measures, organizations can significantly enhance their network security posture and protect against a wide range of threats.

This section provides an overview of secure network components, their operations, and the mechanisms employed to safeguard them.

Operation of Infrastructure

The operation of network infrastructure plays a pivotal role in ensuring continuous and secure network functionality. Key considerations include:

- **Redundant power:** Ensuring that network devices have access to uninterrupted power supplies through redundant power sources and backup systems is critical for maintaining network availability.
- **Warranty and support:** Establishing comprehensive support agreements and warranties with equipment vendors helps in quick resolution of hardware issues, minimizing downtime and ensuring smooth operation.

Transmission Media

The physical security and quality of transmission media are essential for secure data transmission. Key aspects include:

- **Physical security of media:** Protecting cables and other transmission media from physical tampering or damage is crucial. This includes securing wiring closets and ensuring that cables are not exposed to potential threats.
- **Signal propagation quality:** Ensuring high-quality signal propagation through proper installation and maintenance of transmission media, such as twisted-pair cables and fiber optics, is vital for reliable communication.

Network Access Control Systems

Network access control (NAC) systems are employed to manage and enforce security policies at the point of network entry. They ensure that only authorized devices and users can access the network. NAC systems can be physical or virtual and typically include:

- **Authentication:** Verifying the identity of users and devices before granting network access.
- **Compliance checks:** Ensuring that devices meet security policies, such as having up-to-date antivirus software and security patches, before allowing network access.

Endpoint Security

Endpoints, such as computers, mobile devices, and Internet of things (IoT) devices, are often the first point of contact for potential security threats. Securing these endpoints involves:

- **Host-based security:** Implementing security measures directly on the endpoint devices, such as antivirus software, firewalls, and intrusion detection/prevention systems.
- **Configuration management:** Ensuring that endpoints are configured securely and consistently across the network to prevent vulnerabilities.

Firewalls

Firewalls are critical components in network security, providing a barrier between trusted internal networks and untrusted external networks. Different types of firewalls include:

- **Next-generation firewalls:** These firewalls offer advanced features such as deep packet inspection, intrusion prevention, and application awareness.
- **Web application firewalls:** Designed to protect web applications by filtering and monitoring HTTP traffic.
- **Network firewalls:** Traditional firewalls that control traffic between different network segments based on predefined security rules.

Intrusion Detection and Prevention Systems

Intrusion detection systems (IDS) and intrusion prevention systems (IPS) are essential for detecting and preventing unauthorized access or attacks on the network. They monitor network traffic for suspicious activity and can take proactive measures to block or mitigate threats.

- **Intrusion detection systems:** These systems monitor network traffic and alert administrators to potential security incidents.
- **Intrusion prevention systems:** These systems not only detect but also take action to prevent detected threats from causing harm.

Secure Protocols

Using secure protocols is fundamental to protecting data in transit. Some of the key secure protocols include:

- **Internet Protocol Security (IPsec):** Provides secure communication by authenticating and encrypting IP packets.
- **Secure Shell (SSH):** Ensures secure remote access and command execution over unsecured networks.
- **Secure Sockets Layer (SSL)/Transport Layer Security (TLS):** Protects data exchanged over the Internet, such as in web browsing and email.

Physical and Logical Segmentation

Segmentation is a strategy used to isolate different parts of the network to enhance security and manageability. This can be achieved through:

- **Physical segmentation:** Using separate physical devices or media to isolate network segments, such as in-band and out-of-band management.
- **Logical segmentation:** Creating isolated virtual environments within the same physical infrastructure using technologies such as virtual local area networks (VLANs), virtual private networks (VPNs), and virtual routing and forwarding.

Network Device Security

Securing network devices, such as routers, switches, and access points, is paramount for maintaining overall network security. Key practices include:

- **Configuration management:** Ensuring that network devices are securely configured and regularly updated with the latest firmware and security patches.

- **Access controls:** Implementing strict access controls to prevent unauthorized changes to device configurations.
- **Monitoring and logging:** Continuously monitoring network devices for suspicious activity and maintaining logs for audit and forensic purposes.

Redundancy and Failover

Implementing redundancy and failover mechanisms ensures that network services remain available even in the event of a device failure. This includes:

- **Redundant devices:** Deploying multiple instances of critical network devices to take over in case of failure.
- **Failover protocols:** Using protocols such as Hot Standby Router Protocol (HSRP) and Virtual Router Redundancy Protocol (VRRP) to provide automatic failover capabilities.

Network Segmentation

Network segmentation is a critical strategy in enhancing network security and privacy protections. By dividing a network into smaller, isolated segments, organizations can improve security, manageability, and performance. This approach helps to contain potential security breaches, limit the spread of malware, and ensure that sensitive data is accessed only by authorized users. By leveraging physical and logical segmentation techniques, microsegmentation, and secure network components, organizations can create robust and resilient network architectures that support their security and privacy objectives.

In this section, you will explore the key concepts and benefits of network segmentation, including physical and logical segmentation, microsegmentation, and the implementation of secure network components.

Physical Segmentation

Physical segmentation involves the use of distinct physical hardware to create separate network segments. This can include dedicated switches, routers, and cabling to isolate different parts of the network. Physical segmentation provides a high level of security because it completely separates network traffic, making it difficult for an attacker to move laterally across the network. Examples of physical segmentation include air-gapped networks, where critical systems are entirely disconnected from other networks, and the use of in-band and out-of-band management networks to isolate administrative traffic from regular user traffic.

Logical Segmentation

Logical segmentation leverages network technologies to create virtual separations within a physical network infrastructure. This approach is often more flexible and cost-effective than physical segmentation. Key techniques for logical segmentation include:

- **Virtual local area networks:** Enable administrators to segment a network into different broadcast domains within the same physical infrastructure. This helps to isolate traffic and improve security by restricting access to sensitive areas of the network.
- **Virtual private networks:** Create secure, encrypted tunnels over public or shared networks, enabling remote users to access the internal network securely. VPNs are essential for protecting data in transit and ensuring privacy.
- **Virtual routing and forwarding (VRF):** Allows multiple instances of a routing table to coexist on a single router, enabling the segmentation of network traffic without the need for multiple physical devices.
- **Virtual domains:** Create isolated environments within a network, ensuring that different segments operate independently and securely.

Microsegmentation

Microsegmentation takes network segmentation to a more granular level by creating highly specific, isolated segments down to the individual workload or application level. This is achieved through network overlays, encapsulation, and the use of distributed security controls such as firewalls, routers, and intrusion detection/prevention systems. Microsegmentation supports a zero trust security model by ensuring that only authorized traffic is allowed between segments, regardless of their location within the network. Key benefits of microsegmentation include:

- **Enhanced security:** By isolating workloads and applications, microsegmentation reduces the attack surface and limits the potential impact of a security breach.
- **Improved compliance:** Fine-grained segmentation helps organizations meet regulatory requirements by ensuring that sensitive data is accessed and processed only by authorized entities.
- **Greater visibility and control:** Microsegmentation provides detailed insights into network traffic and enables precise control over communication between segments.

Secure Network Components

To implement effective network segmentation, organizations must deploy and maintain secure network components. This includes ensuring the proper operation of infrastructure, such as redundant power supplies and support services, and securing transmission media to protect against physical tampering and signal degradation. Key network components that support segmentation include:

- **Network access control systems:** NAC systems enforce security policies by controlling access to network resources based on the identity and compliance status of devices. They can be implemented as physical or virtual solutions to ensure that only authorized devices can connect to specific network segments.
- **Endpoint security:** Protecting endpoint devices, such as laptops, mobile phones, and tablets, is crucial for maintaining the integrity of network segments. Endpoint security solutions include antivirus software, endpoint detection and response (EDR) tools, and secure configuration management practices.

Implementing Network Segmentation

Implementing network segmentation requires careful planning and execution. Organizations should start by identifying their critical assets and determining the appropriate level of segmentation needed to protect them. This involves:

- **Assessing network traffic:** Understanding the flow of network traffic is essential for designing effective segmentation. This includes identifying north–south traffic (between the data center and external networks) and east–west traffic (within the data center).
- **Defining security policies:** Establishing clear security policies that dictate how traffic should be segmented and controlled is crucial. These policies should be based on the principle of least privilege, ensuring that users and devices have access only to the resources they need.
- **Deploying segmentation technologies:** Implementing VLANs, VPNs, VRF, and microsegmentation technologies to create the desired network segments. This may involve upgrading network infrastructure and deploying new security appliances.
- **Monitoring and management:** Continuously monitoring network traffic and managing segmentation policies to ensure they remain effective. This includes regular audits and updates to address emerging threats and changing business requirements.

System Hardening

In the realm of network security and privacy protections, system hardening is a critical process that aims to enhance the security of the systems by reducing their vulnerability to threats. This involves a series of measures and best practices designed to minimize potential attack surfaces and mitigate risks associated with cyber threats. The ultimate goal of system hardening is to ensure that systems are robust, resilient, and capable of withstanding various security challenges.

System hardening involves a comprehensive approach to securing systems by minimizing vulnerabilities and implementing strong security controls. By following best practices and continuously maintaining the hardened state of systems, organizations can protect their assets and maintain the integrity, confidentiality, and availability of their information.

Key Techniques in System Hardening

System hardening refers to the process of securing a system by reducing its surface of vulnerability. This is often achieved by configuring system settings, removing unnecessary services, and applying the latest security patches and updates. The process encompasses various techniques and practices, each contributing to the overall security posture of the system:

- **Secure configuration:** Ensuring that all systems are configured securely is a fundamental step in system hardening. This involves setting strong passwords, disabling unnecessary services, and configuring security settings to the highest level of protection feasible.
- **Patch management:** Regularly applying security patches and updates is crucial to protect systems from known vulnerabilities. Patch management ensures that systems are up to date with the latest security fixes, reducing the risk of exploitation.
- **Service minimization:** Disabling or removing unnecessary services and applications reduces the potential attack vectors. By minimizing the number of active services, the system becomes less exposed to potential threats.
- **Access control:** Implementing strict access control measures ensures that only authorized users have access to the system. This includes using role-based access control, multifactor authentication, and regularly reviewing access permissions.
- **Network security:** Employing network security measures such as firewalls, intrusion detection systems, and intrusion prevention systems

helps to monitor and protect the system from malicious activities. Network segmentation can also be used to isolate critical systems and limit the spread of potential attacks.
- **Logging and monitoring:** Enabling logging and continuous monitoring of system activities helps in detecting and responding to security incidents promptly. Logs should be regularly reviewed and analyzed to identify any suspicious activities.
- **Backup and recovery:** Implementing robust backup and recovery procedures ensures that data can be restored in the event of a security breach or system failure. Regular backups should be performed, and recovery plans should be tested periodically.

Implementing System Hardening

Implementing system hardening requires a structured approach that involves the following steps:

- **Assessment:** Conduct a thorough assessment of the current system configuration and identify areas that require hardening. This includes reviewing existing security policies, configurations, and installed services.
- **Planning:** Develop a detailed plan that outlines the steps required to harden the system. The plan should include timelines, responsible personnel, and specific actions to be taken.
- **Execution:** Execute the system hardening plan by making the necessary configuration changes, applying patches, and disabling unnecessary services. Ensure that all actions are documented and changes are tested before deployment.
- **Validation:** Validate the effectiveness of the system hardening measures by conducting security assessments, vulnerability scans, and penetration tests. This helps to ensure that the implemented measures are effective in mitigating the identified risks.
- **Maintenance:** System hardening is an ongoing process that requires regular maintenance. Continuously monitor the system for new vulnerabilities, apply patches promptly, and review security configurations periodically.

System hardening is essential for protecting critical systems and data from cyber threats. By reducing the attack surface and implementing robust security measures, organizations can significantly enhance their security posture. This not only helps in preventing security breaches but also ensures compliance with regulatory requirements and industry best practices.

Firewalls and Intrusion Detection/ Prevention Systems

Firewalls and IDPSs play a crucial role in safeguarding an organization's information assets. These systems serve as the first line of defense against various cyber threats, providing both preventive and detective capabilities to maintain the integrity, confidentiality, and availability of network resources.

Firewalls

Firewalls are essential preventive and technical controls that help protect networks by filtering incoming and outgoing traffic based on predefined security rules. They act as barriers between trusted internal networks and untrusted external networks, such as the Internet. Firewalls can be categorized into several types, each offering different levels of protection and functionality:

- **Basic network firewalls:** These firewalls filter traffic based on IP addresses, ports, and protocols. They are commonly placed at the network's edge to monitor all incoming and outgoing traffic. Basic firewalls use access control lists (ACLs) to allow specific traffic while blocking all other traffic by default. For instance, they can allow web traffic on ports 80 (HTTP) and 443 (HTTPS) while blocking all other ports.
- **Second-generation firewalls:** These include application-level gateway firewalls and circuit-level gateway firewalls. Application-level gateways filter traffic based on specific application requirements, such as HTTP or FTP, ensuring that only legitimate application traffic passes through. Circuit-level gateways filter traffic based on the state of the connection, providing additional security by monitoring the TCP handshake process.
- **Third-generation firewalls:** Also known as stateful inspection firewalls or dynamic packet filtering firewalls, these filter traffic based on its state within a stream of traffic, providing more granular control over network communications. They maintain a table of active connections and make decisions based on the context of the traffic flow, allowing for more intelligent filtering.
- **Application firewalls:** These control traffic going to or from specific applications or services. For example, a web application firewall (WAF) protects web servers by inspecting all incoming traffic and blocking malicious activities such as SQL injection and cross-site scripting (XSS) attacks. WAFs are essential for protecting web applications from common vulnerabilities and ensuring the integrity of web services.

- **Next-generation firewalls (NGFWs):** These advanced firewalls function as unified threat management (UTM) devices, combining multiple security features into a single solution. NGFWs include traditional firewall capabilities like packet filtering and stateful inspection, along with advanced features such as deep packet inspection, malware filtering, and intrusion detection/prevention. They provide comprehensive protection by integrating multiple security functions into one device, simplifying management and improving overall security posture.

To maximize the effectiveness of firewalls, organizations should follow these basic guidelines:

- **Block directed broadcasts on routers:** Directed broadcasts can be used to flood targeted networks with traffic. Blocking them helps prevent such attacks.
- **Block private IP addresses at the border:** Traffic from the Internet with a source address in a private IP range is likely spoofed and should be blocked by the firewall.
- **Block ICMP traffic:** Many attackers use ping (ICMP) to discover systems or launch denial-of-service (DoS) attacks. Blocking ICMP traffic at border firewalls can mitigate these risks.

Intrusion Detection and Prevention Systems

Intrusion detection and prevention systems are critical components of a comprehensive network security strategy. These systems monitor network traffic for signs of malicious activity and can take action to prevent or mitigate attacks. IDPS can be classified into two main types:

- **Intrusion detection systems (IDSs):** IDSs monitor network traffic and generate alerts when suspicious activity is detected. They do not take direct action to block or stop attacks but provide valuable information for security analysts to investigate and respond to potential threats. IDSs can be further divided into two categories:
    - **Network-based IDS (NIDS):** These systems monitor traffic across the entire network, providing visibility into potential threats targeting multiple devices.
    - **Host-based IDS (HIDS):** These systems monitor traffic and activities on individual hosts or devices, providing detailed insights into potential threats affecting specific systems.
- **Intrusion prevention systems:** IPSs not only detect malicious activity but also take proactive measures to block or stop attacks in real time.

This can include dropping malicious packets, resetting connections, or blocking traffic from specific IP addresses. IPS can be deployed in two modes:

- **In-band (inline) deployment:** The IPS is placed directly on the network path, allowing it to block malicious traffic before it reaches its destination. This setup provides real-time protection but can introduce a single point of failure.
- **Out-of-band (passive) deployment:** The IPS monitors traffic through a mirrored port on a switch, analyzing copies of the traffic without directly interfering with the flow. This setup reduces the risk of network disruption but may not provide immediate blocking capabilities.

Key features of IDPS include:

- **Signature-based detection:** This method relies on predefined patterns of known threats (signatures) to identify malicious activity. While effective against known threats, it may not detect new or unknown attacks.
- **Anomaly-based detection:** This method establishes a baseline of normal network behavior and detects deviations from this baseline. It can identify new or unknown threats but may generate more false positives.
- **Heuristic-based detection:** This method uses algorithms and machine learning to identify patterns of malicious activity. It can adapt to new threats and provide more accurate detection over time.

In addition to traditional IDS and IPS, organizations can enhance their security posture with advanced tools such as:

- **Passlisting/blocklisting:** These techniques allow or block traffic based on predefined lists of trusted or untrusted sources. Passlisting permits only approved traffic, while blocklisting blocks known malicious sources.
- **Sandboxing:** This technique isolates suspicious files or code in a controlled environment to analyze their behavior without risking the main network. Sandboxing is particularly useful for detecting zero-day exploits and advanced persistent threats (APTs).
- **Honeypots/honeynets:** These decoy systems attract attackers, allowing security teams to study their tactics and gather intelligence without compromising real assets. Honeypots simulate vulnerable systems to lure attackers, while honeynets are networks of honeypots designed to capture more extensive data on attack methods.
- **Antimalware:** Up-to-date antimalware software is essential for detecting and removing malicious code, such as viruses and worms. Antimalware solutions should be regularly updated with the latest signatures to ensure effective protection.

- **Machine learning and AI-based tools:** These advanced technologies can analyze vast amounts of data to identify patterns and predict potential threats, enhancing the overall effectiveness of IDPS. Machine learning algorithms can improve detection accuracy over time by learning from past incidents and adapting to new attack vectors.

Virtual Private Networks and Secure Access Service Edge

In the ever-evolving landscape of network security and privacy, virtual private networks and secure access service edge (SASE) have emerged as critical components. These technologies provide robust mechanisms to secure data in transit and ensure that users can access network resources securely, regardless of their location.

While VPNs provide a proven method for securing remote access, SASE offers a more comprehensive and scalable solution that addresses the challenges of modern network security. By understanding and implementing these technologies, organizations can enhance their security posture and ensure secure, efficient access to their network resources.

Virtual Private Networks

A *virtual private network* is a technology that creates a secure, encrypted connection over a less secure network, such as the Internet. This secure connection, often referred to as a tunnel, allows remote users to access resources on a private network as if they were directly connected to it. VPNs are widely used to secure remote access to corporate networks, protect data transmissions, and maintain privacy.

Key Features of VPNs   There are four critical components of a VPN:

- **Encryption:** VPNs use encryption protocols to secure data in transit, ensuring that even if the data is intercepted, it cannot be read without the decryption key. Common encryption protocols include IPsec (Internet Protocol Security) and SSL/TLS (Secure Sockets Layer/Transport Layer Security). These protocols create a secure tunnel through which data travels, protecting it from eavesdroppers and hackers.
- **Authentication:** VPNs require users to authenticate themselves before establishing the secure connection. This can be achieved through various methods, such as passwords, digital certificates, or multifactor

authentication. Authentication ensures that only authorized users can access the VPN, adding an additional layer of security.
- **Integrity:** VPNs ensure data integrity by using hashing algorithms to verify that data has not been altered during transmission. This means that any changes to the data in transit can be detected, preventing tampering and ensuring that the data received is the same as the data sent.
- **Confidentiality:** By encrypting data, VPNs maintain the confidentiality of sensitive information, preventing unauthorized access. This is particularly important for protecting personal information, financial data, and other confidential communications.

Types of VPNs   There are two main types of VPN:

- **Remote access VPN:** This type of VPN allows individual users to connect to a private network from a remote location. It is commonly used by telecommuters and mobile workers to access corporate resources securely. Remote access VPNs enable employees to work from anywhere while maintaining a secure connection to the company's network.
- **Site-to-site VPN:** This type of VPN connects entire networks to each other, typically used to link branch offices to a central office. It can be further divided into intranet-based (connecting internal networks) and extranet-based (connecting to external partner networks). Site-to-site VPNs are essential for organizations with multiple locations, ensuring secure communication between different sites.

VPNs are essential for securing remote access, but they are not without challenges. VPNs can introduce latency, require significant management overhead, and may not scale well with the increasing use of cloud services and mobile devices. Additionally, VPNs can create a single point of failure, and misconfigurations can lead to security vulnerabilities.

Secure Access Service Edge

SASE is a network architecture that combines wide-area networking (WAN) capabilities with comprehensive security functions, delivered as a cloud-based service. SASE addresses the limitations of traditional VPNs by providing a more flexible, scalable, and efficient approach to secure network access.

Key Components of SASE   To understand how SASE works, you need to familiarize yourself with the following important components of SASE:

- **Software-defined wide-area network (SD-WAN):** SD-WAN technology enables the dynamic routing of traffic across multiple WAN connections, optimizing performance and reliability. SD-WAN can prioritize critical applications and provide failover capabilities, ensuring continuous connectivity even if one link fails.

- **Security functions:** SASE integrates various security services, such as secure web gateways (SWG), cloud access security brokers, firewall as a service (FWaaS), and zero trust network access (ZTNA). These services work together to provide comprehensive security, protecting against threats and ensuring secure access to resources.
- **Cloud-based delivery:** SASE leverages the cloud to deliver security and networking services, allowing for easier scalability, simplified management, and reduced latency. Cloud-based delivery means that organizations can quickly adapt to changing needs and scale their services up or down as required.
- **Identity-driven access:** SASE uses identity and context to enforce security policies, ensuring that access is granted based on user identity, device, location, and other contextual factors. This approach aligns with the zero trust security model, where no entity is trusted by default, and access is granted based on continuous verification.

Benefits of SASE When you implement SASE, you gain the following benefits:

- **Improved performance:** By optimizing traffic routing and reducing the need for backhauling traffic through a central data center, SASE can enhance application performance and user experience. This is particularly important for cloud-based applications and services, which require low latency and high reliability.
- **Scalability:** SASE's cloud-based architecture allows organizations to scale their network and security services easily, accommodating the growing number of remote users and cloud applications. This flexibility is crucial for modern businesses that need to adapt quickly to changing demands.
- **Simplified management:** SASE consolidates multiple security and networking functions into a single platform, reducing complexity and administrative overhead. This unified approach makes it easier for IT teams to manage and monitor the network, ensuring consistent security policies and performance.
- **Enhanced security:** With integrated security services and a zero trust approach, SASE provides robust protection against threats and ensures secure access to resources. Continuous monitoring and adaptive security measures help detect and respond to threats in real time, maintaining a strong security posture.

Implementing SASE Implementing SASE involves the following steps:

- **Assessment and planning:** Organizations should begin by assessing their current network and security infrastructure, identifying gaps and areas for improvement. This assessment will help determine the specific needs and goals for implementing SASE.
- **Vendor selection:** Choosing the right SASE provider is crucial. Organizations should evaluate vendors based on their ability to deliver comprehensive security services, performance, scalability, and ease of management. It's essential to select a vendor that aligns with the organization's requirements and long-term strategy.
- **Integration:** Integrating SASE with existing systems and processes is essential for a smooth transition. This may involve reconfiguring network devices, updating security policies, and training staff. Proper integration ensures that the SASE solution works seamlessly with the organization's infrastructure.
- **Monitoring and optimization:** Continuous monitoring and optimization are necessary to ensure that the SASE solution delivers the desired performance and security outcomes. Regularly reviewing and adjusting the configuration can help maintain optimal performance and address any emerging threats or changes in the network environment.

Secure Wireless Network Management

In today's interconnected world, wireless networks play a crucial role in providing flexibility and mobility for organizations. However, they also introduce unique security challenges that must be addressed to protect sensitive information and maintain network integrity. This section provides an overview of various wireless technologies and outlines best practices for managing wireless networks securely.

Securing the SSID

The service set identifier (SSID) is the name assigned to a wireless network. Changing the default SSID to something unique can help prevent unauthorized access. While disabling SSID broadcasting may seem like an additional security measure, it does not significantly enhance security, as attackers can still detect the SSID using wireless sniffers. Instead, focus on using strong encryption methods such as WPA2 or WPA3.

Wireless Channels

Wireless networks operate on different channels to avoid interference and optimize performance. Selecting the appropriate channel can minimize interference from other wireless networks and devices. In environments with multiple access points, channel planning is essential to ensure optimal coverage and performance.

Conducting a Site Survey

A site survey involves assessing wireless signal strength, quality, and interference within a physical environment. This process helps determine the optimal placement of wireless access points (WAPs) to maximize coverage for authorized users while minimizing the potential for unauthorized access. Site surveys often result in heat maps that guide adjustments to WAP placement, antenna type, orientation, and signal strength.

Wireless Security

Wireless networks must be secured to prevent unauthorized access and data breaches. Key security measures include:

- **Wi-Fi Protected Access (WPA):** WPA, WPA2, and WPA3 provide robust encryption and authentication mechanisms to protect wireless communications.
- **802.1X authentication:** This network access control protocol provides an authentication mechanism for devices attempting to connect to the network.
- **Virtual private networks:** VPNs create secure tunnels for data transmission over wireless networks, ensuring confidentiality and integrity.

Wi-Fi Protected Setup (WPS)

WPS is designed to simplify the process of adding new devices to a secured wireless network. However, WPS has known vulnerabilities that can be exploited by attackers. It is recommended to disable WPS and manually configure network settings to enhance security.

Wireless MAC Filter

MAC filtering allows administrators to specify which devices are allowed to connect to the wireless network based on their MAC addresses. While this adds an extra layer of security, it is not foolproof, as MAC addresses can be spoofed by determined attackers.

Wireless Antenna Management

Proper antenna management is crucial for optimizing wireless network performance and security. Different types of antennas, such as omnidirectional and directional antennas, serve various purposes. Guidelines for optimal antenna placement include using a central location, avoiding physical obstructions, and minimizing interference from reflective surfaces and electrical equipment.

Using Captive Portals

Captive portals redirect newly connected clients to a web-based access control page, where users may be required to provide login credentials, payment information, or agree to an acceptable use policy. Captive portals are commonly used in public wireless networks, such as those in hotels, airports, and cafes, to limit access to authorized users.

Wireless Attacks

Wireless networks are susceptible to various attacks, including:

- **War driving:** Using detection tools to locate wireless networks, often with the intent of unauthorized access.
- **Rogue access points:** Unauthorized access points that can intercept or manipulate network traffic.
- **Evil twin attacks:** Creating a fraudulent access point that mimics a legitimate one to trick users into connecting.
- **Denial-of-service (DoS) attacks:** Flooding the network with traffic to disrupt normal operations.
- **Key reinstallation attacks (KRACK):** Exploiting vulnerabilities in WPA2 to decrypt traffic.

By understanding these threats and implementing robust security measures, organizations can effectively manage and protect their wireless networks from potential attacks.

General Wi-Fi Security Procedure

A comprehensive Wi-Fi security procedure includes the following steps:

- Update firmware.
- Change the default administrator password.
- Enable WPA2 or WPA3 encryption.
- Use strong, complex passwords.
- Change the SSID.
- Consider changing the wireless MAC address.
- Decide whether to disable SSID broadcast based on deployment requirements.
- Enable MAC filtering for small, static pools of wireless clients.
- Use static IP addresses or configure DHCP with reservations for small deployments.
- Separate the WAP from the wired network using a firewall.
- Monitor WAP-to-wired-network communications with a network intrusion detection system (NIDS).
- Deploy a wireless intrusion detection system (WIDS) and a wireless intrusion prevention system (WIPS).
- Consider requiring VPN use across Wi-Fi links.
- Implement a captive portal.
- Track and log all wireless activities and events.

Securing the Cloud

Cloud computing has revolutionized the way organizations manage and store data, offering scalability, flexibility, and cost-efficiency. However, it also introduces unique security challenges that must be addressed to protect sensitive information and ensure the integrity and availability of cloud-based systems. By understanding the unique security challenges of cloud computing and implementing these best practices, organizations can effectively secure their cloud environments and protect their sensitive data from potential threats. This section provides an overview of key security considerations and best practices for securing cloud environments.

Understanding Cloud Security

Cloud security involves a shared responsibility model, where both the cloud service provider (CSP) and the customer have distinct roles in maintaining security. The CSP is typically responsible for the security of the cloud infrastructure, including physical data centers, hardware, and the foundational software that runs the cloud services. Customers, on the other hand, are responsible for securing their data, applications, and any configurations they implement within the cloud environment.

Key Security Considerations

When securing cloud environments, several critical aspects must be taken into account:

- **Data protection:** Ensuring the confidentiality, integrity, and availability of data is paramount. This includes:
    - Implementing encryption for data at rest and in transit.
    - Using strong access controls.
    - Regularly backing up data to prevent loss.
- **Access management:** Properly managing access to cloud resources is critical. This involves:
    - Using identity and access management tools to enforce the principle of least privilege.
    - Implementing multifactor authentication to add an extra layer of security.
    - Monitoring access logs for suspicious activity.
- **Compliance and legal issues:** Organizations must ensure that their use of cloud services complies with relevant laws, regulations, and industry standards. This may involve:
    - Conducting regular audits.
    - Maintaining detailed records of data handling practices.
    - Working with CSPs that offer compliance certifications.
- **Security controls:** Implementing robust security controls is essential to protect cloud environments. This includes:
    - Network security measures such as firewalls and intrusion detection/prevention systems.
    - Application security practices like secure coding and regular vulnerability assessments.
- **Incident response:** Developing and maintaining an incident response plan specific to cloud environments is crucial. This plan should:
    - Outline procedures for detecting, responding to, and recovering from security incidents.
    - Be regularly tested and updated.

- **Vendor management:** Evaluating and managing the security practices of CSPs is an important aspect of cloud security. Organizations should:
  - Perform due diligence when selecting a CSP.
  - Review service level agreements (SLAs) to ensure they meet security requirements.
  - Continuously monitor the CSP's security posture.

Best Practices for Cloud Security

To effectively secure cloud environments, organizations should adopt the following best practices:

- **Adopt a zero trust model:** This security approach assumes that threats can exist both inside and outside the network, and therefore, no entity should be trusted by default. Implementing a zero trust model involves:
  - Strict access controls.
  - Continuous monitoring.
  - Verification of all users and devices.
- **Use automated security tools:** Leveraging automated tools for tasks such as configuration management, vulnerability scanning, and incident detection can help improve the efficiency and effectiveness of cloud security efforts.
- **Regularly update and patch systems:** Keeping cloud-based systems and applications up to date with the latest security patches is essential to protect against known vulnerabilities and exploits.
- **Educate and train employees:** Ensuring that employees are aware of cloud security best practices and potential threats is critical. Regular training sessions and awareness programs can help build a security-conscious culture within the organization.
- **Implement strong encryption:** Encrypting sensitive data both at rest and in transit helps protect it from unauthorized access and breaches. Organizations should:
  - Use strong encryption algorithms.
  - Manage encryption keys securely.
- **Monitor and audit cloud environments:** Continuous monitoring and regular audits of cloud environments help detect and respond to security incidents promptly. Organizations should:
  - Use logging and monitoring tools to track activity.
  - Identify anomalies.

Network Monitoring

Network monitoring is a critical component of an organization's security infrastructure, ensuring that security controls are functioning as intended and providing the necessary protection. Effective network monitoring involves the collection, analysis, and response to security events and anomalies within a network. This section explores the key elements of network monitoring, including logging, intrusion detection and prevention systems, security information and event management systems, continuous monitoring, and threat intelligence.

Logging and Monitoring Activities

Logging and monitoring activities are foundational to network security. Logs provide a record of events occurring within an organization's systems and networks, which can be analyzed to detect and respond to security incidents. Effective log management includes the following components:

- **Intrusion detection and prevention systems:** IDPSs monitor network traffic for suspicious activity. Intrusion detection systems alert administrators when they detect potential threats, while intrusion prevention systems can take immediate action to block or mitigate the threat. These systems are crucial for identifying and responding to attacks in real time.
- **Security information and event management (SIEM):** SIEM systems aggregate and analyze log data from various sources, providing a centralized view of security events. They help identify patterns and anomalies that may indicate security incidents. SIEMs include features such as correlation and aggregation of data, advanced analytics, and automated responses to potential threats.
- **Continuous monitoring and tuning:** Continuous monitoring involves the ongoing collection and analysis of security data to detect and respond to threats in real time. Regular tuning of monitoring systems ensures they remain effective in detecting new and evolving threats. This proactive approach helps maintain a robust security posture and quickly address any vulnerabilities.
- **Egress monitoring:** Egress monitoring focuses on outbound network traffic to detect and prevent data exfiltration and other malicious activities. By monitoring data leaving the network, organizations can identify and block unauthorized transfers of sensitive information, helping to protect against data breaches.

- **Log management:** Proper log management practices, including the collection, storage, and analysis of logs, are essential for effective network monitoring. This includes ensuring logs are timestamped and synchronized using protocols like Network Time Protocol (NTP). Secure log storage and regular review of logs help detect and investigate security incidents.
- **Threat intelligence:** Incorporating threat intelligence feeds and engaging in threat hunting activities can enhance the effectiveness of network monitoring by providing insights into emerging threats and attack patterns. Threat intelligence helps organizations stay informed about the latest threats and vulnerabilities, allowing them to proactively defend against potential attacks.

Conducting Incident Management

When a security incident occurs, it is crucial to have a well-defined incident management process in place. The primary goal of incident management is to minimize the impact of incidents on the organization. The key phases of incident management include:

- **Detection:** Identifying potential security incidents through monitoring and analysis of logs and other data sources. Detection methods can include automated tools, alerts from IDPS, and reports from end users.
- **Response:** Taking immediate action to contain and mitigate the impact of the incident. This may involve isolating affected systems, blocking malicious traffic, and initiating communication with relevant stakeholders.
- **Mitigation:** Implementing measures to prevent the incident from causing further harm. Mitigation strategies can include patching vulnerabilities, updating security configurations, and enhancing monitoring capabilities.
- **Reporting:** Documenting the incident and reporting it to relevant stakeholders. Reporting ensures that all necessary parties are informed and that regulatory and compliance requirements are met.
- **Recovery:** Restoring affected systems and services to normal operation. Recovery efforts focus on minimizing downtime and ensuring that systems are secure and functioning properly.
- **Remediation:** Addressing the root cause of the incident to prevent recurrence. Remediation may involve conducting a thorough investigation, implementing long-term fixes, and updating security policies and procedures.

- **Lessons learned:** Analyzing the incident to identify improvements in security controls and processes. The lessons learned phase helps organizations refine their incident management practices and enhance their overall security posture.

Operating and Maintaining Detection and Preventative Measures

Besides IDS and IPS, effective network monitoring requires the operation and maintenance of various detection and preventative measures, including:

- **Passlisting/blocklisting:** Controlling access to network resources by allowing (*passlisting*) or blocking (*blocklisting*) specific entities. Passlisting ensures that only approved software and users can access the network, while blocklisting blocks known malicious entities.
- **Third-party provided security services:** Utilizing external security services to enhance monitoring capabilities. Third-party services can offer specialized expertise, advanced technologies, and additional resources to support an organization's security efforts.
- **Sandboxing:** Isolating and analyzing suspicious files and activities in a controlled environment. Sandboxing allows security professionals to safely examine potential threats without risking the integrity of the live network.
- **Honeypots/honeynets:** Deploying decoy systems to attract and analyze malicious activity. Honeypots and honeynets serve as traps for attackers, providing valuable insights into their tactics and techniques.
- **Antimalware:** Implementing antimalware solutions to detect and prevent malicious software. Regular updates to malware signatures and heuristic analysis help protect against a wide range of threats.
- **Machine learning and artificial intelligence (AI)-based tools:** Leveraging advanced technologies to enhance the detection and analysis of security threats. Machine learning and AI can identify patterns and anomalies that traditional methods might miss, improving the overall effectiveness of network monitoring.

CHAPTER 8

Security Assessment and Testing

Maintaining a robust security posture requires continuous vigilance and proactive measures. As a security and privacy professional, your role involves not just implementing security controls but also ensuring their ongoing effectiveness. This chapter provides a comprehensive guide to security assessment and testing, essential practices that help you identify, evaluate, and mitigate vulnerabilities within your organization's IT environment.

By delving into this chapter, you will gain insights into building a structured security assessment and testing program that aligns with your organization's unique requirements. You will explore the intricacies of vulnerability management, understand the nature of security vulnerabilities, and learn how to conduct penetration testing to simulate real-world attacks. Additionally, the chapter covers the importance of testing software to uncover hidden flaws and the vital role of training and exercises in preparing your team for potential security incidents. By mastering these concepts, you will enhance your ability to safeguard your organization's assets, ensure compliance with regulatory standards, and ultimately protect sensitive information from malicious threats.

Building a Security Assessment and Testing Program

Building a comprehensive security assessment and testing program is fundamental for any information security team. This program ensures that an organization has adequate security controls and that these controls are functioning properly and effectively safeguarding information assets.

By regularly testing and assessing security controls, organizations can identify and remediate vulnerabilities, ensuring that their security measures remain effective over time. This program should be continuously reviewed and updated to adapt to changing business needs and the evolving threat landscape.

The program includes three major components: security tests, security assessments, and security audits.

Security Testing

Security tests verify that a control is functioning correctly. These tests can be automated scans, tool-assisted penetration tests, or manual attempts to undermine security. Security testing should be conducted regularly, with attention given to each key security control protecting the organization. When scheduling security controls for review, factors such as the availability of security testing resources, the criticality of the systems and applications, the sensitivity of the information, and the risk of attack should be considered. A comprehensive strategy may include frequent automated tests supplemented by less frequent manual tests to ensure thorough coverage.

Security Assessments

Security assessments are detailed reviews of the security of a system, application, or other environments. They involve a risk assessment to identify vulnerabilities and make recommendations for remediation. Unlike security testing, assessments go beyond automated scanning and manual penetration tests, including a thoughtful review of the threat environment, current and future risks, and the value of the targeted environment. The main product of a security assessment is typically a report addressed to management, summarizing the findings in nontechnical language and providing specific recommendations for improving security.

Security Audits

Security audits are systematic evaluations of the security of a system or organization. They can be internal or external and may involve third-party auditors. Audits review compliance with policies, standards, and regulations, ensuring that security controls are properly implemented and maintained. Audits can be conducted on-premise, in the cloud, or in hybrid environments, and they provide an objective assessment of the security posture of the organization.

Designing and Validating Assessment, Test, and Audit Strategies

When designing a security assessment, testing, and audit program, it is crucial to ensure that it will be effective across all locations where the organization operates, including on-premise, cloud, and hybrid environments. A well-designed program considers the criticality and sensitivity of the systems and information, the likelihood of technical failures or misconfigurations, and the risk of attacks. It should also account for the rate of change in the technical environment and the difficulty and time required to perform control tests.

Reviewing Test Results

It is not enough to simply perform security tests; the results must be carefully reviewed to ensure that each test was successful. Reviews can be manual or automated, with automated tools verifying the successful completion of tests and alerting administrators to significant findings. Manual reviews require trained analysts to interpret the results and verify the effectiveness of the controls.

Vulnerability Management

Organizations must continuously identify, prioritize, and remediate vulnerabilities to protect their environments from potential threats. Vulnerability management is a critical component of a comprehensive security assessment and testing program. This process involves regular vulnerability scanning, analysis, and remediation to ensure that security controls are functioning correctly and that no exploitable weaknesses exist within the environment.

By systematically identifying, analyzing, and remediating vulnerabilities, organizations can reduce their risk of exploitation and ensure that their security controls remain effective over time. Regular vulnerability assessments, combined with other security testing and assessment techniques, provide a comprehensive approach to safeguarding information assets in an ever-changing threat landscape.

Vulnerability Management Process

Vulnerabilities are weaknesses in systems, applications, or configurations that can be exploited by attackers to compromise the confidentiality, integrity, or availability of information. These weaknesses can arise from various sources, including improper patch management, weak configurations, default accounts, and the use of insecure protocols and ciphers. Recognizing the potential entry points for attackers is the first step in fortifying an organization's defenses.

A robust vulnerability management program includes several key steps:

- **Identifying scan targets:** The first step in vulnerability management is to identify which systems, applications, and devices will be included in the scanning process. Organizations must consider factors such as data classification, exposure to public networks, and the environment (production, test, or development) when selecting scan targets. Automated tools can assist in discovering connected systems and building an asset inventory. This step ensures that all critical assets are accounted for and assessed regularly.
- **Conducting vulnerability scans:** Vulnerability scanning tools are used to detect known vulnerabilities within the identified scan targets. These scans can be performed in a credentialed or noncredentialed manner and may be intrusive or nonintrusive, depending on the organization's needs. Scans should be scheduled regularly and after significant changes to the environment, such as system upgrades or new deployments. Regular scans help in identifying new vulnerabilities that may have been introduced since the last assessment.
- **Analyzing scan results:** Once a scan is complete, the results must be analyzed to identify and prioritize vulnerabilities. Analysts should review logs and configurations for additional context and verify the accuracy of the findings to avoid false positives and false negatives. Vulnerabilities are then categorized based on their severity and potential impact on the organization. This step involves a detailed examination of the scan data to ensure that the most critical issues are addressed first.
- **Remediation and mitigation:** The next step is to develop and implement a remediation plan to address the identified vulnerabilities. This may involve applying patches, reconfiguring systems, disabling unnecessary services, or implementing additional security controls. High-priority vulnerabilities should be addressed first to minimize the risk of exploitation. Effective remediation requires coordination across various teams, including IT operations and security.
- **Verification and reporting:** After remediation efforts are completed, follow-up scans should be conducted to verify that the vulnerabilities have been effectively addressed. Regular reporting on the status of vulnerabilities and remediation efforts is essential to keep stakeholders informed and ensure accountability. Verification ensures that the remediation actions were successful, and reporting provides transparency and helps in tracking progress over time.

Vulnerability Assessment Techniques

Several techniques can be employed during vulnerability assessments to identify and address security weaknesses:

- **Network discovery:** Identifies systems on the network with open ports and services, providing a baseline for further scanning. This technique helps in mapping the network and understanding the scope of the assessment.
- **Network vulnerability scans:** Detect known security flaws in operating systems, applications, and devices. These scans can identify issues such as missing patches, outdated software, and misconfigurations.
- **Web vulnerability scans:** Probe web applications for vulnerabilities such as SQL injection, cross-site scripting (XSS), and insecure authentication mechanisms. Web applications are a common target for attackers, making this an essential part of vulnerability management.
- **Code review and testing:** Involves peer review of code and automated tools to identify security flaws before deployment. This technique helps in catching vulnerabilities early in the development process.
- **Penetration testing:** Simulates real-world attacks to identify vulnerabilities that may not be detected by automated scans. Penetration tests can be white box (full knowledge), black box (no knowledge), or gray box (partial knowledge) depending on the scope and objectives. Penetration testing provides a deeper understanding of how vulnerabilities can be exploited in practice.

Best Practices for Managing Vulnerabilities

Vulnerability management is not a one-time activity but an ongoing process that requires continuous improvement. Organizations should regularly review and update their vulnerability management policies and procedures to adapt to new threats and changes in the environment. Training and awareness programs for staff can also help improve the overall effectiveness of vulnerability management efforts. Continuous improvement ensures that the organization stays ahead of emerging threats and maintains a robust security posture.

Your organization can also benefit from following these best practices for vulnerability management:

- **Regular scanning and testing:** Conduct regular vulnerability scans and penetration tests to identify and address vulnerabilities before they can be exploited.

- **Patch management:** Implement a robust patch management process to ensure that all software and hardware are regularly updated with the latest security patches.
- **Configuration management:** Regularly review and update system configurations to ensure they adhere to security best practices and do not expose unnecessary vulnerabilities.
- **Security training and awareness:** Conduct regular security training and awareness programs for employees to ensure they understand the importance of security and how to identify and report potential vulnerabilities.
- **Incident response planning:** Develop and maintain an incident response plan to quickly and effectively respond to security incidents and mitigate the impact of exploited vulnerabilities.

Understanding Security Vulnerabilities

Security vulnerabilities are inherent weaknesses or flaws in a system that can be exploited by threats to gain unauthorized access or cause harm. These vulnerabilities can exist in various forms and can be found in software, hardware, configurations, or processes. Understanding and managing security vulnerabilities is a critical aspect of any organization's security program. By identifying and addressing vulnerabilities in software, hardware, configurations, and processes, organizations can significantly reduce their risk of exploitation and enhance their overall security posture.

Software Vulnerabilities

Software vulnerabilities are flaws or weaknesses in software code that can be exploited by attackers to gain unauthorized access, disrupt operations, or steal sensitive information. These vulnerabilities often arise from coding errors, inadequate testing, or the use of outdated software components. Common types of software vulnerabilities include:

- **Buffer overflows:** Occur when a program writes more data to a buffer than it can hold, leading to adjacent memory locations being overwritten. This can result in arbitrary code execution, system crashes, or data corruption.
- **SQL injection:** Involves injecting malicious SQL code into a query to manipulate the database, allowing attackers to view, modify, or delete database records. This vulnerability is common in web applications that do not properly sanitize user inputs.

- **Cross-site scripting:** Occurs when an attacker injects malicious scripts into web pages viewed by other users. These scripts can steal session cookies, deface websites, or redirect users to malicious sites. XSS vulnerabilities arise from improper validation or encoding of user inputs.
- **Insecure coding practices:** Include the use of hardcoded credentials, lack of input validation, and improper error handling. These practices can create exploitable vulnerabilities that attackers can leverage to compromise systems.

Hardware Vulnerabilities

Hardware vulnerabilities are weaknesses in physical devices that can be exploited to gain unauthorized access or cause damage to systems. These vulnerabilities can result from design flaws, manufacturing defects, or inadequate security controls. Common types of hardware vulnerabilities include:

- **Side-channel attacks:** Exploit indirect information, such as power consumption, electromagnetic emissions, or timing information, to infer sensitive data. Examples include power analysis attacks and electromagnetic eavesdropping.
- **Firmware vulnerabilities:** Arise from flaws in the firmware, the low-level software that controls hardware devices. These vulnerabilities can be exploited to gain control over the hardware, install persistent malware, or bypass security controls.
- **Hardware backdoors:** Deliberate or accidental hidden features in hardware that allow unauthorized access or control. These backdoors can be exploited to bypass security measures, steal data, or disrupt operations.
- **Physical tampering:** Involves physically manipulating hardware components to compromise their security. Examples include inserting malicious chips, modifying circuit boards, or accessing debug interfaces.

Configuration Vulnerabilities

Configuration vulnerabilities arise from improper or insecure configurations of systems, applications, or network devices. These vulnerabilities can result from default settings, misconfigurations, or lack of adherence to security best practices. Common types of configuration vulnerabilities include:

- **Default passwords:** Many devices and applications come with default usernames and passwords that are well-known to attackers. Failure to change these defaults can lead to unauthorized access.

- **Open ports:** Unnecessary open ports on network devices or systems can expose services to attackers. These open ports can be used to launch attacks, such as port scanning, exploitation of vulnerable services, or denial-of-service attacks.
- **Unnecessary services:** Running unnecessary services on systems can increase the attack surface and provide additional entry points for attackers. Disabling or removing these services can reduce the risk of exploitation.
- **Weak encryption:** Using outdated or weak encryption algorithms can compromise the confidentiality and integrity of data. Ensuring the use of strong, up-to-date encryption standards is essential for protecting sensitive information.

Process Vulnerabilities

Process vulnerabilities are weaknesses in organizational processes or procedures that can be exploited by attackers. These vulnerabilities often result from inadequate security policies, lack of employee training, or insufficient incident response capabilities. Common types of process vulnerabilities include:

- **Lack of access controls:** Inadequate access controls can allow unauthorized users to access sensitive data or systems. Implementing strong access control mechanisms, such as RBAC and MFA, can help mitigate this risk.
- **Inadequate incident response plans:** Without a well-defined incident response plan, organizations may struggle to effectively respond to security incidents. Developing and regularly testing an incident response plan is crucial for minimizing the impact of security breaches.
- **Poor security awareness:** Employees who are not aware of security best practices can inadvertently expose the organization to risks. Conducting regular security training and awareness programs can help employees recognize and respond to potential threats.
- **Insufficient monitoring and logging:** Lack of adequate monitoring and logging can prevent organizations from detecting and responding to security incidents in a timely manner. Implementing comprehensive monitoring and logging solutions can help identify and mitigate threats.

Penetration Testing

Penetration testing involves simulating real-world attacks on systems, applications, and networks to identify vulnerabilities that could be exploited by malicious actors. The goal of penetration testing is to uncover security weaknesses before attackers can exploit them, allowing organizations to take corrective actions to strengthen their defenses. By simulating real-world attacks, penetration tests provide valuable insights into the effectiveness of security controls and help organizations strengthen their defenses against potential threats.

Types of Penetration Testing

Penetration tests can be categorized based on the level of information provided to the testers prior to the test:

- **White-box penetration test:** Also known as *known environment* tests, white-box penetration tests provide the attackers with detailed information about the systems they are targeting. This approach bypasses many of the reconnaissance steps that typically precede attacks, reducing the time required for the test and increasing the likelihood of identifying security flaws.
- **Gray-box penetration test:** Also known as *partial knowledge* tests, gray-box penetration tests provide the testers with some information about the target environment. This approach balances the advantages and disadvantages of white-box and black-box tests, allowing for a more efficient and targeted assessment while still simulating some aspects of an external attack.
- **Black-box penetration test:** Also known as *unknown environment* tests, black-box penetration tests do not provide the attackers with any prior information about the target environment. This approach simulates an external attack, where the tester must first gather information about the target before attempting to exploit vulnerabilities.

Penetration Testing Process

The penetration testing process typically follows several key steps:

- **Planning and reconnaissance:** This phase involves defining the scope and objectives of the test, obtaining authorization from senior management, and gathering information about the target environment.

Reconnaissance activities may include footprinting (the process of gathering information about a target system or network to identify potential vulnerabilities that can be exploited by attackers), war driving (described in Chapter 7), and open-source intelligence (OSINT) gathering.

- **Scanning:** During this phase, testers use automated tools to identify open ports, services, and potential vulnerabilities in the target environment. Scanning helps to create a map of the target systems and identify potential entry points for exploitation.
- **Gaining access:** In this phase, testers attempt to exploit identified vulnerabilities to gain access to the target systems. This may involve techniques such as SQL injection, XSS, buffer overflows, and other common attack vectors.
- **Maintaining access:** Once access is gained, testers may attempt to establish a persistent presence on the target systems. This phase simulates the actions of an attacker who seeks to maintain long-term access to the compromised environment.
- **Analysis and reporting:** After the testing is complete, the results are analyzed to identify the security weaknesses discovered during the test. A detailed report is prepared, outlining the vulnerabilities, the methods used to exploit them, and recommendations for remediation.
- **Remediation and retesting:** Based on the findings of the penetration test, the organization takes corrective actions to address the identified vulnerabilities. After remediation, a follow-up test may be conducted to ensure that the issues have been resolved.

Tools and Techniques

Penetration testers use a variety of tools and techniques to conduct their assessments. Some commonly used tools include:

- **Metasploit framework:** An open-source tool that automates the execution of common attacks, saving testers time by eliminating many routine steps involved in exploiting vulnerabilities.
- **Nmap:** A network scanning tool used to discover hosts and services on a network, creating a map of the target environment.
- **Burp Suite:** A web application security testing tool that includes features for scanning, crawling, and exploiting web application vulnerabilities.
- **Wireshark:** A network protocol analyzer used to capture and analyze network traffic, helping testers identify potential security issues.

Breach and Attack Simulations

Breach and attack simulation (BAS) platforms automate some aspects of penetration testing by injecting threat indicators into systems and networks to trigger security controls. BAS platforms may place suspicious files on servers, send beaconing packets over networks, or probe systems for known vulnerabilities. These simulations help organizations identify deficiencies in their detection and prevention controls, allowing for timely updates and enhancements.

Considerations and Best Practices

When conducting penetration tests, organizations should be aware of the potential risks and disruptions associated with testing. It is essential to clearly outline the rules of engagement, obtain proper authorization, and ensure that the testing does not negatively impact business operations. Additionally, organizations should consider using industry-standard methodologies, such as the Open Worldwide Application Security Project (OWASP) Web Security Testing Guide, NIST 800-115, or the PCI DSS Penetration Test Guidance, to ensure comprehensive and consistent testing practices.

Testing Software

Software testing is an essential practice to ensure that applications are not only functional but also secure against potential threats. Software applications often have privileged access to the operating system, handle sensitive information, and perform business-critical functions. Therefore, security professionals must integrate robust testing methodologies into the software development life cycle (SDLC) to safeguard the confidentiality, integrity, and availability of information assets.

By integrating security testing into the SDLC, organizations can proactively identify and mitigate vulnerabilities, ensuring that their software applications remain secure and reliable. Regular code reviews, compliance checks, and robust exception handling are essential components of a comprehensive software testing strategy that protects against the ever-evolving threat landscape.

Importance of Software Testing

Software testing is crucial because it helps identify and mitigate vulnerabilities that could be exploited by malicious actors. Applications, particularly those exposed to the public, must undergo rigorous testing to ensure they meet security requirements. Testing should be integrated from the early stages of development to avoid the complexities and higher costs associated with adding security measures to already developed systems.

Types of Software Testing

Various testing methodologies can be employed to assess the security of software applications. These include:

- **Static application security testing (SAST):** This involves analyzing the source code for security vulnerabilities without executing the program. SAST tools can identify issues such as buffer overflows, SQL injection, and cross-site scripting vulnerabilities early in the development process.
- **Dynamic application security testing (DAST):** Unlike SAST, DAST tests the application in its running state. It simulates attacks on the application to identify vulnerabilities that could be exploited in a live environment. DAST is particularly useful for identifying runtime issues such as authentication problems and server misconfigurations.
- **Interactive application security testing (IAST):** IAST combines elements of both SAST and DAST by analyzing the application in real time during its execution. It provides more context-aware results, making it easier to identify and fix vulnerabilities.
- **Software composition analysis (SCA):** This testing method examines the third-party components and libraries used in the application to identify known vulnerabilities. SCA is essential for managing the risks associated with open-source software.

Code Review

Code review is a foundational practice in software assessment programs. It involves the systematic examination of source code by developers other than the author to identify defects and ensure compliance with security standards. Code review processes can vary in formality, ranging from informal peer reviews to structured methodologies:

- **Fagan inspection:** A formal process that includes six steps: planning, overview, preparation, inspection, rework, and follow-up. Each step is meticulously documented to ensure thorough examination and remediation of identified issues.

- **Pair programming:** An agile software development technique that places two developers at one workstation. One developer writes code while the other reviews it in real time, providing immediate feedback and ensuring that multiple developers are familiar with the code. Developers frequently switch roles to gain a comprehensive understanding of the code.
- **Over-the-shoulder review:** The developer who wrote the code explains it to another developer. This method allows for peer review and helps both developers understand the code better. It also facilitates knowledge sharing and the identification of potential issues.
- **Pass-around review:** Also known as *email pass-around reviews*, this method involves sending the completed code to one or more reviewers who check it for issues. This approach allows flexibility in timing but may lack the immediate interaction and learning opportunities provided by other methods.
- **Tool-assisted review:** Leverages software tools to automate parts of the code review process. Tools like Atlassian's Crucible, Codacy, and Phabricator can identify coding errors, enforce coding standards, and streamline the review process. Tool-assisted reviews can complement manual reviews by quickly identifying common issues.

Automated Versus Manual Code Review

Both automated and manual code reviews play vital roles in software testing:

- **Automated code review:** Tools can quickly scan large codebases to identify common security issues and coding errors. These tools provide a first line of defense by catching obvious defects that might be overlooked during manual reviews.
- **Manual code review:** Human reviewers can provide deeper insights into the context and logic of the code, identifying complex vulnerabilities that automated tools might miss. Manual reviews also foster knowledge sharing and adherence to coding standards within the development team.

Security Testing in the SDLC

Integrating security testing into the SDLC ensures that security is considered at every stage of software development. This integration is often referred to as *shift-left* testing, meaning that testing is integrated from the initial stages of development rather than being deferred until later stages—that is, testing is "moved to the left" on the project timeline. This approach aims to identify and address security issues as early as possible. Key practices include:

- **Threat modeling:** Identifying potential threats and vulnerabilities during the design phase.
- **Secure coding practices:** Adhering to coding standards and guidelines that promote security.
- **Continuous integration/continuous deployment (CI/CD):** Incorporating automated security tests into the CI/CD pipeline to ensure that new code changes do not introduce vulnerabilities.

Compliance Checks

Compliance checks are an essential part of security testing programs, especially for organizations subject to regulatory requirements. These checks verify that the security controls implemented in the software meet regulatory standards and are functioning as intended. Regular compliance checks help maintain the health of the organization's compliance program and avoid regulatory issues.

Exception Handling

Proper exception handling is a critical aspect of secure software design. Software should be designed to handle unexpected inputs and errors gracefully without exposing sensitive information or compromising security. Effective exception handling can prevent many common vulnerabilities, such as buffer overflows and injection attacks.

Training and Exercises

Training and exercises ensure that an organization's personnel are well-prepared to respond to security incidents and that security controls are functioning effectively. This section provides an overview of the importance of training and exercises, types of training, and various exercises that can be conducted to enhance security readiness.

Training and exercises help in building a security-conscious culture within an organization. They ensure that employees are aware of security policies, procedures, and their roles in maintaining security. Regular training helps in keeping the staff updated on the latest security threats and best practices. Exercises, on the other hand, provide a practical approach to test the effectiveness of security controls and the readiness of personnel to respond to incidents.

Types of Training

Effective security training programs must cater to the diverse roles and responsibilities within an organization. By tailoring training to the specific needs of different employee groups, organizations can ensure that all personnel are equipped with the knowledge and skills necessary to maintain security. Following are the main types of training that should be considered:

- **Security awareness training:** This type of training is designed to educate employees about the basic principles of information security, such as recognizing phishing attempts, creating strong passwords, and understanding the importance of data protection. It is typically conducted for all employees regardless of their role within the organization.
- **Role-based training:** This training is tailored to the specific roles and responsibilities of different employees. For example, IT staff may receive training on secure coding practices and network security, while management may focus on risk management and compliance requirements.
- **Technical training:** Technical training is aimed at IT and security professionals. It includes in-depth sessions on topics such as vulnerability management, incident response, and advanced security technologies. This type of training ensures that technical staff have the skills necessary to implement and maintain security controls effectively.
- **Compliance training:** Compliance training ensures that employees are aware of the legal and regulatory requirements relevant to their organization. This includes training on data protection laws, industry standards, and internal policies to ensure compliance with external and internal mandates.

Types of Exercises

Exercises are practical activities designed to test and improve the organization's security posture. They simulate real-world scenarios to assess the effectiveness of security controls, the readiness of personnel, and the overall incident response process. By conducting various types of exercises, organizations can identify vulnerabilities, enhance coordination among team members, and ensure continuous improvement in their security practices. Following are the main types of exercises that should be considered:

- **Tabletop exercises:** These are discussion-based sessions where team members walk through a hypothetical security incident scenario. The goal is to evaluate the effectiveness of the incident response plan and identify any gaps or weaknesses. Tabletop exercises help in improving coordination and communication among team members.

- **Functional exercises:** These exercises involve a more hands-on approach where participants perform their roles in response to a simulated incident. Functional exercises test the actual implementation of security controls and the ability of the team to respond to real-world scenarios.
- **Full-scale exercises:** These are comprehensive exercises that simulate a real incident as closely as possible. They involve multiple teams and departments and test the entire incident response process from detection to resolution. Full-scale exercises help in validating the overall effectiveness of the security program and identifying areas for improvement.
- **Red team/blue team exercises:** In these exercises, the red team simulates an attack on the organization's systems, while the blue team defends against the attack. This type of exercise helps in identifying vulnerabilities and testing the effectiveness of security controls. It also provides valuable insights into the tactics, techniques, and procedures used by attackers.
- **Purple team exercises:** These exercises involve collaboration between the red and blue teams to improve the overall security posture of the organization. The red team shares insights on potential vulnerabilities, while the blue team works on enhancing defenses. Purple team exercises foster a culture of continuous improvement and knowledge sharing.
- **Capture the flag (CTF) exercises:** CTF exercises are a fun and engaging way to achieve training objectives. In a CTF exercise, the red team begins with set objectives, such as disrupting a website, stealing a file from a secured system, or causing other security failures. The exercise is scored based on how many objectives the red team was able to achieve compared to how many the blue team prevented them from executing. CTF exercises provide practical, hands-on experience in both offensive and defensive security techniques, helping participants to better understand the tactics used by attackers and how to counter them.

Conducting Effective Training and Exercises

To ensure the effectiveness of training and exercises, organizations should follow these best practices:

- **Regular scheduling:** Training and exercises should be conducted regularly to ensure that employees remain aware of current threats and best practices. A consistent schedule helps in maintaining a high level of security readiness.
- **Realistic scenarios:** Exercises should be based on realistic scenarios that reflect the actual threats faced by the organization. This helps in ensuring that the exercises are relevant and provide valuable insights.

- **Post-exercise reviews:** After each exercise, a thorough review should be conducted to evaluate performance and identify areas for improvement. Feedback from participants should be collected and used to enhance future training and exercises.
- **Continuous improvement:** Training and exercise programs should be continuously updated to reflect changes in the threat landscape and advancements in security practices. This ensures that the organization remains prepared to handle new and emerging threats.

CHAPTER 9

Endpoint and Device Security

Endpoint and device security has become a critical component of any comprehensive cybersecurity strategy. As a security or privacy professional, understanding the complexities and nuances of protecting endpoint devices, network hardware, and mobile devices is essential to safeguarding your organization's sensitive information. This chapter provides an overview of the various technologies, methodologies, and best practices that are pivotal in fortifying the security of these critical assets. By delving into this chapter, you will gain valuable insights into the mechanisms and tools that can help you detect, respond to, and mitigate threats targeting your endpoints and devices.

The importance of robust endpoint and device security cannot be overstated, as these are often the first line of defense against cyber threats. This chapter will equip you with the knowledge needed to effectively manage and secure a diverse array of devices, from traditional desktop computers to mobile phones and network equipment. You'll learn about the latest advancements in malware detection and prevention, the critical role of patch management, and the strategies for maintaining secure configurations across your device landscape. By the end of this chapter, you will be better prepared to implement and oversee security measures that protect your organization from a wide range of potential vulnerabilities and threats.

Endpoint Detection and Response

Endpoint detection and response (EDR) is a critical component of an organization's cybersecurity strategy. EDR solutions are designed to monitor and manage endpoint devices such as laptops, desktops, mobile phones, and tablets. These devices are often the first line of defense against cyber threats and, consequently, are at high risk of being targeted by malicious actors. Effective endpoint security requires a combination of proactive measures to prevent attacks and reactive measures to detect and respond to incidents when they occur.

Endpoint devices are particularly vulnerable to cyberattacks because they are used by end users who may unintentionally or intentionally compromise security mechanisms. This makes it essential for cybersecurity professionals to focus on the secure configuration, monitoring, and management of these systems. The goal is to maintain the confidentiality, integrity, and availability of the data and resources accessed through these endpoints.

Key Components of EDR Solutions

EDR platforms provide a comprehensive approach to endpoint security by integrating several key components:

- **Continuous monitoring and detection:** EDR solutions continuously monitor endpoint activities to detect suspicious behavior or anomalies that may indicate a security threat. This includes monitoring system processes, network connections, and user activities.
- **Incident response:** When a potential threat is detected, EDR platforms facilitate a swift response to contain and mitigate the impact. This may involve isolating affected devices, terminating malicious processes, and removing malware.
- **Investigation and analysis:** EDR tools provide detailed forensic capabilities to investigate security incidents. This helps in understanding the root cause of an attack, the extent of the compromise, and the tactics, techniques, and procedures (TTPs) used by attackers.
- **Remediation and recovery:** After an incident is contained, EDR solutions assist in remediating affected systems and restoring them to a secure state. This includes applying patches, updating configurations, and ensuring that no residual threats remain.
- **Threat intelligence integration:** EDR platforms often integrate with threat intelligence feeds to stay updated on the latest threats and vulnerabilities. This enhances the ability to detect and respond to emerging threats promptly.
- **Automation and orchestration:** Many EDR solutions incorporate automation to streamline incident response processes. Automated workflows can handle routine tasks, allowing security teams to focus on more complex issues.

Prevention Mechanisms

To complement detection and response capabilities, EDR solutions also include preventive measures to reduce the likelihood of successful attacks:

- **Antimalware software:** Antimalware tools use signature detection and heuristic detection to identify and block malicious software. Signature detection relies on known malware signatures, while heuristic detection analyzes the behavior of unknown software to identify potential threats.
- **Data loss prevention:** DLP systems prevent the unauthorized exfiltration of sensitive data from endpoint devices. They monitor data transfers and enforce policies to ensure that sensitive information is not leaked.
- **Patch management:** Regularly applying security patches is crucial to protect endpoints from known vulnerabilities. Patch management systems ensure that updates are consistently applied across all devices.
- **System hardening:** Hardening involves configuring systems to reduce their attack surface. This includes disabling unnecessary services, enforcing strong authentication mechanisms, and applying security best practices.
- **Secure configuration management:** Maintaining secure configurations for endpoint devices is essential. Configuration management tools help enforce security policies and ensure that devices remain compliant with organizational standards.

Challenges in Endpoint Security

Despite the advanced capabilities of EDR solutions, organizations face several challenges in securing their endpoints:

- **User behavior:** End users can be a weak link in the security chain. Educating users about security best practices and promoting a security-aware culture is vital to prevent accidental or intentional security breaches.
- **Device diversity:** Organizations often have a wide variety of endpoint devices with different operating systems, configurations, and security requirements. Managing security across this diverse landscape can be complex.
- **Remote work:** The rise of remote work has increased the number of endpoints operating outside the traditional corporate network. This requires robust security measures to protect devices that may not be directly managed by the organization's IT team.

- **Advanced threats:** Cyber threats are constantly evolving, with attackers using sophisticated techniques to bypass traditional security measures. EDR solutions must continuously adapt to detect and respond to these advanced threats.

Best Practices for Implementing EDR

To maximize the effectiveness of EDR solutions, organizations should follow these best practices:

- **Comprehensive coverage:** Ensure that all endpoint devices are covered by the EDR solution. This includes not only corporate-owned devices but also personal devices used for work purposes.
- **Integration with other security tools:** EDR should be integrated with other security tools such as firewalls, IDS, and SIEM systems to provide a holistic view of the security landscape.
- **Regular updates and maintenance:** Keep the EDR solution and its components up to date with the latest patches and threat intelligence. Regular maintenance ensures that the solution remains effective against new threats.
- **Incident response planning:** Develop and regularly update an incident response plan that outlines the steps to be taken in the event of a security incident. This plan should be tested through regular drills and simulations.
- **User training and awareness:** Conduct regular training sessions to educate users about the importance of endpoint security and the role they play in maintaining it. Awareness programs can help reduce the risk of user-related security incidents.

EDR is a vital aspect of endpoint and device security, providing the tools and capabilities needed to detect, respond to, and mitigate security threats. By implementing robust EDR solutions and following best practices, organizations can enhance their security posture and protect their critical assets from cyber threats.

Network Device Security

Network devices, such as routers, switches, and firewalls, play a pivotal role in managing and directing data traffic across enterprise networks. Securing these devices is essential to prevent unauthorized access, data breaches, and other security incidents that could compromise the integrity and availability of network services.

Key Concepts in Network Device Security

Before examining the techniques, you can use to secure specific devices, here are a few important security concepts that apply to all network devices:

- **Physical security:** Ensuring that network devices are physically secure is the first line of defense. This involves restricting physical access to network infrastructure through secure locations like locked server rooms or data centers. Unauthorized physical access can lead to device tampering, theft, or damage.
- **Configuration management:** Proper configuration of network devices is essential for security. This includes setting strong administrative passwords, disabling unnecessary services, and applying the principle of least privilege. Regular reviews and updates to configurations help maintain security posture.
- **Firmware and software updates:** Keeping the firmware and software of network devices up to date is crucial. Manufacturers frequently release updates that patch security vulnerabilities. An effective patch management process ensures that all devices are running the latest, most secure versions of their software.
- **Access control:** Implementing robust access control measures helps ensure that only authorized personnel can access network devices. This can be achieved by using ACLs, RBAC, and NAC systems.
- **Network segmentation:** Dividing the network into segments can limit the spread of potential security incidents. By isolating sensitive systems and devices in different segments, organizations can contain and mitigate the impact of a breach.
- **Monitoring and logging:** Continuous monitoring and logging of network device activity are essential for detecting and responding to security incidents. SIEM systems can aggregate and analyze logs to identify suspicious activities and potential threats.
- **Encryption:** Using encryption protocols to secure data in transit helps protect sensitive information from interception and tampering. Protocols such as IPsec, SSL/TLS, and SSH provide secure communication channels for data transmission across the network.
- **Regular audits and assessments:** Conducting regular security audits and assessments of network devices helps identify vulnerabilities and ensure compliance with security policies and standards. These assessments can include vulnerability scans, penetration testing, and configuration reviews.
- **Incident response:** Having a well-defined incident response plan in place is crucial for addressing security incidents involving network devices. This plan should outline the steps to be taken in the event of a breach, including containment, eradication, and recovery procedures.

- **Training and awareness:** Educating network administrators and other relevant personnel about the importance of network device security and best practices is vital. Regular training sessions and awareness programs can help reinforce security policies and procedures.

Securing Switches

Switches are essential for connecting devices within a network. They require specific security measures to ensure they are not exploited by malicious actors:

- **Switch physical security:** Switches are often distributed throughout an organization, making them more vulnerable to physical tampering. It is crucial to keep switches in locked, secure locations where only authorized personnel have access. If someone gains physical access to a switch, they could potentially take control of that portion of the network.
- **VLAN security:** Virtual local area networks (VLANs) are used to segment network traffic. To secure VLANs:
  - **Implement VLAN pruning:** This practice ensures that only necessary VLANs are trunked to each switch, reducing the risk of a compromised switch affecting other parts of the network.
  - **Block VLAN hopping:** Malicious users might attempt to switch from their authorized VLAN to another by pretending to be a switch. To prevent this, configure switches to deny automatic VLAN trunking negotiation and only trunk VLANs when explicitly authorized by a network administrator.
- **Port security:** Port security prevents unauthorized devices from connecting to the network by limiting the MAC addresses that can use a particular switch port. This can be implemented in two modes:
  - **Static mode:** Administrators manually configure each port with allowable MAC addresses, providing the highest level of security but requiring significant administrative effort.
  - **Dynamic or "sticky" mode:** The switch memorizes the first MAC address it sees on a port and restricts access to that address. This method is faster to configure but can be risky if there are unused, active ports.

Securing Routers

Routers serve as the backbone for connecting different networks and play a crucial role in network security.

- **Access control lists:** Routers can be configured with ACLs to filter incoming and outgoing traffic, allowing only legitimate traffic to pass

through. This helps in reducing the load on firewalls and other network devices by blocking unwanted traffic early.
- **Quality of service (QoS):** Routers can prioritize traffic to ensure that critical applications receive the necessary bandwidth. This is particularly important for applications like videoconferencing, which require consistent and reliable network performance.
- **Router hardening:** This involves disabling unnecessary services, changing default passwords, and applying security patches regularly. It also includes configuring secure management protocols like SSH instead of Telnet and ensuring that remote management interfaces are not exposed to untrusted networks.
- **Monitoring and logging:** Just like switches, routers should be continuously monitored for unusual activity. Logs should be regularly reviewed to detect and respond to potential security incidents promptly.

By implementing these key concepts and specific measures for securing switches and routers, organizations can significantly enhance the security of their network infrastructure. Effective network device security requires a combination of technical controls, administrative measures, and ongoing vigilance to adapt to the evolving threat landscape.

Mobile Device Management

Mobile devices, including smartphones, tablets, and laptops, have become integral to modern business operations, providing flexibility and productivity benefits. However, their portability and connectivity also introduce significant security risks. Effective mobile device management (MDM) is crucial for protecting sensitive information and maintaining the security of an organization's network.

Security Challenges of Mobile Devices

Mobile devices face unique security challenges due to their mobility, diverse operating systems, and the variety of applications they run. Key challenges include:

- **Physical security:** Mobile devices are easily lost or stolen, which can lead to unauthorized access to sensitive data.
- **Malware and malicious apps:** Mobile devices are susceptible to malware and malicious applications that can compromise data and system integrity.

- **Network security:** Mobile devices often connect to various networks, including unsecured public Wi-Fi, increasing the risk of data interception and unauthorized access.
- **Data leakage:** The use of personal devices for work purposes can lead to data leakage if proper security measures are not in place.

Mobile Device Management Solutions

MDM solutions help organizations manage and secure mobile devices by providing a centralized platform for monitoring, managing, and securing mobile endpoints. Key features of MDM solutions include:

- **Device enrollment and provisioning:** MDM solutions streamline the process of enrolling and provisioning devices, ensuring that all devices comply with organizational security policies.
- **Policy enforcement:** MDM solutions enforce security policies, such as password requirements, encryption, and device lockout, to protect sensitive data.
- **Application management:** MDM solutions control the installation and use of applications on mobile devices, preventing the use of unauthorized or potentially harmful apps.
- **Remote management:** MDM solutions enable administrators to remotely manage devices, including the ability to lock or wipe devices that are lost or stolen.
- **Monitoring and reporting:** MDM solutions provide monitoring and reporting capabilities to track device compliance, usage, and security incidents.

Mobile Device Security Features

Mobile devices come with a variety of security features designed to protect sensitive information and maintain the integrity of the device. Here are some key security features:

- **Device authentication:** Authentication mechanisms, such as passwords, PINs, biometrics (fingerprint, facial recognition, iris scan), and proximity devices (NFC, RFID), ensure that only authorized users can access the device.
- **Full-device encryption:** Encrypts all data stored on the device, protecting it from unauthorized access even if the device is lost or stolen. Encryption is often combined with device authentication to enhance security.

- **Communication protection:** Encrypts voice, video, text, and data transmissions to prevent eavesdropping and unauthorized access. This includes using secure protocols and apps that support encrypted communications.
- **Remote wiping:** Allows administrators to remotely delete all data and configuration settings on a lost or stolen device, reducing the risk of data breaches. This feature is most effective when combined with full-device encryption.
- **Screen locks:** Prevents unauthorized access by requiring a PIN, password, or biometric authentication to unlock the device. Screen locks should be configured to activate automatically after a period of inactivity.
- **Device lockout:** Temporarily or permanently locks the device after a set number of failed authentication attempts, preventing brute force attacks. Some devices may also trigger a data wipe after multiple failed attempts.
- **GPS and location services:** Enables tracking of the device's location, which can be useful for locating lost or stolen devices and enforcing location-based security policies.
- **Content management:** Controls access to and management of data and applications on the device, ensuring that only authorized users can access sensitive information and install approved apps.
- **Sideloading:** Refers to the installation of applications from sources other than the official app store. Organizations should restrict or monitor sideloading to prevent the installation of potentially harmful apps.
- **Credential management:** Securely stores and manages user credentials, such as passwords and encryption keys, often using a password vault or similar tool. These solutions typically employ strong encryption and multifactor authentication to protect credentials.

By leveraging these security features, organizations can significantly enhance the security of their mobile devices and protect sensitive information from unauthorized access and potential breaches.

Mobile Device Deployment Policies

Implementing a mobile device deployment policy is essential for managing the use of mobile devices within an organization. These policies help balance security concerns with user convenience and productivity. Here are some common deployment models:

- **Bring your own device (BYOD):** Allows employees to use their personal mobile devices for work purposes. While this model can improve employee satisfaction and reduce hardware costs for the organization, it also introduces significant security risks due to the wide variety of devices and potential lack of security controls on personal devices.

- **Choose your own device (CYOD):** Provides employees with a list of approved devices from which to select. This model ensures that all devices meet the organization's security requirements while giving employees some choice. However, it can still present challenges in managing device security and support.
- **Corporate-owned, personally enabled (COPE):** The organization purchases and provides devices to employees, who can then use them for both work and personal activities. This model allows the organization to maintain control over device security and compliance while offering employees the convenience of using a single device for both work and personal tasks.
- **Corporate-owned mobile strategy (COMS):** Also known as corporate-owned, business-only (COBO), this model involves the organization purchasing and providing devices solely for work purposes. Employees are not allowed to use these devices for personal activities. This approach offers the highest level of security and control but may require employees to carry separate devices for work and personal use.

By carefully selecting and implementing a mobile device deployment policy, organizations can effectively manage the security risks associated with mobile devices while accommodating the needs and preferences of their employees.

Best Practices for Mobile Device Security

To effectively manage and secure mobile devices, organizations should implement the following best practices:

- **Develop a comprehensive mobile device policy:** Establish clear guidelines for the use of mobile devices, including acceptable use, security requirements, and incident reporting procedures.
- **Implement strong authentication and encryption:** Require strong passwords or biometric authentication and ensure that data stored on mobile devices is encrypted.
- **Regularly update and patch devices:** Keep mobile device operating systems and applications up to date with the latest security patches to protect against known vulnerabilities.

- **Use secure communication channels:** Ensure that mobile devices use secure communication channels, such as VPNs, for accessing corporate resources.
- **Educate users:** Provide training and awareness programs to educate users about mobile device security risks and best practices for protecting their devices and data.

Mobile devices offer significant benefits to organizations but also introduce substantial security risks. By implementing robust mobile device management solutions and following best practices, organizations can mitigate these risks and protect their sensitive information. Effective MDM is essential for maintaining the security and integrity of an organization's mobile endpoints and ensuring that mobile devices contribute to, rather than compromise, overall cybersecurity.

Understanding Malware

Malware, or malicious software, represents a broad category of software threats that exploit various vulnerabilities in the network, operating system, software, and physical security to spread harmful payloads to computer systems. These malicious code objects can significantly compromise the security of systems, making it essential for information security professionals to understand and mitigate these threats effectively.

Types of Malware

Malware comes in many forms, each with unique characteristics and methods of propagation. Understanding these different types is crucial for developing effective defenses against them. Here are some of the most common types of malware:

- **Viruses:** These are malicious code objects that attach themselves to legitimate software or files. When the infected program runs, the virus activates, potentially spreading to other programs and files. Viruses can cause a range of damage, from corrupting data to rendering systems inoperable. They often rely on user action to spread, such as opening an infected email attachment or running an infected executable.
- **Worms:** Unlike viruses, worms can spread independently without user intervention. They exploit vulnerabilities in operating systems or applications to propagate through networks. Worms can cause extensive damage by consuming bandwidth, overloading systems, and facilitating further attacks by creating backdoors.

- **Trojan horses:** These malicious programs disguise themselves as legitimate software. Once executed, they can create backdoors, steal data, or cause other harm. Trojans often appear as harmless applications or utilities, tricking users into installing them. They do not replicate like viruses or worms but can be just as destructive.
- **Logic bombs:** These are pieces of code intentionally inserted into software that will execute a malicious function when specific conditions are met. For example, a logic bomb might be programmed to delete files on a particular date or when a specific user logs in. Logic bombs can remain dormant for long periods, making them difficult to detect.
- **Ransomware:** This type of malware encrypts the victim's files, demanding a ransom to restore access. It can cause significant operational disruptions and financial losses. Ransomware attacks often begin with phishing emails or exploit vulnerabilities in software. Once the malware encrypts the data, the attacker demands payment, usually in cryptocurrency, in exchange for the decryption key.
- **Spyware:** This software secretly monitors user activity and collects information without the user's knowledge or consent. Spyware can track keystrokes, capture screenshots, and record browsing habits, often sending the collected data to a remote attacker. It can be used for identity theft, corporate espionage, or other malicious purposes.
- **Adware:** While primarily designed to display advertisements, adware can also collect user data and slow down system performance. Adware often comes bundled with free software and can be difficult to remove. It can track user behavior to display targeted ads, leading to privacy concerns and potential security risks.
- **Rootkits:** These are highly sophisticated malware designed to gain unauthorized root-level access to a system and hide their presence. Rootkits can modify the operating system and security software to avoid detection, making them extremely difficult to detect and remove. They can be used to maintain persistent access to a compromised system, allowing attackers to control it remotely.
- **Botnets:** A botnet is a network of infected computers, known as bots or zombies, controlled by an attacker. Botnets are often used to conduct large-scale attacks, such as distributed denial-of-service (DDoS) attacks, spam campaigns, and credential stuffing. The individual bots in a botnet can be controlled remotely, allowing the attacker to coordinate their actions.
- **Keyloggers:** This type of malware records keystrokes on an infected system, capturing sensitive information such as passwords, credit card

numbers, and personal messages. Keyloggers can be hardware-based or software-based and are often used in conjunction with other malware to steal data.
- **Fileless malware:** Unlike traditional malware, fileless malware does not rely on files to infect a system. Instead, it exploits existing software, applications, or protocols to execute malicious activities. Fileless malware can reside in memory, making it difficult to detect and remove with traditional antivirus solutions.
- **Malvertising:** This involves injecting malicious advertisements into legitimate online advertising networks. When users click on these ads, they are redirected to malicious websites or exposed to drive-by downloads that automatically install malware on their systems. Malvertising can affect even reputable websites, making it a widespread and insidious threat.

Understanding the various types of malware and their characteristics is essential for developing robust cybersecurity defenses. By recognizing the different methods malware uses to propagate and execute its payload, security professionals can implement targeted measures to prevent, detect, and respond to these threats effectively.

Malware Characteristics

Malware can exhibit a variety of characteristics that make it challenging to detect and remove. Understanding these characteristics is essential for developing effective countermeasures:

- **Polymorphism:** Polymorphic malware changes its code each time it infects a new system. This characteristic helps it evade signature-based detection methods used by traditional antivirus software. Polymorphic viruses maintain the same functionality but alter their appearance, making it difficult for antivirus solutions to recognize them.
- **Metamorphism:** Metamorphic malware goes a step further than polymorphic malware by completely rewriting its code with each infection. This makes it even more challenging to detect, as the malware can appear entirely different each time it infects a new system.
- **Stealth techniques:** Stealth malware uses various methods to hide its presence on an infected system. For example, it may modify system files and processes to avoid detection by antivirus software. Stealth techniques can include rootkits that hide the existence of other malware and alter system behavior to prevent detection.

- **Encryption:** Encrypted malware uses cryptographic techniques to conceal its code. This can make it difficult for security software to analyze and detect the malware. Encrypted malware typically includes a decryption routine that decrypts the main payload when executed.
- **Zero-day exploits:** Zero-day malware takes advantage of previously unknown vulnerabilities in software or hardware. These exploits are particularly dangerous because there are no existing patches or defenses against them at the time of the attack. Zero-day attacks can cause significant damage before security vendors develop and distribute patches.
- **Fileless execution:** Fileless malware operates without writing any files to disk, making it difficult to detect using traditional file-based antivirus methods. Instead, it resides in memory or leverages legitimate system tools and processes to execute its payload. This characteristic allows fileless malware to evade many security controls.
- **Persistence:** Persistent malware is designed to remain on an infected system even after reboots or attempts to remove it. It may use various techniques to achieve persistence, such as modifying system startup processes, creating hidden files, or exploiting vulnerabilities in system software.
- **Command and control (C&C):** Some malware establishes a connection with a remote server to receive instructions and updates from the attacker. This C&C infrastructure allows the attacker to control the infected system, exfiltrate data, and deploy additional payloads. C&C communication can be encrypted and obfuscated to avoid detection.
- **Propagation methods:** Malware can use various methods to spread from one system to another. Common propagation methods include exploiting network vulnerabilities, using infected removable media, sending malicious email attachments, and leveraging social media platforms. Understanding these methods helps in developing strategies to contain and prevent the spread of malware.

Understanding the various types of malware and their characteristics is essential for developing robust cybersecurity defenses. By recognizing the different methods malware uses to propagate and execute its payload, security professionals can implement targeted measures to prevent, detect, and respond to these threats effectively.

Malware Prevention

Professionals in information security must not only understand the various types of malware and their characteristics but must also be familiar with effective strategies for prevention and mitigation.

Basic Preventive Measures

To protect against malware, organizations should implement a combination of technical controls, user education, and policy enforcement. Here are some fundamental steps to prevent malware infections:

- **Keep systems and applications up to date:** Regularly apply patches and updates to fix security vulnerabilities.
- **Remove or disable unneeded services and protocols:** Minimize the attack surface by disabling unnecessary features.
- **Use intrusion detection and prevention systems (IDS/IPS):** Monitor network traffic for signs of malicious activity and block potential threats.
- **Use up-to-date antimalware software:** Install and maintain antimalware solutions on all endpoints to detect and prevent infections.
- **Use firewalls:** Implement network and host-based firewalls to filter traffic and block unauthorized access.
- **Implement configuration and system management processes:** Ensure systems are securely configured and maintained throughout their life cycle.

Advanced Malware Prevention Techniques

For a more robust defense against malware, organizations should consider advanced techniques and tools:

- **Endpoint detection and response:** EDR platforms provide comprehensive monitoring, detection, and response capabilities for endpoint security incidents.
- **Data loss prevention:** DLP systems prevent unauthorized data exfiltration by monitoring and controlling data transfers.
- **Sandboxing:** Isolate and analyze suspicious files in a controlled environment to detect and prevent malware execution.
- **Honeypots and honeynets:** Deploy decoy systems to attract and analyze attackers, gaining insights into their methods and tools.
- **Machine learning and AI-based tools:** Utilize advanced algorithms to detect and respond to malware based on patterns and behaviors.

Educating Users

User education is a critical component of malware prevention. Employees should be trained to recognize and avoid common malware delivery methods, such as phishing emails and malicious links. Key educational topics include:

- **Social engineering tactics:** Understand how attackers use deception to trick users into installing malware.
- **Safe browsing practices:** Avoid clicking on suspicious links or downloading unverified software.
- **Email hygiene:** Be cautious with email attachments and links, especially from unknown sources.

Policy and Governance

Organizations should establish and enforce policies that promote secure practices and reduce the risk of malware infections. Important policy areas include:

- **Access control:** Implement the principle of least privilege to limit user permissions and reduce the impact of malware.
- **Software installation:** Restrict the installation of unauthorized software to prevent the introduction of malware.
- **Incident response:** Develop and maintain an incident response plan to quickly address and mitigate malware infections.

Malware prevention requires a multifaceted approach that combines technical controls, user education, and strong policies. By implementing these strategies, organizations can significantly reduce the risk of malware infections and protect their systems and data from harm. Effective malware prevention not only safeguards the organization's assets but also ensures the continuity of operations and the protection of sensitive information.

Patching and Vulnerability Remediation

Patching and vulnerability remediation are critical components of maintaining a secure environment. These processes ensure that systems remain protected against known vulnerabilities and threats, which can be exploited by malicious actors if left unaddressed. This section provides an overview of the key concepts and practices involved in managing patches and reducing vulnerabilities.

The Importance of Patch Management

Patch management is the process of identifying, acquiring, installing, and verifying patches for software and systems. Patches are pieces of code designed to fix security vulnerabilities, improve functionality, or address other software issues. Effective patch management is essential for maintaining the security and stability of IT systems.

Key reasons for patch management include:

- **Security:** Patches often address security vulnerabilities that could be exploited by attackers. Applying patches promptly helps protect systems from potential breaches.
- **Functionality:** Patches can improve the performance and functionality of software, ensuring that systems run efficiently.
- **Compliance:** Many regulatory frameworks require organizations to maintain up-to-date systems, making patch management a critical component of compliance efforts.

Patch Management Process

A robust patch management process involves several key steps to ensure that patches are applied effectively and efficiently:

1. **Inventory systems and software:** Maintain an up-to-date inventory of all systems and software within the organization. This inventory helps identify which systems require patches and ensures that no critical systems are overlooked.
2. **Identify vulnerabilities:** Regularly scan systems for known vulnerabilities using automated tools. These tools compare the current state of systems against a database of known vulnerabilities and identify any gaps that need to be addressed.
3. **Evaluate patches:** Once vulnerabilities are identified, evaluate the available patches to determine their relevance and priority. Consider factors such as the severity of the vulnerability, the potential impact on the organization, and the availability of the patch.
4. **Test patches:** Before deploying patches to production systems, test them in a controlled environment to ensure they do not introduce new issues or conflicts. This step helps prevent disruptions to business operations.
5. **Deploy patches:** After successful testing, deploy patches to production systems. This deployment should be carefully managed to minimize downtime and ensure that critical systems remain operational.

6. **Verify and monitor:** After deploying patches, verify that they have been applied correctly and monitor systems for any issues. Regular monitoring helps ensure that patches are effective and that no new vulnerabilities have been introduced.

Reducing Vulnerabilities

In addition to patch management, reducing vulnerabilities involves several proactive measures to strengthen the security posture of an organization:

- **Configuration management:** Ensure that systems are configured securely according to best practices. Regularly review and update configurations to address any potential weaknesses.
- **Access controls:** Implement strict access controls to limit the exposure of sensitive systems and data. Use principles such as least privilege and need-to-know to restrict access to only those who require it.
- **Security training:** Provide regular security training and awareness programs for employees. Educated users are less likely to fall victim to social engineering attacks and more likely to follow security best practices.
- **Incident response:** Develop and maintain an incident response plan to quickly address and mitigate the impact of security incidents. Regularly test and update the plan to ensure its effectiveness.

Vulnerability Remediation Workflow

A comprehensive vulnerability remediation workflow helps organizations systematically address identified vulnerabilities. The workflow typically includes the following steps:

1. **Detection:** Use vulnerability scanning tools to detect vulnerabilities in systems and software.
2. **Prioritization:** Assess the severity and potential impact of detected vulnerabilities to prioritize remediation efforts.
3. **Remediation:** Apply patches, updates, or other mitigation measures to address detected vulnerabilities.
4. **Verification:** Verify that remediation efforts have been successful and that vulnerabilities have been effectively addressed.
5. **Documentation:** Document the remediation process and maintain records for compliance and auditing purposes.

Challenges and Best Practices

Organizations may face several challenges in patch management and vulnerability remediation, including the complexity of IT environments, limited resources, and the need to balance security with operational requirements. To address these challenges, consider the following best practices:

- **Automate processes:** Use automated tools for vulnerability scanning, patch deployment, and monitoring to improve efficiency and accuracy.
- **Establish policies:** Develop clear patch management and vulnerability remediation policies to guide efforts and ensure consistency.
- **Audit regularly:** Conduct regular audits and assessments to identify gaps in patch management processes and to ensure compliance with regulatory requirements.
- **Collaborate:** Foster collaboration between IT, security, and business teams to ensure that patch management efforts align with organizational goals and priorities.

By implementing a structured approach to patch management and vulnerability remediation, organizations can significantly reduce their risk exposure and enhance their overall cybersecurity posture.

CHAPTER 10

Application Security

Ensuring the security of applications is paramount. As a security and privacy professional, you are on the front lines of defending against a myriad of threats that target applications, which are often the gateway to sensitive data and critical systems. This chapter is designed to equip you with the knowledge and tools necessary to fortify your applications against these threats. By understanding and implementing secure software development practices, integrating security into DevOps processes, and recognizing common attack vectors, you can significantly enhance the resilience of your applications.

Throughout this chapter, you will gain insights into the Secure Software Development Life Cycle, which is essential for building robust and secure applications from the ground up. You will explore the integration of security into DevOps, a practice that ensures security is not an afterthought but a continuous process embedded in the development workflow. Additionally, you will learn about various application attacks, including injection and authorization vulnerabilities, and how to defend against them. By mastering application security controls and adhering to secure coding best practices, you will be well-equipped to protect your applications from potential exploits. This chapter aims to provide you with a comprehensive understanding of application security, empowering you to safeguard your organization's digital assets effectively.

Secure Software Development Life Cycle

The Secure Software Development Life Cycle (SDLC) is a critical framework for ensuring that security is embedded into every phase of software development.

This approach helps mitigate risks, meet compliance requirements, and protect sensitive data from potential threats. In this section, we will explore the essential components and best practices for integrating security into the SDLC.

Introduction to Systems Development Controls

Many organizations rely on custom-developed software to achieve their unique business objectives. However, these custom solutions can present significant security vulnerabilities due to malicious or careless developers who might introduce backdoors, buffer overflow vulnerabilities, or other weaknesses. To protect against these vulnerabilities, it is crucial to introduce security controls throughout the entire system's development life cycle.

An organized, methodical process ensures that solutions meet both functional requirements and security guidelines. Security should be considered at every stage of a system's development, including the software development process. Programmers should strive to build security into every application they develop, with greater levels of security provided to critical applications and those that process sensitive information. It is much easier to build security into a system during development than to add security to an existing system.

Phases of the Secure Software Development Life Cycle

The following are the essential phases of the Secure Software Development Life Cycle, along with key security considerations for each phase:

- **Planning and requirements analysis:** This phase involves understanding the project's goals, gathering requirements, and conducting a thorough risk assessment to identify potential threats and vulnerabilities. Key security considerations:
    - **Security requirements:** Identify and document security requirements based on the organization's policies, industry standards, and regulatory requirements. This includes confidentiality, integrity, availability, and privacy considerations.
    - **Risk assessment:** Conduct a thorough risk assessment to identify potential threats and vulnerabilities. This helps prioritize security efforts and allocate resources effectively.

- **Design:** In this phase, the system architecture is designed with security in mind, incorporating secure design principles and threat modeling techniques. Key security considerations:
  - **Threat modeling:** Use threat modeling techniques to identify potential security threats and design countermeasures. This involves understanding the system architecture, data flows, and potential attack vectors.
  - **Secure design principles:** Implement secure design principles such as least privilege, defense in depth, and fail securely. These principles help create a robust security foundation.
- **Development:** During the development phase, secure coding practices are followed to prevent common vulnerabilities, and regular code reviews are conducted to ensure adherence to security standards. Key security considerations:
  - **Secure coding practices:** Follow secure coding guidelines to prevent common vulnerabilities such as SQL injection, cross-site scripting (XSS), and buffer overflows. Use static code analysis tools to identify and fix security issues early in the development process.
  - **Code reviews:** Conduct regular code reviews to ensure adherence to secure coding practices and identify potential security flaws. Peer reviews and automated tools can be used to enhance the effectiveness of this process.
- **Testing:** This phase involves rigorous security testing to identify vulnerabilities and ensure that security controls are functioning as intended. Key security considerations:
  - **Security testing:** Perform various security testing techniques, including static application security testing (SAST), dynamic application security testing (DAST), and interactive application security testing (IAST). These tests help identify vulnerabilities and ensure that security controls are functioning as intended.
  - **Penetration testing:** Conduct penetration testing to simulate real-world attacks and identify weaknesses that could be exploited by malicious actors. This helps validate the effectiveness of security controls and uncover hidden vulnerabilities.
- **Deployment:** Secure deployment practices are followed to ensure that the application is configured securely and that the deployment environment is hardened. Key security considerations:
  - **Secure configuration:** Ensure that the application is deployed with secure configurations, including appropriate access controls, encryption settings, and logging mechanisms. Avoid default configurations that could expose the application to unnecessary risks.

- o **Environment hardening:** Harden the deployment environment by securing servers, databases, and network components. This includes applying patches, disabling unnecessary services, and implementing firewall rules.
- **Maintenance and operations:** Continuous monitoring and regular patch management are essential to maintaining the security posture of the application over time. Key security considerations:
  - o **Continuous monitoring:** Implement continuous monitoring to detect and respond to security incidents in real time. This involves monitoring logs, network traffic, and system behavior for signs of malicious activity.
  - o **Patch management:** Regularly update and patch the application and its dependencies to address known vulnerabilities. This helps maintain the security posture of the application over time.
- **Disposal:** When an application reaches the end of its life cycle, secure decommissioning practices are followed to ensure that sensitive data is securely deleted and access credentials are revoked. Key security consideration:
  - o **Secure decommissioning:** When an application reaches the end of its life cycle, ensure that it is securely decommissioned. This includes securely deleting sensitive data, revoking access credentials, and removing the application from production environments.

Best Practices for Secure Software Development

To further enhance the security of the software development process, it is essential to follow best practices that promote security awareness, collaboration, and efficiency. Here are some key best practices for secure software development:

- **Security training and awareness:** Provide ongoing security training and awareness programs for developers, testers, and other stakeholders. This helps ensure that everyone involved in the SDLC understands the importance of security and follows best practices.
- **Automation:** Leverage automation tools for security testing, code analysis, and deployment. Automation helps streamline security processes, reduce human error, and improve efficiency.
- **Collaboration:** Foster collaboration between development, security, and operations teams. This helps ensure that security is integrated into the SDLC and that potential issues are addressed promptly.
- **Documentation:** Maintain comprehensive documentation of security requirements, design decisions, testing results, and deployment

configurations. This helps ensure consistency and provides a reference for future development efforts.

By integrating security into every phase of the SDLC, organizations can develop robust, secure applications that protect sensitive data and meet compliance requirements. Following these best practices helps mitigate risks and ensures that security is a fundamental aspect of the software development process.

DevSecOps and DevOps Integration

The integration of development, security, and operations—commonly referred to as DevSecOps—has become essential for organizations seeking to maintain robust security postures while achieving rapid software delivery. This approach builds on the principles of DevOps, which aims to streamline and automate the processes between software development and IT operations to shorten the development life cycle and deliver high-quality software continuously.

The DevOps Approach

DevOps is closely aligned with the Agile development methodology, focusing on reducing the time required to develop, test, and deploy software changes. Traditional software development models often resulted in major software deployments occurring infrequently, sometimes only once a year. In contrast, organizations adopting the DevOps model strive to deploy code several times per day, with some aiming for continuous integration and continuous delivery (CI/CD). This frequent deployment cycle necessitates a high degree of automation, including the integration of code repositories, software configuration management processes, and the movement of code between development, testing, and production environments.

The DevOps approach emphasizes collaboration between development and operations teams, breaking down silos and fostering a culture of shared responsibility. This collaboration is crucial for achieving the primary goals of DevOps: improved deployment frequency, faster time to market, lower failure rates of new releases, and shortened lead time between fixes.

Continuous Integration and Continuous Deployment

Continuous integration (CI) and continuous deployment (CD) are fundamental practices within the DevOps and DevSecOps frameworks, designed to enhance the efficiency and reliability of software development and deployment processes. Together, they form a pipeline that automates the integration, testing, and deployment of code changes, ensuring that software can be delivered rapidly and with high quality.

Continuous Integration   CI is a development practice where developers frequently integrate their code changes into a shared repository, typically multiple times a day. Each integration is verified by an automated build process, which includes compiling the code, running tests, and performing other quality checks. The primary goals of CI are to detect integration issues early, reduce the time required to identify and fix defects, and improve the overall quality of the software.

Key components of CI include:

- **Automated builds:** Every code change triggers an automated build process, ensuring that the code compiles correctly and is free of syntax errors.
- **Automated testing:** Automated tests are run as part of the build process to verify the functionality and quality of the code. This includes unit tests, integration tests, and other types of automated tests.
- **Code quality checks:** Tools such as static code analyzers and linters are used to enforce coding standards and detect potential issues in the code.
- **Continuous feedback:** Developers receive immediate feedback on the status of their code changes, allowing them to quickly address any issues that arise.

Continuous Deployment   CD extends the principles of CI by automating the deployment of code changes to production environments. In a CD pipeline, code changes that pass all automated tests and quality checks are automatically deployed to production without manual intervention. This practice ensures that software can be released quickly and reliably, enabling organizations to respond to market demands and customer feedback more effectively.

Key components of CD include:

- **Automated deployment:** Code changes are automatically deployed to production environments once they pass all tests and quality checks. This reduces the risk of human error and speeds up the release process.
- **Environment consistency:** Automated deployment processes ensure that code is deployed consistently across different environments, reducing the likelihood of environment-specific issues.
- **Rollback mechanisms:** Automated rollback mechanisms are in place to quickly revert to a previous version of the software in case of issues with the new deployment.
- **Monitoring and logging:** Continuous monitoring and logging are essential to detect and diagnose issues in production environments. This includes performance monitoring, error tracking, and security monitoring.

Benefits of CI/CD   Implementing CI/CD practices, particularly with integrated security, offers several benefits:

- **Increased deployment frequency:** Automated build, test, and deployment processes enable organizations to release software more frequently, providing faster delivery of new features and bug fixes.
- **Improved code quality:** Continuous testing and quality checks help identify and address issues early, resulting in higher-quality software.
- **Reduced deployment risk:** Automated deployment processes and rollback mechanisms reduce the risk of deployment failures and minimize downtime.
- **Enhanced security:** Integrating security into the CI/CD pipeline ensures that security checks are performed continuously, reducing the likelihood of security vulnerabilities in production.

Continuous integration and continuous deployment are essential practices within the DevOps and DevSecOps frameworks, enabling organizations to deliver high-quality software rapidly and reliably. By integrating security into the CI/CD pipeline, organizations can ensure that security is maintained throughout the development and deployment processes, enhancing their overall security posture and driving business value.

Integrating Security into DevOps: DevSecOps

As organizations increasingly adopt DevOps practices, the need to integrate security into this rapid development and deployment cycle becomes apparent. This integration is where DevSecOps comes into play. DevSecOps extends the DevOps philosophy by embedding security practices into every phase of the SDLC, ensuring that security is not an afterthought but a fundamental component of the development process.

Key elements of DevSecOps include:

- **Security as code:** Security controls and tests are automated and integrated into the CI/CD pipeline, allowing for continuous security validation. This approach ensures that security checks are performed consistently and at scale without slowing down the development process.
- **Shift-left security:** Security practices and testing are moved to the earliest stages of the development process. By identifying and addressing security issues early, organizations can reduce the cost and complexity of remediating vulnerabilities later in the SDLC.
- **Collaboration and training:** Effective DevSecOps requires close collaboration between development, operations, and security teams.

Additionally, developers need to be trained in secure coding practices and made aware of common security threats and vulnerabilities.
- **Continuous monitoring and feedback:** Security is monitored continuously, and feedback loops are established to ensure that security issues are promptly addressed. This continuous monitoring helps organizations quickly detect and respond to security incidents.

Implementing DevSecOps

Implementing DevSecOps involves several steps:

- **Culture shift:** Organizations must foster a culture that values security as a shared responsibility. This cultural shift often requires strong leadership and a commitment to ongoing training and education.
- **Automation:** Automation is critical to the success of DevSecOps. Security tools and processes must be integrated into the CI/CD pipeline to enable continuous security testing and validation.
- **Tool integration:** Selecting and integrating the right tools is essential for effective DevSecOps. These tools should support automated security testing, vulnerability scanning, and compliance checks.
- **Metrics and reporting:** Establishing metrics and reporting mechanisms helps organizations track the effectiveness of their DevSecOps practices and identify areas for improvement.
- **Policy and governance:** Clear policies and governance frameworks are necessary to ensure that security practices are consistently applied across the organization.

Benefits of DevSecOps

The integration of security into the DevOps process offers several benefits:

- **Improved security posture:** By embedding security into the development process, organizations can identify and address vulnerabilities early, reducing the risk of security breaches.
- **Faster time to market:** Automated security testing and validation allow for rapid deployment of secure software, enabling organizations to respond quickly to market demands.
- **Cost savings:** Addressing security issues early in the development process can significantly reduce the cost of remediation compared to fixing vulnerabilities in production.

- **Enhanced compliance:** Continuous security monitoring and automated compliance checks help organizations meet regulatory requirements and industry standards.

DevSecOps represents a significant evolution in the way organizations approach software development and security. By integrating security into every phase of the SDLC and fostering a culture of collaboration and shared responsibility, organizations can achieve both rapid software delivery and robust security. This approach not only enhances an organization's security posture but also drives business value by enabling faster, more reliable software releases.

Application Attacks

Understanding various application attack vectors is crucial for safeguarding systems and data. Application attacks exploit vulnerabilities in software to compromise security, and they come in many forms. This section will cover four common types of application attacks: buffer overflows, time of check to time of use (TOCTTOU), backdoors, and privilege escalation and rootkits.

Buffer Overflows

Buffer overflows occur when an application writes more data to a buffer than it can hold. This excess data can overwrite adjacent memory, leading to erratic program behavior, crashes, or execution of malicious code. Attackers often exploit buffer overflows to inject and execute arbitrary code with the same privileges as the running application. To mitigate these risks, developers should use bounds-checking techniques, employ safe functions, and apply compiler-based protections like stack canaries and address space layout randomization (ASLR).

Time of Check to Time of Use

TOCTTOU vulnerabilities arise when a program checks a condition before performing an operation, but the condition changes before the operation is executed. This race condition can be exploited by attackers to manipulate the timing of operations, leading to unauthorized actions. For example, an attacker might replace a file after it has been checked but before it is used.

Preventing TOCTTOU vulnerabilities involves using atomic operations, locking mechanisms, and ensuring that checks and operations are performed as closely together as possible.

Backdoors

Backdoors are hidden methods of bypassing normal authentication and gaining unauthorized access to a system. They are often inserted intentionally by developers for maintenance purposes or by attackers to maintain persistent access. Backdoors can be embedded in software, firmware, or hardware. Detecting and removing backdoors requires thorough code reviews, regular security audits, and using tools to scan for unexpected network connections or changes in system behavior.

Privilege Escalation and Rootkits

Privilege escalation occurs when an attacker gains elevated access to resources that are normally protected from an application or user. This can be achieved through exploiting vulnerabilities or misconfigurations. Rootkits are a type of malware designed to hide the presence of malicious processes or files, allowing attackers to maintain privileged access undetected. Rootkits can operate at the user level or kernel level, making them particularly difficult to detect and remove. Effective defenses against privilege escalation and rootkits include applying the principle of least privilege, regular patching, using intrusion detection systems, and employing rootkit detection tools that analyze system behavior and integrity.

Injection Vulnerabilities

Injection vulnerabilities are a significant threat to application security, as they allow attackers to introduce malicious code into a program, potentially compromising the entire system. These vulnerabilities can lead to unauthorized access, data breaches, and other malicious activities. This section explores three common types of injection vulnerabilities: SQL injection attacks, code injection attacks, and command injection attacks.

SQL Injection Attacks

SQL injection attacks are a prevalent form of injection vulnerability where attackers insert malicious SQL code into a query. This type of attack targets databases and can lead to unauthorized access, data manipulation, or even deletion of data. SQL injection typically occurs when user inputs are not adequately validated or sanitized before being incorporated into SQL queries.

For example, consider a web application that asks a user to enter a username and password. If a legitimate user enters the username `jane_doe` and the password `mypassword`, the query becomes

```
SELECT * FROM users WHERE username = 'jane_doe' AND password = 'mypassword';
```

If the credentials match a record in the users table, the user is authenticated.

An attacker exploits this by inputting malicious SQL. For instance, the attacker might input the username `admin'` -- and the password: `anything`. The query becomes

```
SELECT * FROM users WHERE username = 'admin' --' AND password = 'anything';
```

The -- starts an SQL comment, ignoring everything after it in the query. The resulting query is equivalent to

```
SELECT * FROM users WHERE username = 'admin';
```

This effectively bypasses password verification, granting unauthorized access to the admin account.

To mitigate SQL injection risks, developers should use prepared statements, parameterized queries, and input validation techniques to ensure that user inputs are treated as data rather than executable code.

Code Injection Attacks

Code injection attacks involve inserting attacker-written code into the legitimate code created by a web application developer. These attacks can occur in various environments where user-supplied input is incorporated into the application's code execution.

One common example of a code injection attack is an LDAP injection, where attackers embed commands in text sent as part of a Lightweight Directory Access Protocol (LDAP) query. If a web server uses a script to craft LDAP statements based on user input without proper validation, attackers can manipulate the input to execute arbitrary commands on the LDAP directory service.

Another example is XML injection, where the target is an XML application. Attackers can insert malicious XML content to manipulate the application's behavior. Similarly, DLL injection attacks involve loading malicious dynamic-link libraries (DLLs) into an application, allowing attackers to execute arbitrary code.

To defend against code injection attacks, developers should implement input validation and escaping, ensuring that user inputs are properly sanitized before being processed by the application. Defensive coding practices and thorough testing can also help identify and mitigate potential vulnerabilities.

Command Injection Attacks

Command injection attacks occur when an application passes unsafe user-supplied input to a system shell or operating system command. This type of attack is particularly dangerous because it allows attackers to execute arbitrary commands on the host operating system, potentially gaining full control over the system.

For instance, consider a web application with a "Username" text box that creates directories for new users by executing a command. On a Linux system, the application might use a `system()` call to send the directory creation command to the underlying operating system. For example, if someone fills in the text box with

`mchapple`

the application might use the function call

`system('mkdir /home/students/mchapple')`

to create a home directory for that user. An attacker examining this application might guess that this is how the application works and then supply the input:

`mchapple & rm -rf /home`

which the application then uses to create the system call

`system('mkdir /home/students/mchapple & rm -rf /home')`

This sequence of commands deletes the `/home` directory along with all files and subfolders it contains.

To prevent command injection attacks, developers should avoid using system calls that incorporate user input. Instead, they should use safer alternatives, such as built-in functions or libraries that do not require shell access. Additionally, input validation and sanitization are crucial to ensure that user inputs do not contain malicious commands.

Authorization Vulnerabilities

Authorization vulnerabilities in applications can have severe consequences, allowing unauthorized access to sensitive data and system functionalities.

Authorization Vulnerabilities   195

These vulnerabilities often stem from improper handling of user permissions and access controls. In this section, you explore three common types of authorization vulnerabilities: insecure direct object references, directory traversal, and file inclusion.

Insecure Direct Object References

Insecure direct object references (IDOR) occur when an application exposes a reference to an internal object, such as a file, directory, or database key, without proper access control checks. This vulnerability allows attackers to manipulate the reference to access unauthorized resources. For example, if an application uses a URL parameter to access user account information,

```
https://example.com/user?account=12345
```

an attacker could change the account number to access another user's account.

To prevent IDOR, use the following mitigation strategies:

- **Implement access control checks:** Ensure that every request for an object includes proper authorization checks to verify that the user has permission to access the requested resource.
- **Use indirect references:** Instead of exposing direct references to internal objects, use indirect references, such as unique tokens or hashes, that map to the actual objects on the server side.
- **Validate input:** Always validate and sanitize user input to prevent manipulation of object references.

Directory Traversal

Directory traversal, also known as *path traversal*, is a vulnerability that allows attackers to access files and directories stored outside the web root folder. By manipulating file paths, attackers can navigate the directory structure and access sensitive files, such as configuration files, password files, and application source code.

To prevent directory traversal, use the following mitigation strategies:

- **Validate and sanitize input:** Ensure that user input used in file paths is properly validated and sanitized to remove any malicious characters or sequences (such as ../).

- **Use secure APIs:** Employ secure file handling functions and APIs that prevent directory traversal attacks by restricting file access to specific directories.
- **Implement access controls:** Enforce strict access controls on the server to limit access to sensitive files and directories.

File Inclusion

File inclusion vulnerabilities occur when an application dynamically includes files based on user input. There are two types of file inclusion vulnerabilities: local file inclusion (LFI) and remote file inclusion (RFI). LFI allows attackers to include files from the local server, while RFI enables the inclusion of files from remote servers. These vulnerabilities can lead to arbitrary code execution, information disclosure, and other malicious activities.

To prevent file inclusion, use the following mitigation strategies:

- **Validate and sanitize input:** Ensure that any user input used in file inclusion is thoroughly validated and sanitized to prevent the inclusion of unauthorized files.
- **Use passlisting:** Implement passlisting to restrict file inclusion to a predefined set of allowed files.
- **Disable remote file inclusion:** If not required, disable the ability to include remote files in the application's configuration settings.

By understanding and addressing these common authorization vulnerabilities, security professionals can significantly enhance the security of their applications and protect sensitive data from unauthorized access.

Web Application Attacks

Web applications are a critical component of modern business operations, but they also present significant security challenges. The complexity of these applications, combined with their public-facing nature, makes them attractive targets for attackers. This section explores three common types of web application attacks: cross-site scripting (XSS), request forgery, and session hijacking.

Cross-Site Scripting

Cross-site scripting attacks occur when attackers inject malicious HTML or JavaScript code into a web page viewed by other users. This can lead to various malicious activities, such as stealing session cookies, redirecting users to phishing sites, or executing arbitrary actions on behalf of the user.

There are two primary types of XSS attacks:

- **Stored/persistent XSS:** In this type of attack, the malicious code is stored on the target server, such as in a database, and is served to users whenever they request the stored content. For example, an attacker might post a message containing a script on a message board, which then executes whenever any user views the message.
- **Reflected XSS:** This occurs when the malicious code is reflected off a web server, such as in an error message or search result, and is immediately executed by the user's browser. This type of XSS is typically delivered via a URL crafted by the attacker.

Both types of XSS attacks can be mitigated through proper input validation, escaping user input, and employing content security policy (CSP) headers.

Request Forgery

Request forgery attacks exploit trust relationships to trick users into performing actions they did not intend. There are two main forms of request forgery:

- **Cross-site request forgery (CSRF):** In CSRF attacks, an attacker tricks a user into submitting a request to a web application in which the user is authenticated. This can lead to unauthorized actions being performed on behalf of the user, such as changing account details or making transactions. Mitigation techniques include using anti-CSRF tokens, requiring reauthentication for sensitive actions, and checking the HTTP Referer header.
- **Server-side request forgery (SSRF):** SSRF attacks occur when an attacker can manipulate a server to make requests to unintended locations, potentially accessing internal services or sensitive data. To prevent SSRF attacks, developers should validate and sanitize user inputs that are used to generate requests and implement network segmentation to limit the server's ability to interact with internal resources.

Session Hijacking

Session hijacking involves an attacker taking over a user's session to impersonate them and gain unauthorized access to resources. Common techniques include:

- **Session fixation:** The attacker sets a user's session ID to a known value, then waits for the user to log in, allowing the attacker to use the same session ID to gain access.

- **Session sidejacking:** The attacker intercepts and captures session cookies over an unencrypted connection, such as public Wi-Fi, and uses them to hijack the session.
- **Cross-site script attacks:** Using XSS vulnerabilities, attackers can steal session cookies directly from the user's browser.

Mitigation strategies for session hijacking include using secure cookies (with the Secure and HttpOnly flags), implementing session timeout and regeneration mechanisms, and ensuring all communication is encrypted using HTTPS.

By understanding and addressing these common web application attacks, security professionals can better protect their applications and users from potential threats.

Application Security Controls

Application security is a critical aspect of maintaining the overall security posture of an organization. It involves implementing measures to protect applications from threats that can compromise the confidentiality, integrity, and availability of data. This section will cover key application security controls and the importance of software security testing in ensuring the effectiveness of these controls.

Key Application Security Controls

Application security controls are essential measures designed to protect applications from various threats that can compromise the confidentiality, integrity, and availability of data. This section delves into four critical application security controls: input validation, web application firewalls, database security, and code security.

Input Validation

Input validation is a fundamental security control that ensures user inputs conform to expected formats and values before processing them. Proper input validation helps prevent injection attacks, such as SQL injection and XSS, which can exploit vulnerabilities in applications.

- **Passlisting and blocklisting:** Passlisting involves defining a set of acceptable inputs, while blocklisting identifies known malicious inputs. Passlisting is generally more secure as it only allows known good inputs.

- **Escaping inputs:** Escaping inputs involves converting special characters into a safe format to prevent them from being interpreted as code. This is particularly important for preventing XSS attacks.
- **Parameterized queries:** Using parameterized queries ensures that user inputs are treated as data rather than executable code. This approach is effective in preventing SQL injection attacks.

Web Application Firewalls

Web application firewalls (WAFs) play a crucial role in protecting web applications from attacks by filtering and monitoring HTTP traffic between a web application and the Internet. WAFs operate at the application layer of the OSI model and provide an additional layer of defense against web application vulnerabilities.

- **Input validation:** WAFs perform input validation by scrutinizing incoming traffic and blocking malicious inputs before they reach the application server.
- **Passlisting and blocklisting:** Similar to input validation techniques, WAFs can use passlisting and blocklisting to allow or block specific types of traffic based on predefined rules.
- **Protection against injection flaws:** WAFs help protect against injection flaws by detecting and blocking malicious payloads that attempt to exploit vulnerabilities in the application.

Database Security

Secure applications rely on secure databases to store and manage data. Database security encompasses various practices and controls to protect databases from unauthorized access, data breaches, and other threats.

- **Parameterized queries and stored procedures:** Parameterized queries and stored procedures help prevent SQL injection attacks by ensuring that user inputs are treated as data rather than executable code.
- **Encryption:** Encrypting sensitive data both at rest and in transit is crucial for protecting it from unauthorized access. Strong encryption algorithms and proper key management practices are essential for effective database security.
- **Obfuscation and camouflage:** Techniques such as data minimization, tokenization, and hashing help protect sensitive information by reducing the amount of data stored, replacing identifiers with unique tokens, and using irreversible hash values.

Code Security

Code security involves implementing secure coding practices to ensure that applications are resistant to common vulnerabilities. By following guidelines and standards, developers can write code that is more secure and less prone to exploitation.

Key software security testing methods include:

- **Secure coding practices:** Adhering to secure coding practices, such as avoiding hard-coded credentials, using secure libraries, and performing regular code reviews, helps reduce the risk of vulnerabilities in the code.
- **Static application security testing (SAST):** SAST tools analyze the application's source code or binary code without executing it to identify vulnerabilities such as insecure coding practices and buffer overflows early in the development process.
- **Dynamic application security testing (DAST):** DAST tools test the application in its running state to identify vulnerabilities that are only apparent during runtime, such as authentication and authorization issues.
- **Interactive application security testing (IAST):** IAST combines elements of both SAST and DAST by analyzing the application's behavior during runtime while also inspecting the source code. This approach provides a more comprehensive view of the application's security posture.
- **Software composition analysis (SCA):** SCA focuses on identifying vulnerabilities in third-party components and libraries used within the application. This is important because many applications rely on open-source or commercial components that may have known vulnerabilities.
- **Penetration testing:** This involves simulating real-world attacks on the application to identify and exploit vulnerabilities. This type of testing provides valuable insights into how an attacker might compromise the application and helps prioritize remediation efforts.
- **Threat modeling:** Threat modeling is a proactive approach to identifying and mitigating potential threats to the application. It involves analyzing the application's architecture, data flows, and potential attack vectors to develop strategies for mitigating identified risks.
- **Security code reviews:** These reviews involve manually inspecting the application's source code to identify security vulnerabilities. This process can be conducted by internal security teams or external experts and is often used in conjunction with automated testing tools.

Importance of Continuous Testing and Monitoring

Application security is not a one-time effort but an ongoing process. Continuous testing and monitoring are essential to maintain the security of applications over time. This includes:

- **Regular security assessments:** Conducting periodic security assessments to identify new vulnerabilities and ensure that existing controls are effective.
- **Continuous integration and continuous deployment:** Integrating security testing into the CI/CD pipeline to ensure that security is considered at every stage of the development process.
- **Monitoring and incident response:** Implementing monitoring solutions to detect and respond to security incidents in real time. This includes setting up alerts for suspicious activities and having an incident response plan in place.

Application security controls and software security testing are critical components of an organization's overall security strategy. By implementing robust security controls and continuously testing and monitoring applications, organizations can significantly reduce the risk of security breaches and protect their valuable data and assets.

Coding Best Practices

Coding best practices are pivotal in ensuring that software is resilient against potential threats and vulnerabilities. This section delves into four critical aspects of secure coding practices: source code comments, error handling, hard-coded credentials, and memory management. By adhering to these best practices, developers can significantly enhance the security posture of their applications.

Source Code Comments

Source code comments are essential for maintaining code readability and aiding future developers in understanding the logic and functionality of the code. However, comments should be crafted with security in mind to avoid inadvertently disclosing sensitive information. Best practices for source code comments include:

- **Avoid sensitive information:** Never include passwords, cryptographic keys, or any other sensitive information in comments.

- **Descriptive but concise:** Ensure comments are descriptive enough to explain the code's purpose but concise enough to avoid clutter.
- **Relevant updates:** Regularly update comments to reflect any changes in the code, ensuring accuracy and relevance.

Error Handling

Proper error handling is crucial for maintaining the stability and security of an application. Inadequate error handling can expose applications to various attacks, such as information leakage and denial of service. Effective error handling practices include:

- **Generic error messages:** Provide users with generic error messages that do not reveal internal application details or stack traces.
- **Logging errors securely:** Log detailed error information internally for debugging purposes but ensure logs are stored securely and access is restricted.
- **Graceful degradation:** Ensure the application can handle errors gracefully without crashing or exposing sensitive information.

Hard-Coded Credentials

Hard-coded credentials, such as usernames and passwords embedded directly in the source code, pose a significant security risk. If attackers gain access to the source code, they can easily retrieve these credentials and compromise the application. To mitigate this risk, follow these practices:

- **Externalize credentials:** Store credentials in secure external storage, such as environment variables or secure vaults, rather than embedding them in the source code.
- **Use configuration management:** Implement configuration management tools to handle credentials securely and ensure they are not exposed in version control systems.
- **Regularly rotate credentials:** Regularly update and rotate credentials to minimize the risk of unauthorized access.

Memory Management

Memory management is a critical aspect of secure coding, as improper handling can lead to vulnerabilities such as buffer overflows, memory leaks, and other exploits. To ensure secure memory management, developers should adhere to the following practices:

- **Avoid buffer overflows:** Validate input lengths and use safe functions that prevent buffer overflows.
- **Use automatic memory management:** Leverage programming languages and frameworks that provide automatic memory management, such as garbage collection, to reduce the risk of memory-related vulnerabilities.
- **Free allocated memory:** Ensure that dynamically allocated memory is properly freed after use to prevent memory leaks and potential exploitation.

By incorporating these coding best practices into the development process, developers can create more secure and robust applications, reducing the risk of vulnerabilities and enhancing overall application security.

CHAPTER 11

Cryptography Essentials

Understanding the core principles and applications of cryptography is essential for any professional in the fields of information security and privacy. Cryptography serves as the cornerstone for securing sensitive information, ensuring confidentiality, integrity, authentication, and nonrepudiation. By mastering these concepts, you will be better equipped to protect data from unauthorized access and manipulation, both in transit and at rest. This chapter provides a comprehensive overview of the fundamental cryptographic techniques and their practical applications, empowering you with the knowledge needed to implement robust security measures.

Throughout this chapter, you will delve into the intricacies of both symmetric and asymmetric cryptography, exploring their unique strengths and use cases. You will also gain insight into the critical role of hash functions and digital signatures in maintaining data integrity and authenticity. Additionally, the chapter covers the essential components of public key infrastructure and key management best practices, which are vital for the secure generation, distribution, and destruction of cryptographic keys. By understanding the various cryptographic attacks and how to defend against them, you will be able to enhance the security posture of your organization. This chapter is designed to provide you with the foundational knowledge and practical skills necessary to navigate the complex world of cryptography effectively.

Core Cryptography Concepts

The study of cryptography begins with understanding its fundamental principles. *Cryptography* is the science of encoding and decoding information to protect its confidentiality, integrity, and authenticity. It relies on complex mathematical algorithms and protocols to transform readable data (*plaintext*) into an unreadable format (*ciphertext*) and vice versa.

Cryptography is built upon a set of core concepts and principles that form the foundation of secure communication and data protection. Understanding these concepts is crucial for designing and implementing effective cryptographic systems. This section provides a summary of key cryptography concepts, including encryption and decryption, cryptographic algorithms, keys, and cryptographic protocols.

Goals of Cryptography

Cryptographic systems are designed to achieve four primary goals:

- **Confidentiality:** Ensures that information is accessible only to those authorized to have access. It protects data from unauthorized disclosure both in storage and during transmission. Confidentiality is typically achieved using encryption algorithms that transform plaintext into ciphertext, which can only be decrypted by someone with the appropriate key.
- **Integrity:** Ensures that information remains accurate and unaltered during storage and transmission. Integrity is maintained by using cryptographic hash functions, which generate a unique hash value based on the input data. Any alteration in the data will result in a different hash value, signaling a potential integrity breach.
- **Authentication:** Verifies the identity of users and systems, ensuring that entities are who they claim to be. Authentication mechanisms often involve cryptographic techniques such as digital signatures and certificates, which provide proof of identity and origin.
- **Nonrepudiation:** Prevents entities from denying their actions, ensuring accountability. Nonrepudiation is typically achieved through digital signatures, which provide undeniable proof that a particular entity performed a specific action, such as sending a message or approving a transaction.

Encryption and Decryption

Encryption is the process of converting plaintext (readable data) into ciphertext (unreadable data) using a cryptographic algorithm and a key. *Decryption* is the reverse process, transforming ciphertext back into plaintext using the appropriate key. The primary purpose of encryption and decryption is to protect the confidentiality of information, ensuring that only authorized parties can access the original data.

Cryptographic Algorithms

Cryptographic algorithms are mathematical functions used for encryption and decryption. They are categorized into two main types:

- **Symmetric algorithms:** Use the same key for both encryption and decryption. They are efficient and suitable for encrypting large amounts of data. Examples include the Advanced Encryption Standard (AES) and the Data Encryption Standard (DES).
- **Asymmetric algorithms:** Use a pair of keys—a *public key* for encryption and a *private key* for decryption. They provide enhanced security features and solve the key distribution problem inherent in symmetric algorithms. Examples include Rivest–Shamir–Adleman (RSA) and elliptic-curve cryptography (ECC).

Keys

Keys are secret values used in cryptographic algorithms to encrypt and decrypt data. The security of a cryptographic system relies heavily on the secrecy and strength of its keys. Key management practices, such as key generation, distribution, storage, rotation, and destruction, are critical components of a secure cryptographic system.

In asymmetric cryptography, each user has a pair of keys: a public key and a private key. The public key is available to anyone and is used to encrypt data or verify digital signatures. The private key is kept confidential and is used to decrypt data or create digital signatures. This key pair ensures secure communication and authentication without the need for a shared secret key.

Cryptographic Protocols

Cryptographic protocols define the rules and procedures for secure communication and data exchange. They specify how cryptographic algorithms and keys are used to achieve security goals such as confidentiality, integrity, authentication, and nonrepudiation. Common cryptographic protocols include:

- **Secure Sockets Layer (SSL)/Transport Layer Security (TLS):** Protocols for securing web communications.
- **Pretty Good Privacy (PGP):** A protocol for securing email communications.
- **Internet Protocol Security (IPsec):** A protocol suite for securing network communications.

Hash Functions

Hash functions are mathematical algorithms that generate a fixed-size hash value (or digest) based on input data. They are used to ensure data integrity by detecting any changes to the original data. Hash functions are one-way operations, meaning it is computationally infeasible to reverse the process and obtain the original input from the hash value. Common hash functions include the Secure Hash Algorithm (SHA) family and Message Digest Algorithm 5 (MD5).

Digital Signatures

Digital signatures provide a mechanism for verifying the authenticity and integrity of digital messages, software, or documents. They use asymmetric cryptography to create a unique signature based on the sender's private key, which can be verified by anyone using the corresponding public key. Digital signatures ensure that the message has not been altered and that it originates from the claimed sender.

Public Key Infrastructure

Public key infrastructure (PKI) is a framework that manages digital certificates and public–private key pairs. It includes components such as certificate authorities (CAs), registration authorities (RAs), and repositories for storing and distributing certificates. PKI supports secure key exchange, digital signatures, and certificate-based authentication, enabling secure communication and data exchange in various applications.

Cryptography is an essential tool for securing information in the digital age. By understanding the core concepts, goals, and modern techniques of cryptography, security professionals can design and implement robust systems that protect sensitive data from unauthorized access and tampering. Whether through symmetric or asymmetric methods, cryptography remains a cornerstone of information security, ensuring the confidentiality, integrity, authentication, and nonrepudiation of data.

Symmetric Cryptography

Symmetric cryptography, also known as *secret key* or *private key* cryptography, is a fundamental concept in the realm of cryptographic systems. This method relies on a shared secret key that is used for both encryption and decryption of messages. The same key is distributed to all parties involved in the communication, ensuring that both the sender and the receiver possess a copy of the shared key. This section provides an overview of symmetric cryptography, its key algorithms, as well as its strengths and weaknesses.

How Symmetric Cryptography Works

Symmetric key algorithms utilize a single secret key for both encryption and decryption processes. When a sender wishes to encrypt a message, they use the shared secret key to transform the plaintext into ciphertext. The receiver, who also possesses the shared key, uses it to decrypt the ciphertext back into plaintext. This process ensures that the message remains confidential during transmission.

The primary advantage of symmetric cryptography is its speed. Symmetric encryption algorithms are significantly faster than their asymmetric counterparts, often operating 1,000–10,000 times faster. This high speed makes symmetric cryptography suitable for bulk encryption tasks and hardware implementations, where rapid processing is essential.

Common Symmetric Key Algorithms

Several symmetric key algorithms are widely used in cryptographic systems today. Some of the most common include:

- **Advanced Encryption Standard (AES):** AES is the most used symmetric encryption algorithm, known for its robustness and efficiency. It supports key sizes of 128, 192, and 256 bits.
- **Data Encryption Standard (DES):** DES was once a widely used symmetric algorithm but is now considered insecure due to its 56-bit key length, which is vulnerable to brute-force attacks.
- **Triple DES (3DES):** An enhancement of DES, 3DES applies the DES algorithm three times with different keys, effectively increasing the key length and security.
- **Rivest Cipher (RC6):** RC6 is a symmetric key algorithm that supports key sizes of 128, 192, and 256 bits.
- **CAST-128 and CAST-256:** These algorithms (named after their creators, Carlisle Adams and Stafford Tavares) offer flexible key sizes and are known for their security and efficiency.

Strengths and Weaknesses of Symmetric Cryptography

Symmetric cryptography has several strengths:

- **Speed:** Symmetric encryption is very fast, making it suitable for encrypting large volumes of data.
- **Simplicity:** The use of a single key for both encryption and decryption simplifies the process and reduces computational overhead.

However, symmetric cryptography also has notable weaknesses:

- **Key distribution:** One of the major challenges is the secure distribution of the secret key. Parties must have a secure method of exchanging the key before communication can commence. If a secure electronic channel is unavailable, offline key distribution methods, such as physical exchange, must be used, which can be cumbersome and insecure.
- **Nonrepudiation:** Symmetric cryptography does not provide nonrepudiation. Since any party with the shared key can encrypt and decrypt messages, it is impossible to prove the origin of a message.
- **Scalability:** The algorithm is not scalable for large groups. Secure communication between individuals in a group requires each pair of users to share a unique secret key, resulting in a complex key management scenario.
- **Key regeneration:** Keys must be regenerated frequently, especially when a participant leaves the group. This ensures that the departed participant can no longer decrypt messages intended for the group.

Symmetric cryptography is a vital component of modern cryptographic systems, offering high-speed encryption and simplicity. However, it presents challenges in key distribution, nonrepudiation, scalability, and key management. Understanding and addressing these challenges is essential for implementing secure and efficient symmetric cryptosystems.

Asymmetric Cryptography

Asymmetric cryptography, also known as *public key cryptography*, is a fundamental component of modern cryptographic systems. It addresses the key distribution problem inherent in symmetric cryptography by using pairs of keys: a public key and a private key. This method allows secure communication between parties who have not previously shared a secret key, making it highly scalable and suitable for various applications.

Public and Private Keys

In asymmetric cryptography, each user generates a pair of keys: a public key, which is shared openly, and a private key, which is kept secret. The public key is used to encrypt messages, while the private key is used to decrypt them. This key pair is mathematically related, ensuring that a message encrypted with the public key can only be decrypted with the corresponding private key.

The process of asymmetric cryptography can be summarized as follows:

1. **Key generation:** Each user generates a pair of keys—public and private.
2. **Key distribution:** The public key is distributed to anyone who wants to send a secure message to the key owner.
3. **Encryption:** The sender encrypts the plaintext message using the recipient's public key.
4. **Decryption:** The recipient decrypts the ciphertext message using their private key.

This process ensures that even if the public key is known to everyone, only the intended recipient can decrypt the message, maintaining confidentiality.

Strengths of Asymmetric Cryptography

Asymmetric cryptography offers several advantages:

- **Scalability:** Adding new users requires only the generation of a new key pair, making the system highly scalable.
- **Key revocation:** Users can be easily removed by revoking their keys without affecting other users.
- **Nonrepudiation:** Digital signatures created using private keys can authenticate the origin of a message and prevent the sender from denying it later.
- **Confidentiality and integrity:** Ensures that only the intended recipient can read the message and that the message has not been altered during transmission.

Weaknesses of Asymmetric Cryptography

Despite its strengths, asymmetric cryptography has some limitations:

- **Slower speed:** Asymmetric algorithms are computationally intensive and slower compared to symmetric algorithms, making them less suitable for bulk data encryption.
- **Complexity:** The mathematical operations involved are more complex, requiring more processing power and resources.

Common Asymmetric Algorithms

Several asymmetric algorithms are widely used in cryptographic systems:

- **Rivest-Shamir-Adleman:** One of the most popular public key algorithms, RSA is based on the difficulty of factoring large prime numbers. It is used for secure data transmission and digital signatures.
- **Diffie-Hellman:** This algorithm allows two parties to securely exchange cryptographic keys over a public channel. It is primarily used for key exchange rather than direct encryption.
- **ElGamal:** Based on the Diffie-Hellman key exchange, ElGamal is used for both encryption and digital signatures.
- **Elliptic-curve cryptography (ECC):** ECC offers the same level of security as RSA but with smaller key sizes, making it more efficient. It is increasingly used in mobile devices and other environments with limited processing power.

Hybrid Cryptography

Due to the slower speed of asymmetric algorithms, *hybrid cryptography* is often used. This approach combines the strengths of both symmetric and asymmetric cryptography. Typically, asymmetric cryptography is used to establish a secure connection and exchange a symmetric key, which is then used for the remainder of the session. This method leverages the speed of symmetric encryption for bulk data while maintaining the secure key exchange of asymmetric encryption.

Quantum Cryptography

Quantum cryptography is an emerging field that leverages the principles of quantum mechanics to enhance cryptographic systems. Unlike classical cryptographic methods, quantum cryptography uses quantum bits, or qubits, which can exist in multiple states simultaneously. This property allows for the development of potentially unbreakable encryption methods.

One of the most promising applications of quantum cryptography is *quantum key distribution* (QKD). QKD enables two parties to generate a shared, secret key using the principles of quantum mechanics. The key advantage of QKD is its ability to detect any eavesdropping attempts. If a third party tries to intercept the key, the quantum state of the qubits will change, alerting the communicating parties to the presence of an intruder.

While quantum cryptography is still largely theoretical and not yet widely implemented, it holds the potential to revolutionize secure communications by providing a level of security that is theoretically immune to computational attacks, including those posed by future quantum computers.

Hash Functions

Hash functions are a fundamental component of cryptographic systems, playing a crucial role in ensuring data integrity and authenticity. At their core, hash functions take an input, which can be of any length, and produce a fixed-length output known as a *message digest* or *hash value*. This output serves as a unique representation of the input data, enabling various security applications, such as digital signatures and data integrity checks.

The primary purpose of a hash function is to generate a unique output for a given input, ensuring that even the slightest change in the input results in a significantly different hash value. This property is essential for verifying the integrity of data, as any alteration, intentional or accidental, will produce a different hash value, indicating that the data has been compromised.

In practical terms, hash functions are integral to the implementation of digital signatures. When a sender wishes to sign a message, they first generate a hash value of the message using a cryptographically secure hash function. This hash value is then encrypted with the sender's private key, creating a digital signature. The recipient of the message can verify its authenticity by decrypting the digital signature with the sender's public key and comparing the resulting hash value with one they generate from the received message. If the hash values match, the message is confirmed to be authentic and unaltered.

Key Requirements for Hash Functions

For a hash function to be considered cryptographically secure, it must satisfy several key requirements:

- **Variable input length:** The hash function should be capable of processing input data of any length, providing flexibility in its application across different types of data.
- **Fixed output length:** Regardless of the input size, the hash function must produce a consistent, fixed-length output. This uniformity simplifies the process of comparing hash values and ensures compatibility across various systems.

- **Ease of computation:** The hash function should be computationally efficient, allowing for rapid processing of data and generation of hash values. This efficiency is crucial for applications that require real-time data processing and verification.
- **One-way function:** A secure hash function must be one-way, meaning it should be computationally infeasible to reverse-engineer the original input from the hash value. This property ensures that sensitive data remains protected, even if the hash value is exposed.
- **Collision resistance:** The hash function must be designed to minimize the likelihood of collisions, where two different inputs produce the same hash value. Collision resistance is vital for maintaining the uniqueness of hash values and preventing potential security vulnerabilities.

Secure Hash Algorithm (SHA)

The SHA family, developed by the National Institute of Standards and Technology (NIST), is a set of cryptographic hash functions widely used for data integrity and authentication. The family includes several versions, with SHA-2 and SHA-3 being the most prevalent in modern applications.

- **SHA-1:** Once popular, SHA-1 produces a 160-bit hash value. However, due to vulnerabilities, it has been deprecated and is no longer recommended for secure applications.
- **SHA-2:** This version includes several variants, such as SHA-256 and SHA-512, which produce 256-bit and 512-bit hash values, respectively. SHA-2 is considered secure and is widely used in digital signatures and certificate generation.
- **SHA-3:** Released as a backup to SHA-2, SHA-3 uses a different computational approach but offers similar security levels with hash lengths of 224, 256, 384, and 512 bits.

Message Digest (MD5)

Developed by Ronald Rivest in 1992, MD5 was once a widely used hash function producing a 128-bit hash value. It processes data in 512-bit blocks and uses four rounds of computation. Despite its historical significance, MD5 is now considered insecure due to vulnerabilities that allow for collision attacks, where two different inputs produce the same hash value. As a result, it is no longer recommended for applications requiring data integrity and security.

RACE Integrity Primitives Evaluation Message Digest (RIPEMD)

RIPEMD is a family of cryptographic hash functions that serves as an alternative to the SHA family. It includes several variants:

- **RIPEMD-128:** Produces a 128-bit hash value but is no longer considered secure.
- **RIPEMD-160:** The most widely used variant, producing a 160-bit hash value and considered secure.
- **RIPEMD-256 and RIPEMD-320:** These variants produce longer hash values but do not offer additional security over RIPEMD-160.

Comparison of Hash Function Value Lengths

The following table compares the hash value lengths for various well-known hashing functions:

Hash Function Name	Hash Value Length (bits)
HAVAL	128, 160, 192, 224, 256
HMAC	Variable
MD5	128
SHA-1	160
SHA2-224/SHA3-224	224
SHA2-256/SHA3-256	256
SHA2-384/SHA3-384	384
SHA3-512/SHA3-512	512
RIPEMD-128	128
RIPEMD-160	160
RIPEMD-256	256 (but with equivalent security to 128)
RIPEMD-320	320 (but with equivalent security to 160)

Hash functions are indispensable tools in the realm of cryptography, providing a means to ensure data integrity and authenticity. By generating unique, fixed-length outputs from variable-length inputs, hash functions enable secure data verification and play a critical role in the implementation of digital signatures and other cryptographic protocols. Their properties, such as one-way functionality and collision resistance, are essential for maintaining the security and reliability of modern information systems.

Digital Signatures

Digital signatures are a fundamental component of cryptographic systems, providing a robust mechanism to verify the authenticity and integrity of messages and documents. These signatures achieve specific security objectives by using hashing algorithms and asymmetric cryptography. Below, we examine the goals of digital signatures and detail the processes involved in their creation and verification using Alice and Bob as an example.

Goals of Using Digital Signatures

Digital signatures serve several key security goals:

- **Authentication:** Digital signatures confirm the identity of the sender. By using the sender's private key to create the signature, recipients can be confident that the message genuinely originates from the claimed sender.
- **Integrity:** Digital signatures ensure that the message has not been altered during transit. Any modification to the message will result in a mismatch between the hash values, alerting the recipient to potential tampering.
- **Nonrepudiation:** Digital signatures prevent the sender from denying the authenticity of their message. Since the digital signature is created using the sender's private key, it provides undeniable proof that the sender was responsible for the message.

Digitally Signing a Message

When Alice wants to digitally sign a message to Bob, she follows these steps:

1. **Generate a message digest:** Alice starts by creating a hash value of the original plaintext message using a cryptographic hash function, such as SHA-3. This hash value, known as a message digest, acts as a unique fingerprint of the message.

2. **Encrypt the message digest:** Alice encrypts the message digest using her private key. This step ensures that the digital signature can only be generated by Alice, as she is the sole possessor of her private key.
3. **Create the digital signature:** The encrypted message digest becomes the digital signature. This digital signature is unique to both the message content and Alice's private key.
4. **Append the signature to the message:** Alice appends the digital signature to the original plaintext message. This combined package is what Alice sends to Bob.
5. **Transmit the message and signature:** Alice sends the message along with the digital signature to Bob, ensuring that the integrity and authenticity of the message can be verified upon receipt.

Process: Bob Verifying the Digital Signature from Alice

Upon receiving a digitally signed message from Alice, Bob undertakes the following steps to verify it:

1. **Receive the message and signature:** Upon receiving the message, Bob separates the plaintext message from the digital signature.
2. **Decrypt the digital signature:** Bob uses Alice's public key to decrypt the digital signature. This step is crucial because it reveals the original message digest that Alice encrypted with her private key.
3. **Generate a message digest:** Bob then uses the same cryptographic hash function that Alice used to generate a hash value of the full plaintext message he received.
4. **Compare hash values:** Bob compares the decrypted message digest obtained from the digital signature with the message digest he computed himself. If the two digests match, it confirms that the message was indeed sent by Alice and has not been altered during transit.
5. **Confirm authenticity and integrity:** A match between the two hash values assures Bob that the message is authentic and intact, having been sent by Alice without any modifications.

Digital signatures are a vital tool in secure communications, enabling parties to verify the authenticity and integrity of messages. By following these processes, Alice and Bob can ensure that their communication remains trustworthy and secure, fulfilling the primary goals of digital signature technology.

Public Key Infrastructure

PKI is an essential framework used to secure communications and data exchanges over untrusted networks. It leverages cryptographic techniques to ensure confidentiality, integrity, authentication, and nonrepudiation. At the heart of PKI is the use of asymmetric cryptography, which involves the use of public and private key pairs. This section delves into the fundamental components and operations of PKI, focusing on its role in managing digital certificates and the trust model it establishes.

Certificates

Digital certificates are electronic documents that serve as a key component of PKI by providing a mechanism to associate a public key with an entity's identity, ensuring secure communication. They are formatted according to the X.509 standard and contain specific identifying information. This includes the certificate holder's name, the public key, the CA's name, and the certificate's validity period. The digital signature of the issuing CA is also included, which allows others to verify the authenticity of the certificate. Essentially, digital certificates ensure that the public key contained within them belongs to the entity to which it was issued.

Public Key Infrastructure Overview

PKI is a system designed to create, manage, distribute, use, store, and revoke digital certificates. It allows users and systems to securely exchange data over the Internet and verify the identity of each party involved in the communication process. The core components of PKI include CAs, RAs, digital certificates, and a central directory.

- **Certificate authority (CA):** The CA is a trusted entity responsible for issuing and managing digital certificates. It verifies the identity of entities requesting a certificate and signs the certificates with its private key, thereby vouching for their authenticity. The CA's public key is used by others to verify the certificates it issues.
- **Registration authority (RA):** The RA acts as a mediator between the user and the CA. It is responsible for accepting requests for digital certificates and authenticating the entity making the request. Once verified, the RA forwards the request to the CA for certificate issuance.

- **Central directory:** This is a secure repository for storing and distributing digital certificates and certificate revocation lists (CRLs). It allows users to access and verify the validity of certificates.

Certificate Life Cycle

The life cycle of a digital certificate comprises several stages, from creation to eventual expiration or revocation. Understanding this cycle is crucial for maintaining secure communications.

- **Enrollment:** The process begins with the entity generating a public-private key pair and submitting a certificate signing request (CSR) to the CA. The CA verifies the entity's identity and issues the certificate.
- **Validation:** Once issued, the certificate can be used for secure communications. Recipients validate the certificate by checking the CA's digital signature and ensuring the certificate is not revoked.
- **Renewal:** As the certificate approaches its expiration date, the entity may need to renew it. This involves generating a new CSR and undergoing the validation process again to obtain a new certificate.
- **Revocation:** A certificate may be revoked before its expiration if it is compromised or if the entity's credentials change. The CA updates the CRL to reflect this change.
- **Expiration:** Certificates have a predefined validity period. Once expired, they can no longer be used for secure communications unless renewed.

Trust Model in PKI

PKI operates on a hierarchical trust model, where trust is established through a chain of certificates. At the top of this hierarchy is the root CA, which issues certificates to subordinate CAs. These subordinate CAs, in turn, issue certificates to end entities. Each certificate in the chain is signed by the CA above it, creating a path of trust from the root CA to the end entity.

- **Root CA:** The most trusted entity in the PKI hierarchy. Its public key is widely distributed and trusted by all parties within the PKI. The security of the entire PKI depends on the integrity of the root CA's private key.
- **Intermediate CAs:** Subordinate CAs that exist between the root CA and end entities. They distribute the trust of the root CA by issuing certificates to other CAs or directly to end entities.

- **End entities:** These are the users, devices, or services that hold digital certificates issued by the CAs. They rely on the trust chain established by the PKI to authenticate and encrypt communications.

Applications of PKI

PKI is utilized in various applications to enhance security and trust in digital communications. Some common applications include:

- **Secure email:** PKI is used to encrypt emails and authenticate the sender's identity using digital signatures. Protocols like S/MIME and PGP rely on PKI to provide secure email communication.
- **Secure web traffic:** The use of Hypertext Transfer Protocol Secure (HTTPS) for secure web browsing is made possible by PKI. Web servers present digital certificates to authenticate themselves to users, ensuring the confidentiality and integrity of data exchanged over the Internet.
- **Virtual private networks (VPNs):** PKI enables secure remote access to networks by authenticating users and encrypting data traffic. VPNs use digital certificates to establish trust between clients and servers.

Public key infrastructure is a vital component in securing digital communications by providing a structured approach to managing digital certificates and establishing trust among entities. Through its hierarchical trust model and robust cryptographic techniques, PKI ensures the confidentiality, integrity, and authenticity of data exchanged over untrusted networks.

Key Management Best Practices

At the heart of effective cryptographic implementations lies the crucial process of key management. Proper key management ensures that cryptographic keys are generated, distributed, stored, and destroyed in a secure manner, safeguarding the entire cryptographic system from potential vulnerabilities. This section explores best practices in key management, focusing on both symmetric and asymmetric cryptographic systems, to provide a comprehensive understanding of how to effectively manage cryptographic keys.

Symmetric Key Management

Symmetric cryptography relies on a single shared secret key for both encryption and decryption processes. This simplicity, however, introduces challenges in key distribution and management. The following best practices are critical for managing symmetric keys:

- **Secure key creation and distribution:** Keys should be generated using a secure, random process to ensure unpredictability. Distribution of symmetric keys can be achieved through offline methods, public key encryption, or the Diffie–Hellman key exchange algorithm. Offline distribution, though straightforward, is prone to interception and loss, making it less practical for geographically dispersed users. Using public key encryption to establish a secure channel for exchanging symmetric keys combines the speed of symmetric encryption with the secure distribution capabilities of asymmetric cryptography.
- **Key storage and protection:** Symmetric keys must be stored securely to prevent unauthorized access. This involves using hardware security modules (HSMs) or similar secure storage solutions that provide physical and logical protection of keys.
- **Key rotation and lifetime management:** Regularly rotating keys minimizes the risk of exposure and limits the potential damage from a compromised key. Organizations should establish policies defining the lifespan of keys and the frequency of key rotation based on the sensitivity of the data being protected.
- **Key destruction and disposal:** When a key is no longer needed, it should be securely destroyed to prevent its recovery and misuse. This involves overwriting the key data in memory and on storage devices to ensure it cannot be reconstructed.

Asymmetric Key Management

Asymmetric cryptography uses a pair of keys: a public key, which is openly shared, and a private key, which is kept secret. This dual-key system simplifies key distribution but introduces its own set of management challenges. Best practices for managing asymmetric keys include:

- **Public and private key generation:** As with symmetric keys, asymmetric keys should be generated using a secure, random process. The strength of the cryptographic system is directly related to the key length and randomness.
- **Public key distribution:** Public keys should be distributed through trusted channels to ensure their authenticity. This can be achieved using digital certificates issued by a trusted certificate authority, which vouches for the validity of the public key.

- **Private key protection:** The security of an asymmetric cryptosystem heavily depends on the confidentiality of the private key. Private keys should be stored in secure environments, such as HSMs, and protected by strong access controls and encryption.
- **Key rotation and revocation:** Like symmetric keys, asymmetric keys should be rotated periodically to mitigate potential risks. Additionally, mechanisms must be in place to revoke keys that are compromised or no longer in use. Certificate revocation lists and online certificate status protocols (OCSPs) are commonly used to manage key revocation.
- **Key escrow and recovery:** In some cases, it may be necessary to recover a lost key to access encrypted data. Key escrow arrangements allow a trusted third party to hold a copy of the private key, enabling recovery while maintaining security. Careful consideration should be given to the trustworthiness and security of the escrow arrangement.

Effective key management is essential for maintaining the security and integrity of cryptographic systems. By adhering to these best practices for both symmetric and asymmetric key management, organizations can ensure that their cryptographic keys are handled securely throughout their life cycle, protecting sensitive information from unauthorized access and ensuring the reliability of their security infrastructure.

Cryptographic Attacks

Cryptographic attacks pose a significant threat to the security of information systems, targeting the cryptographic techniques used to protect data. Understanding these attacks is crucial for information security professionals to implement effective safeguards and respond appropriately. This section provides an overview of various cryptographic attacks and strategies to defend against them.

Brute-Force Attacks

A *brute-force attack* involves systematically trying every possible key until the correct one is found. These attacks are computationally intensive but can succeed if the key length is short. To defend against brute-force attacks, it is essential to use sufficiently long and complex keys, making it infeasible to try all possibilities within a reasonable time frame.

Ciphertext-Only Attacks

A *ciphertext-only attack* occurs when an attacker has access only to the ciphertext and attempts to deduce the plaintext or the key. Frequency analysis is a common method, examining the frequency of characters or patterns in the ciphertext to infer the underlying plaintext, particularly effective against substitution ciphers. Using complex and modern encryption algorithms can mitigate these attacks.

Known Plaintext Attacks

A *known plaintext attack* happens when the attacker has access to both the plaintext and its corresponding ciphertext, using this information to deduce the encryption key or algorithm. Defending against this type of attack involves using encryption algorithms that remain secure even when portions of the plaintext are known.

Chosen Plaintext and Chosen Ciphertext Attacks

A *chosen plaintext attack* or *chosen ciphertext attack* requires the attacker to encrypt or decrypt arbitrary plaintexts or ciphertexts. This ability allows the attacker to gather information about the encryption key or algorithm. Robust encryption algorithms and protocols that do not reveal information about the key or algorithm, even when arbitrary data is encrypted or decrypted, can mitigate these attacks.

On-Path Attacks

An *on-path attack* (also known as a *man-in-the-middle attack*) involves an attacker intercepting and potentially altering communications between two parties without their knowledge. The attacker may impersonate each party to the other, gaining access to sensitive information. Implementing strong mutual authentication and encryption protocols can help prevent on-path attacks.

Birthday Attacks

A *birthday attack* exploits the mathematics of probability in hash functions to find two different inputs that produce the same hash value, known as a collision.

This attack is named after the birthday paradox, which illustrates that collisions are more likely than intuitively expected. Using hash functions with longer output lengths and collision-resistant properties can defend against birthday attacks.

Replay Attacks

A *replay attack* involves capturing a legitimate communication session and replaying it to trick the system into granting unauthorized access. Implementing session tokens, timestamps, and nonces (random numbers used only once) can help prevent replay attacks by ensuring that each session is unique and cannot be reused.

Implementation Attacks

An *implementation attack* exploits weaknesses in the way cryptographic algorithms are implemented, such as software bugs or hardware flaws. This type of attack focuses on exploiting the hardware or software code, not just errors and flaws but also the methodology employed to program the encryption system. Ensuring that cryptographic implementations are thoroughly tested and validated can help mitigate these attacks.

Side-Channel Attacks

A *side-channel attack* gathers information from the physical implementation of a cryptosystem, such as changes in processor utilization, electricity consumption, or electromagnetic radiation, to deduce cryptographic keys. This type of attack leverages the characteristic footprints of system activity. To defend against side-channel attacks, cryptographic systems should implement countermeasures such as masking and hiding techniques.

Timing Attacks

A *timing attack* is a subset of side-channel attacks where the attacker measures precisely how long cryptographic operations take to complete, gaining information about the cryptographic process that may be used to undermine its security. Ensuring that cryptographic operations take a constant amount of time can help mitigate timing attacks.

Fault Injection Attacks

A *fault injection attack* involves causing external faults, such as high-voltage electricity or extreme temperatures, to compromise the integrity of a cryptographic device. These attacks exploit vulnerabilities in the hardware to induce malfunctions that undermine the security of the device. Designing hardware to withstand such external conditions can help mitigate fault injection attacks.

Statistical Attacks

A *statistical attack* exploits statistical weaknesses in a cryptosystem, such as the inability to produce truly random numbers. These attacks may also target vulnerabilities in the hardware or operating system hosting the cryptography application. Ensuring the use of strong random number generators and addressing hardware vulnerabilities can help defend against statistical attacks.

Security professionals must remain vigilant against the evolving landscape of cryptographic attacks and continuously update their defenses. This involves staying informed about the latest cryptographic research, using well-vetted cryptographic algorithms and protocols, and ensuring that implementations are secure against both theoretical and practical attacks. By understanding these attack vectors and implementing robust countermeasures, organizations can protect their sensitive data and maintain the integrity of their cryptographic systems.

CHAPTER 12

Physical and Environmental Security

As a security and privacy professional, you know that safeguarding digital assets is only one part of the equation; ensuring the physical protection of these assets is equally critical. This chapter delves into the essential elements of physical and environmental security, providing you with a comprehensive understanding of how to fortify your organization's physical infrastructure against potential threats.

The chapter covers key topics including the principles of secure facility design, effective physical access controls, and the critical aspects of maintaining secure data centers and server rooms. You will also explore the importance of environmental controls, such as power management, HVAC systems, and fire suppression, which are vital for maintaining the integrity and availability of your organization's IT infrastructure. By understanding and implementing these security measures, you will be better equipped to protect your organization's assets from both physical and environmental threats, ensuring a robust defense strategy that complements your digital security efforts. This chapter aims to enhance your knowledge and skills, empowering you to design, implement, and manage security solutions that address the full spectrum of potential vulnerabilities.

Security and Facility Design

The design of a facility is a fundamental aspect of ensuring robust security measures are in place. This section will explore the principles of security and facility design, highlighting key considerations and controls necessary to protect physical environments from unauthorized access, natural disasters, and other potential threats.

Secure Facility Plan

A *secure facility plan* is essential for outlining an organization's security needs and identifying the methods or mechanisms to provide comprehensive security. Developed through risk assessment and critical path analysis, this plan creates a complete picture of the interdependencies necessary to sustain the organization. It emphasizes the importance of electricity, environmental controls, and water/sewage as foundational requirements. Additionally, the plan addresses technology convergence, which can lead to efficiency and cost savings but also presents potential single points of failure. Security staff should be involved in site and facility design to ensure that long-term security goals are supported by the building itself, not just policies and personnel.

Site Selection

Choosing the right site for a facility is a critical step in the security design process. Site selection should prioritize security needs over other factors such as cost, location, and size. The proximity to other buildings and businesses, as well as emergency response personnel, must be carefully considered. The site should be able to withstand local extreme weather conditions and deter break-in attempts. Additionally, organizations may consider industrial camouflage to mask or hide a facility's actual function, presenting a façade that conceals its true purpose.

Facility Design

The design of a facility must prioritize the protection of life and safety while complying with applicable laws and regulations. Important considerations include combustibility, fire rating, construction materials, and the placement and control of structural elements such as walls and doors. The concept of crime prevention through environmental design (CPTED) is integral to facility design, as it aims to reduce crime and fear through strategic environmental planning. CPTED is a well-established approach to facility design that aims to reduce crime and the fear of crime through strategic environmental planning. The core principle of CPTED is that the design of the physical environment can influence human behavior and perceptions, thereby enhancing security. Key CPTED recommendations include:

- Keeping planters and decorative elements small or distant from the building to prevent concealment or unauthorized access.
- Locating critical infrastructure, such as data centers, at the core of the building.
- Providing seating areas to encourage natural surveillance by occupants.
- Maintaining clear and open entrances to enhance visibility.
- Minimizing the number of entrances and securing them during off-hours.
- Strategically positioning visitor parking and delivery access to control visibility and access.

Regulatory Compliance and Safety Considerations

Facility designs and physical security controls must comply with applicable laws and regulations, such as health and safety requirements, building codes, and labor restrictions. In the United States, organizations should adhere to guidelines from the Occupational Safety and Health Administration (OSHA) and the Environmental Protection Agency (EPA). Additionally, appointing a facility security officer can aid in the design, implementation, and management of security measures.

The design of a facility is a critical component of physical and environmental security. By applying security principles to site and facility design, organizations can create a secure environment that protects their assets and personnel. Through strategic planning, the implementation of security controls, and adherence to regulatory requirements, organizations can effectively mitigate physical threats and ensure the safety and security of their operations.

Physical Access Controls and Monitoring

Physical access controls and monitoring are essential components that help prevent unauthorized access, ensure the integrity of sensitive information, and protect against environmental threats. This section delves into various aspects of physical security, including equipment failure, wiring closets, intrusion detection systems, cameras, access abuses, media storage facilities, evidence storage, and work area security.

Equipment Failure

Equipment failure is an inevitable occurrence that can compromise the security and functionality of an organization's infrastructure. It is crucial to anticipate and prepare for such failures by implementing a robust maintenance plan and having replacement parts readily available. Organizations should consider service-level agreements with vendors to ensure timely repairs and replacements. Additionally, regular testing and monitoring of equipment can help identify potential issues before they escalate into significant problems.

Wiring Closets

Wiring closets are critical infrastructure components that house networking cables and essential equipment such as patch panels, switches, routers, and backbone channels. These closets require stringent security measures to prevent unauthorized access and potential sabotage. Physical access controls such as locks, smartcards, and proximity readers should be employed to restrict entry. Regular physical inspections and monitoring through surveillance cameras can further enhance the security of wiring closets.

Intrusion Detection Systems

An IDS is vital for detecting and responding to unauthorized access attempts or breaches. These systems can be automated or manual and are designed to alert security personnel of any suspicious activities. An IDS can monitor entry points, detect abnormal events, and trigger alarms to notify security teams of potential threats. Implementing an IDS as part of a comprehensive security strategy can significantly reduce the risk of unauthorized access and ensure timely response to incidents.

Cameras

Surveillance cameras, including closed-circuit television (CCTV) systems, play a crucial role in deterring unwanted activities and providing a digital record of events. Cameras can be overt or hidden, operate in visible or infrared light, and offer features such as pan, tilt, and zoom. They can be triggered by movement and support functionalities like facial recognition and object detection. Monitoring and recording footage from cameras can help identify security breaches and provide evidence for investigations.

Access Abuses

Access abuses, such as impersonation, tailgating, and piggybacking, pose significant security risks. To mitigate these threats, organizations should deploy security guards or monitoring systems to oversee access points and ensure only authorized individuals gain entry. Implementing strict access control measures, such as badges and biometric authentication, can further prevent unauthorized access and reduce the likelihood of access abuses.

Media Storage Facilities

Media storage facilities are designated areas for storing sensitive data and media. These facilities should be equipped with physical security controls such as locks, access restrictions, and environmental controls to protect against unauthorized access and environmental threats. Offline storage and encryption can add additional layers of security. Regular audits and activity tracking can help ensure the integrity and confidentiality of stored media.

Evidence Storage

Evidence storage is crucial for maintaining the integrity and chain of custody of digital and physical evidence. Secure storage facilities with controlled access, activity tracking, and hash management are essential to prevent tampering or unauthorized access. Properly managed evidence storage ensures that evidence remains admissible in legal proceedings and investigations.

Work Area Security

Work area security involves protecting sensitive information and assets within an organization's premises. This includes implementing access controls to restrict entry to critical areas, ensuring clean desk policies, and using privacy screens to prevent unauthorized viewing of sensitive information. Regular security awareness training for employees can reinforce the importance of maintaining work area security and help prevent accidental data breaches.

Physical access controls and monitoring are vital components of a comprehensive security strategy. By addressing equipment failure, securing wiring closets, implementing intrusion detection systems, utilizing cameras, preventing access abuses, and ensuring the security of media, evidence, and work areas, organizations can significantly enhance their physical and environmental security posture.

Security in Data Centers and Server Rooms

Data centers and server rooms play a pivotal role in safeguarding an organization's IT infrastructure. These facilities are the backbone of any organization's operations, housing mission-critical servers and networking devices. Ensuring their security is paramount to maintaining the integrity, availability, and confidentiality of data. This section delves into the essential security considerations for data centers and server rooms, highlighting best practices to protect these vital assets.

Server rooms and data centers are specialized environments designed to support the optimal operation of IT infrastructure while minimizing the risk of unauthorized access or intervention. These facilities are often configured as "lights-out" areas, which prioritize equipment efficiency over human comfort. This design approach typically includes features such as gas-based halon-substitute fire detection and extinguishing systems, walls with a minimum one-hour fire rating, low temperatures, and minimal lighting. The primary goal is to create an environment that supports the continuous operation of IT equipment while mitigating potential risks.

Location and Infrastructure Considerations

The physical location of a server room or data center is a critical factor in its security. Ideally, these facilities should be situated at the core of a building, away from external walls and water, gas, and sewage lines, which pose risks of leakage or flooding. Avoiding placement on the ground floor, top floor, or basement can reduce exposure to environmental threats such as flooding or unauthorized access. Additionally, the structural integrity of the facility should be reinforced to withstand natural disasters and other physical threats.

Access Control Measures

Implementing robust access control measures is essential to prevent unauthorized entry into server rooms and data centers. This includes the use of secure locks, smartcards for authentication, proximity devices, and readers. Intrusion detection systems, surveillance cameras, and regular physical inspections further enhance security by monitoring and recording access attempts. Access should be limited to authorized personnel only, and a comprehensive logging system should be in place to track all entries and exits.

Environmental Controls

Maintaining a stable environment within data centers and server rooms is crucial for the proper functioning of IT equipment. This involves regulating temperature, humidity, and airflow to prevent overheating and equipment failure. HVAC systems should be designed to provide consistent environmental conditions and include redundant systems to ensure continuous operation in the event of a failure. Clean power sources and backup generators are also vital to prevent power disruptions that could lead to data loss or system downtime.

Fire Detection and Suppression

Fire poses a significant risk to data centers and server rooms, making fire detection and suppression systems a critical component of their security infrastructure. These systems should be designed to detect fires early and suppress them effectively while minimizing damage to equipment and data. Gas-based fire suppression systems, such as those using halon substitutes, are often preferred due to their ability to extinguish fires without damaging sensitive electronics. Regular testing and maintenance of these systems are essential to ensure their effectiveness in an emergency.

Physical Security Enhancements

Beyond access control and environmental measures, additional physical security mechanisms can further protect data centers and server rooms. These include perimeter breach detection systems, fences, gates, turnstiles, lighting, security guards, and guard dogs. Locks, badges, protected cable distribution, motion detectors, and intrusion alarms add layers of security to deter and detect unauthorized access. Secondary verification mechanisms, such as biometric authentication, can also be employed to enhance security.

The security of data centers and server rooms is a multifaceted endeavor that requires a comprehensive approach integrating physical, environmental, and procedural controls. By implementing these best practices, organizations can safeguard their critical IT infrastructure, ensuring the continuous availability and security of their data and systems.

Environmental Controls

Environmental controls play a critical role in ensuring that the physical infrastructure supporting IT systems remains secure and operational. These controls encompass a range of considerations, including utility management and fire prevention, detection, and suppression. By implementing robust environmental controls, organizations can mitigate risks associated with utility disruptions and fire hazards, thereby enhancing the overall security posture.

Utility Considerations

Utility considerations are a vital aspect of environmental controls. Organizations must ensure that critical systems have a reliable and continuous power supply. This involves implementing redundant power sources, such as uninterruptible power supplies (UPS) and backup generators, to maintain operations during power outages. Additionally, clean power sources are essential to prevent voltage fluctuations and power surges that could damage sensitive equipment. Power distribution units (PDUs) and surge protectors can help manage and stabilize power delivery to critical systems.

Managing utilities also extends to HVAC systems. Proper HVAC management is crucial for maintaining optimal temperature and humidity levels within data centers and server rooms. Computers and networking equipment generate significant heat, and without adequate cooling, they may overheat and fail. Organizations should ensure that HVAC systems are designed to provide sufficient cooling capacity and are regularly maintained to prevent failures. Humidity levels should be maintained between 20 percent and 80 percent to prevent static electricity and corrosion, which can damage electronic components.

Fire Prevention, Detection, and Suppression

Fire prevention, detection, and suppression are equally critical components of environmental controls. Protecting personnel from harm is the foremost priority, but safeguarding IT infrastructure from fire damage is also essential. Fire prevention measures include designing facilities with fire-resistant materials and ensuring that electrical systems are properly installed and maintained to reduce the risk of electrical fires.

Detection systems, such as smoke detectors and heat sensors, are vital for early identification of fire incidents. These systems should be strategically placed throughout the facility to provide comprehensive coverage and ensure rapid detection. Once a fire is detected, suppression systems must be activated to control and extinguish the fire. Traditional water-based sprinkler systems may not be suitable for data centers due to the risk of water damage to electronic equipment. Instead, organizations can deploy gas-based suppression systems, such as FM-200 or inert gas systems, which effectively extinguish fires without harming sensitive equipment.

In addition to technical measures, organizations should establish and regularly test emergency response procedures to ensure that personnel know how to react in the event of a fire. Fire drills and training sessions can help reinforce these procedures and ensure that employees are prepared to evacuate safely and efficiently.

By integrating comprehensive utility management and fire prevention, detection, and suppression strategies, organizations can enhance their environmental controls and protect their critical infrastructure from potential hazards. These measures, combined with regular maintenance and testing, form a robust framework for ensuring the physical and environmental security of IT systems and safeguarding the continuity of operations.

Implement and Manage Physical Security

Implementing and managing physical security is a vital aspect of an organization's security strategy, focusing on safeguarding physical assets, infrastructure, and personnel from potential threats. This involves deploying a range of security controls to ensure the protection of facilities and their contents. Here, we will focus on perimeter security controls, internal security controls, and key performance indicators (KPIs) that help measure the effectiveness of these security measures.

Perimeter Security Controls

Perimeter security controls serve as the initial line of defense in a physical security framework. These controls are designed to deter, detect, and delay unauthorized access to the facility's premises. Physical barriers such as fences, gates, and bollards are commonly used to restrict access and define the boundaries of the property. Additionally, security lighting is strategically placed to illuminate vulnerable areas, deterring potential intruders and enhancing the effectiveness of surveillance systems. CCTV cameras play a crucial role in monitoring activities around the perimeter, providing real-time alerts and recording evidence of any suspicious activities. These measures work together to create a secure perimeter that prevents unauthorized entry and protects the facility from external threats.

Internal Security Controls

Internal security controls focus on safeguarding the interior of the facility and ensuring that only authorized personnel can access sensitive areas. Access control systems are a key component of internal security, regulating entry to restricted zones within the building. These systems can range from traditional lock-and-key mechanisms to advanced biometric authentication and smart card readers, providing varying levels of security based on the organization's needs. By implementing robust access control measures, organizations can mitigate the risk of internal threats and protect critical operations and assets. Surveillance systems and security personnel may also be deployed within the facility to monitor activities and respond to any security incidents promptly.

Key Performance Indicators

KPIs are essential for evaluating the effectiveness of physical security measures and ensuring continuous improvement. KPIs provide quantifiable metrics that help organizations assess the success of their security program in achieving its objectives. For physical security, KPIs might include metrics such as the number of successful and unsuccessful intrusion attempts, the time taken to detect and respond to incidents, and the level of organizational impact resulting from security breaches. Establishing a baseline for each KPI and maintaining a historical record of measurements enable organizations to perform trend analysis and identify areas for improvement. Reliable KPI assessment allows organizations to pinpoint deficiencies, evaluate response measures, and conduct cost/benefit analyses for physical security controls, ultimately enhancing the overall security posture.

Perimeter and internal security controls are fundamental components of a robust physical security strategy, while KPIs provide valuable insights into the effectiveness of these measures. By implementing these controls and regularly assessing their performance, organizations can create a secure environment that supports their broader security objectives and protects their assets and personnel from potential threats.

CHAPTER 13

Legal and Ethical Considerations

Understanding the legal and ethical dimensions of information security and privacy is paramount for professionals in these fields. As a security or privacy professional, you are responsible not only for safeguarding data and systems but also for ensuring that your practices align with a complex web of laws and ethical standards. This chapter serves as a comprehensive overview of the critical legal frameworks and ethical principles that govern your work.

Navigating the legal landscape requires a nuanced understanding of various laws, from those addressing computer crime and intellectual property to software licensing and import/export regulations. These legalities form the backbone of compliance efforts and are essential for protecting your organization from legal liabilities and reputational damage. Furthermore, privacy laws, which vary significantly across jurisdictions, demand your attention to ensure that personal data is handled with the utmost care and in compliance with applicable regulations.

Beyond legal obligations, ethical considerations play a crucial role in guiding your professional conduct. Adhering to ethical standards not only fosters trust and integrity but also enhances the credibility of your organization. By engaging with this chapter, you will gain valuable insights into the legal and ethical aspects of your role, equipping you to make informed decisions that uphold both the letter and the spirit of the law. This knowledge is indispensable for maintaining the delicate balance between innovation and compliance in the ever-evolving field of information security and privacy.

Computer Crime

In today's digital age, understanding computer crimes and the laws against them is crucial for information security professionals. These laws not only help protect individuals and organizations from various threats but also ensure the ethical use of technology. Computer crime laws encompass a range of activities, from unauthorized access to systems to the theft of sensitive information, and are designed to safeguard the integrity, confidentiality, and availability of data. This section provides an overview of the legal landscape surrounding computer crimes, highlighting the major categories of these crimes and the laws that address them.

Computer Crimes

Computer crimes are generally defined as violations of laws or regulations that involve the use of a computer. These crimes can be categorized into several groups based on their motivations and objectives. Understanding these categories helps security professionals identify potential threats and implement appropriate countermeasures.

- **Military and intelligence attacks:** These attacks aim to obtain secret and restricted information from military or law enforcement sources. The goal is often to gain a strategic advantage or to disrupt the operations of a nation-state.
- **Business attacks:** Similar to military attacks, business attacks target civilian systems to gain unauthorized access to proprietary information. These attacks can lead to industrial espionage, where competitors seek to gain an edge by stealing trade secrets or confidential business data.
- **Financial attacks:** These attacks are motivated by financial gain and often involve unauthorized access to financial systems or data. Examples include transferring funds from unapproved sources, accessing services without payment, or selling compromised data for profit.
- **Terrorist attacks:** In the context of computer crimes, terrorist attacks aim to disrupt normal life by damaging critical infrastructure or communication systems. These attacks often seek to create fear and chaos, affecting the ability of organizations and governments to respond effectively.
- **Grudge attacks:** Motivated by personal vendettas, grudge attacks aim to cause damage by destroying data or using information to embarrass an organization or individual. These attacks are often driven by a desire for revenge or to settle personal scores.

- **Thrill attacks:** Often carried out by inexperienced individuals, thrill attacks are motivated by the excitement of compromising or disabling a system. While these attacks may not be sophisticated, they can still cause significant disruptions and financial losses.
- **Hacktivist attacks:** Hacktivists use their technical skills to promote political or social causes. These attacks often involve defacing websites or releasing sensitive information to draw attention to specific issues.

Computer Crime Laws

To combat these diverse threats, various laws have been enacted to protect society against computer crimes.

To effectively safeguard digital assets and ensure compliance with legal standards, information security professionals must have a thorough understanding of key legislative acts that address computer crimes. Several significant U.S. laws that have been enacted to combat computer-related offenses and protect sensitive information:

- **Computer Fraud and Abuse Act (CFAA):** Enacted in 1984 and amended several times since, the CFAA is a cornerstone of U.S. legislation aimed at combating computer crimes. Initially part of the Comprehensive Crime Control Act, the CFAA was designed to protect federal computers and those involved in interstate commerce. Over the years, its scope has expanded to include a wide range of offenses, such as unauthorized access to computers, trafficking in passwords, and causing damage to computer systems. The CFAA has been instrumental in prosecuting hackers and other cybercriminals, although it has faced criticism for its broad interpretation, which some argue criminalizes minor infractions like violating website terms of service.
- **National Information Infrastructure Protection Act of 1996:** This act amended the CFAA to further extend its protections. It broadened the scope to include computer systems used in international commerce and extended similar protections to critical national infrastructure components, such as railroads, pipelines, and power grids. The act treats any intentional or reckless act that damages critical infrastructure as a felony, reflecting the increasing importance of protecting these assets from cyber threats.
- **Federal Information Security Management Act (FISMA) of 2002:** FISMA was enacted to improve the security of federal information systems. It requires federal agencies to implement comprehensive information security programs covering their operations and those of their contractors. FISMA emphasizes risk assessments, security policies,

and procedures to manage and mitigate information security risks. The National Institute of Standards and Technology (NIST) provides guidelines for FISMA implementation, ensuring that federal agencies maintain robust security postures.

- **Federal Cybersecurity Laws of 2014:** Recognizing the growing threat of cyberattacks, Congress enacted several laws in 2014 to enhance the federal government's cybersecurity capabilities. These laws include the Federal Information Security Modernization Act, which updates FISMA to improve federal information security practices, and the Cybersecurity Enhancement Act, which promotes research and development in cybersecurity technologies. Additionally, the National Cybersecurity Protection Act established the National Cybersecurity and Communications Integration Center (NCCIC) to facilitate information sharing and collaboration between government and private sector entities.
- **Electronic Communications Privacy Act (ECPA) of 1986:** The ECPA was enacted to protect the electronic privacy of individuals by prohibiting unauthorized interception and access to electronic communications. It extends the protections of the Federal Wiretap Act to include electronic communications, such as email and voicemail, and establishes legal standards for law enforcement access to stored communications. The ECPA also addresses the disclosure of electronic communication content by service providers, making it illegal to monitor mobile phone conversations without authorization.
- **Identity Theft and Assumption Deterrence Act (ITADA) of 1998:** This act was established to address the growing issue of identity theft, which involves the unauthorized use of another person's identifying information to commit fraud or other crimes. ITADA criminalizes identity theft and provides penalties for offenders, including fines and imprisonment. The act also designates the Federal Trade Commission (FTC) as the central agency for receiving and processing identity theft complaints, helping victims recover from the impact of identity theft.

These legislative acts form the foundation of the legal framework governing computer crimes in the United States. By understanding the provisions and implications of these laws, information security professionals can better navigate the complex legal landscape, ensuring compliance and protecting their organizations from potential legal liabilities. Moreover, staying informed about ongoing legislative and judicial developments is crucial for adapting to the evolving nature of cyber threats and maintaining a robust security posture. Moreover, it is crucial for professionals to adhere to ethical standards, as they are entrusted with significant authority and responsibility in protecting sensitive information.

Computer Crime Evidence

Security practitioners must also be familiar with the types of evidence that may be used in criminal or civil trials. Evidence can be categorized into real evidence (actual objects brought into the courtroom), documentary evidence (written documents providing insight into the facts), and testimonial evidence (verbal or written statements made by witnesses). Electronic evidence, often gathered through the analysis of hardware, software, storage media, and networks, plays a critical role in computer crime investigations.

Intellectual Property Laws

Understanding intellectual property (IP) laws is crucial for professionals who must navigate the complexities of protecting intangible assets. As economies worldwide shift from manufacturing to service-oriented models, IP has become increasingly valuable. This section provides an overview of the key concepts and legal frameworks surrounding intellectual property, highlighting the importance of safeguarding these assets in the digital age.

Intellectual property encompasses various intangible assets, including copyrights, trademarks, patents, and trade secrets. These assets are vital for businesses, particularly those in creative industries such as publishing, film, and music, where the output is primarily intellectual. Companies rely on IP to maintain competitive advantages and protect their innovations, brand identity, and creative works. Therefore, understanding the legal protections available for IP is essential for information security professionals tasked with safeguarding these valuable assets.

Copyright Law

Copyright law protects creators of "original works of authorship" from unauthorized duplication or use of their work. This protection extends to a wide range of creative works, including the following:

- Literary works
- Musical works
- Dramatic works
- Pantomimes and choreographic works
- Pictorial, graphical, and sculptural works

- Motion pictures and other audiovisual works
- Sound recordings
- Architectural works

Copyright law ensures that creators receive recognition and financial benefits from their creations, thereby encouraging innovation and creativity.

Trademarks

Trademarks protect symbols, names, and slogans used to identify goods or services. They help consumers distinguish between different brands and ensure that companies can build and maintain brand recognition. Trademarks are crucial for businesses seeking to establish a strong market presence and protect their brand identity from infringement.

Patents

Patents provide legal protection for inventions, granting inventors exclusive rights to their creations for a specified period. This protection encourages innovation by allowing inventors to profit from their inventions without the fear of unauthorized use or duplication. Patents cover a wide range of innovations, from technological advancements to new processes and products.

Trade Secrets

Trade secrets encompass confidential business information that provides a competitive edge. This can include formulas, practices, designs, and processes that are not publicly known. Protecting trade secrets requires robust security measures to prevent unauthorized access and disclosure, as legal protection is contingent upon maintaining the secrecy of the information.

The Importance of IP Laws

Information security professionals must be aware of the legal frameworks surrounding IP to ensure compliance and protect their organization's assets. This includes understanding the nuances of IP laws across different jurisdictions, as international variations can complicate enforcement and protection efforts. In regions where IP rights are frequently violated, businesses must take additional precautions and seek legal counsel to navigate the complexities of IP protection.

Intellectual property laws play a vital role in protecting the intangible assets that drive innovation and economic growth. For information security professionals, understanding these laws is essential for safeguarding their organization's IP and ensuring compliance with legal requirements. By implementing robust security measures and staying informed about the evolving legal landscape, professionals can effectively protect their organization's valuable intellectual assets.

Software Licensing Laws

Understanding software licensing laws is crucial for professionals to ensure compliance and protect intellectual property. Software licensing laws govern how software can be used, distributed, and modified, and they play a significant role in maintaining the integrity of software systems and protecting the rights of creators.

Software Licensing Types

Software licensing is a legal framework that defines the permissions and restrictions associated with software use. It ensures that software creators are compensated for their work and that users understand their rights and obligations. There are several types of software licenses, each with varying levels of permissions and restrictions:

- **Perpetual licenses:** These licenses allow users to pay a one-time fee for the software and use it indefinitely without any time limitations. However, support and updates might require additional fees.
- **Subscription licenses:** Unlike perpetual licenses, subscription licenses are time-bound. Users pay a recurring fee, often monthly or annually, to use the software. This type of license typically includes updates and support as part of the subscription.
- **Open-source licenses:** Open-source software is usually free to use, modify, and distribute. However, there are various open-source licenses, each with its conditions, such as the GNU General Public License (GPL) or the MIT License, which may require sharing modifications with the community or maintaining original license terms.
- **Freeware:** This is software available free of charge. It might come with restrictions on usage or lack features available in a paid version but generally does not allow modification or redistribution.

- **Enterprise license agreements (ELAs):** These comprehensive agreements are between software vendors and large organizations. ELAs allow for software deployment throughout the organization under favorable terms, often at a discounted price.
- **End-user license agreements (EULAs):** EULAs define the rights and restrictions that apply when using the software. These agreements are typically presented during the installation or initial setup process, requiring user acceptance before proceeding.
- **Concurrent use licenses:** This type of license allows a set number of users to access the software simultaneously. Once the limit is reached, additional users must wait until a slot becomes available.
- **Named user licenses:** These licenses are tied to specific users, typically identified by their login credentials, ensuring only designated individuals can access the software.
- **Cloud services license agreements:** Pertaining to software as a service (SaaS) provided over the Internet, these agreements require user affirmation before accessing the service, often presenting terms upon registration.

The Importance of Software Licensing Laws

Understanding software licensing laws is essential for organizations to avoid legal issues and ensure compliance. Violating software licenses can result in legal penalties, financial losses, and reputational damage. Organizations must implement proper software asset management practices to track and manage software licenses, ensuring that they comply with licensing agreements and avoid unauthorized software use.

Software licensing laws are a critical component of information security and intellectual property protection. By understanding and adhering to these laws, organizations can protect their software assets, respect the rights of creators, and avoid legal complications.

Import/Export Laws

Import and export laws play a crucial role in regulating the movement of goods, services, and information across borders. These laws are particularly significant in the context of information security and privacy, as they govern the international transfer of technology, data, and intellectual property. Understanding and complying with these laws is essential for businesses operating on a global scale to avoid legal repercussions and ensure smooth cross-border operations.

Import/export laws are designed to control the flow of goods and technology to protect national security, promote economic interests, and enforce international agreements. For information security professionals, these laws primarily concern the transfer of technology and cryptographic tools, which can have dual-use applications—serving both civilian and military purposes. As such, these items are often subject to strict regulations to prevent their misuse.

Export Controls

Export controls are a critical component of import/export laws. These controls are implemented to restrict the dissemination of sensitive technologies and information that could potentially threaten national security if accessed by hostile entities. For instance, cryptographic software and hardware, which are vital for securing communications and data, are often classified under export control regulations. Organizations must obtain the necessary licenses and approvals before exporting these items to certain countries or entities.

Countries of Concern

An important aspect of export controls is the identification of countries of concern, which are designated by regulatory bodies such as the Department of Commerce's Bureau of Industry and Security (BIS). These countries are identified based on various factors, including threats of nuclear proliferation and designation as state sponsors of terrorism. Currently, countries such as Cuba, Iran, North Korea, and Syria fall under this category. Exporting high-performance computing systems or encryption technology to these nations requires special approval, reflecting the increased scrutiny and restrictions placed on transactions involving these regions.

Import Regulations

Import regulations focus on the goods and technologies entering a country. These regulations aim to protect domestic industries, ensure compliance with national standards, and prevent the entry of harmful or substandard products. In the realm of information security, import regulations may apply to foreign software and hardware that could pose security risks, such as those with embedded vulnerabilities or backdoors.

International agreements play a significant role in harmonizing import/export laws across different jurisdictions. Treaties and agreements, such as the Wassenaar Arrangement, establish common standards and guidelines for the transfer of dual-use goods and technologies among member countries. These agreements facilitate international trade while ensuring that security concerns are addressed.

Multinational Companies

For multinational companies, navigating the complex landscape of import/export laws requires a thorough understanding of the legal requirements in each jurisdiction they operate in. Compliance involves not only obtaining the necessary licenses and permits but also implementing robust internal controls and processes to monitor and manage cross-border transactions.

Import/export laws are a critical aspect of legal and ethical considerations in information security and privacy. They regulate the international movement of technology and data, ensuring that these transfers do not compromise national security or violate international agreements. Organizations must diligently comply with these laws, particularly when dealing with countries of concern, to avoid legal penalties and maintain their reputation in the global market.

Privacy Laws

When it comes to privacy, understanding the legal and ethical considerations is paramount for professionals tasked with safeguarding personal data. Privacy laws form the backbone of these considerations, providing a structured framework for protecting individual rights and guiding organizational practices. This section provides an overview of key U.S. privacy laws, emphasizing their importance in the context of information security and privacy management.

Privacy laws are designed to protect individuals' personal information from unauthorized access and misuse. These laws vary significantly across jurisdictions, creating a complex landscape for organizations, especially those operating on a global scale. In the United States, privacy laws are not comprehensive at the federal level, leading to a patchwork of state laws that address various aspects of privacy and data protection.

Enforcement

Understanding the enforcement mechanisms of privacy laws is crucial for compliance. In the United States, enforcement is carried out by various federal and state agencies, each with its own jurisdiction and authority. The Federal Trade

Commission (FTC) plays a significant role in enforcing consumer privacy laws, while state attorneys general may pursue violations of state privacy statutes.

Liability

Legal liability under privacy laws can arise from both criminal and civil actions. Criminal liability involves the prosecution of individuals or organizations for violations of privacy laws, which can result in fines or imprisonment. Civil liability, on the other hand, involves lawsuits brought by individuals or groups seeking damages for privacy violations. Organizations must be aware of both types of liability and take steps to mitigate risks through robust compliance programs and data protection measures.

Negligence

Negligence is a common theory of liability in privacy law, where organizations may be held accountable for failing to take reasonable steps to protect personal information. This underscores the importance of implementing comprehensive security measures and regularly reviewing and updating privacy policies and practices.

Ethical Concerns

Privacy laws also intersect with ethical considerations, as organizations must balance their business interests with the rights and expectations of individuals. Ethical considerations often go beyond legal requirements, prompting organizations to adopt best practices in data protection and transparency. This includes obtaining informed consent from individuals, providing clear and accessible privacy notices, and ensuring accountability in data handling practices.

Key U.S. Privacy Laws

Although the United States has no explicit constitutional guarantee of privacy, a myriad of federal laws (many enacted in recent years) are designed to protect the private information the government maintains about citizens as well as key portions of the private sector such as financial, educational, and healthcare institutions. The following list displays brief descriptions of a number of these federal laws:

- **Fourth Amendment:** Protects individuals from unreasonable searches and seizures, providing a foundational privacy right against government intrusion.

- **Privacy Act of 1974:** Regulates the collection, maintenance, and use of personal information by federal agencies, ensuring transparency and individual rights.
- **Electronic Communications Privacy Act of 1986:** Extends privacy protections to electronic communications, prohibiting unauthorized interception and access.
- **Communications Assistance for Law Enforcement Act (CALEA) of 1994:** Requires telecommunications carriers to facilitate lawful surveillance by law enforcement.
- **Economic Espionage Act of 1996:** Criminalizes the theft of trade secrets, recognizing proprietary economic information as protected property.
- **Health Insurance Portability and Accountability Act (HIPAA) of 1996:** Establishes privacy and security standards for protecting health information.
- **Health Information Technology for Economic and Clinical Health Act (HITECH) of 2009:** Enhances HIPAA by introducing breach notification requirements and extending obligations to business associates.
- **Children's Online Privacy Protection Act (COPPA) of 2009:** Protects the privacy of children under 13 by requiring parental consent for data collection.
- **Gramm–Leach–Bliley Act (GLBA) of 1999:** Mandates financial institutions to protect consumer financial information and provide privacy notices.
- **USA PATRIOT Act of 2001:** Expands law enforcement's surveillance capabilities, including access to electronic communications and financial records.
- **Clarifying Lawful Overseas Use of Data (CLOUD) Act:** Facilitates cross-border data access for law enforcement, addressing jurisdictional challenges.
- **Family Educational Rights and Privacy Act (FERPA):** Protects the privacy of student education records, granting rights to parents and eligible students.
- **Identity Theft and Assumption Deterrence Act:** Criminalizes identity theft and provides mechanisms for victims to recover from its effects.

European Union Privacy Law

The European Union's General Data Protection Regulation (GDPR) is one of the most comprehensive privacy laws globally, setting a high standard for data protection and privacy. It applies to all organizations processing the personal data of EU residents, regardless of where the organization is based. Key provisions of the GDPR include:

- **Lawfulness, fairness, and transparency:** You must have a legal basis for processing personal information, you must not process data in a manner that is misleading or detrimental to data subjects, and you must be open and honest about data processing activities.
- **Purpose limitation:** You must clearly document and disclose the purposes for which you collect data and limit your activity to disclosed purposes.
- **Data minimization:** You must ensure that the data you process is adequate for your stated purpose and limited to what you actually need for that purpose.
- **Accuracy:** You must ensure that the data you collect, create, or maintain is correct and not misleading; you maintain updated records; and you correct or erase inaccurate data.
- **Storage limitation:** You keep data only for as long as it is needed to fulfill a legitimate, disclosed purpose and that you comply with the "right to be forgotten" that allows individuals to require companies to delete their information if it is no longer needed.
- **Integrity and confidentiality:** You must have appropriate security, integrity, and confidentiality controls in place to protect data.
- **Accountability:** You must take responsibility for actions you take with protected data, and the data controller must be able to demonstrate compliance.

The Importance of Privacy Laws

In conclusion, privacy laws provide a critical framework for protecting personal information and guiding organizational practices in the realm of information security and privacy. Understanding the legal and ethical considerations associated with these laws is essential for professionals tasked with safeguarding personal data. By navigating the complex landscape of privacy laws and implementing robust compliance programs, organizations can protect individual rights, mitigate legal risks, and build trust with their stakeholders.

Compliance

From the perspective of information security, *compliance* refers to the adherence to laws, regulations, and standards that govern cybersecurity practices. This complex landscape requires information security professionals to navigate a myriad of legal and regulatory frameworks across multiple jurisdictions. Compliance is particularly challenging for multinational organizations that must reconcile differences between international laws and local regulations.

Cybercrime and data breaches are significant concerns, prompting law enforcement and governments worldwide to address these issues through legislation and specialized investigative units. Compliance involves understanding and implementing measures to prevent cybercrimes and protect data integrity. This includes adhering to licensing and intellectual property requirements, managing import/export controls, and navigating transborder data flows. Privacy issues, such as those addressed by the GDPR and the CCPA, are also critical components of compliance, requiring organizations to protect personal information and uphold individuals' rights.

Organizations must also consider contractual, legal, industry standard, and regulatory requirements as part of their compliance strategy. This involves aligning security practices with business objectives and ensuring that policies and procedures reflect both internal goals and external obligations. Compliance is not just a legal necessity but also a strategic component of security governance, helping organizations mitigate risks and maintain trust with stakeholders. By understanding and implementing these compliance requirements, organizations can effectively manage their security posture and protect their assets against evolving threats.

Ethical Considerations

In the realm of information security, ethical considerations are paramount for professionals who navigate the complex landscape of protecting data and systems. Ethics in information security involves adhering to a set of principles and codes of conduct that guide professionals in making decisions that protect the confidentiality, integrity, and availability of information while respecting the rights and privacy of individuals.

Organizational Code of Ethics

Organizations often develop their own codes of ethics that align with their mission, values, and business practices. These codes are designed to guide employees in making ethical decisions that support organizational goals while adhering to legal and regulatory requirements. Adhering to these organizational codes is crucial for maintaining trust and integrity within the organization and with external stakeholders.

ISC2 Code of Professional Ethics

The ISC2 Code of Professional Ethics provides a framework for ethical behavior among information security professionals. This code emphasizes the importance of acting honorably, honestly, justly, responsibly, and legally. Key canons include protecting society, the commonwealth, and the infrastructure; providing diligent and competent service to principals; and advancing and protecting the profession. By adhering to these principles, professionals ensure that their actions benefit the common good and maintain public trust and confidence.

Ethics and the Internet

With the rapid expansion of the Internet, ethical guidelines have become crucial in guiding digital activities. RFC 1087, titled "Ethics and the Internet," outlines practices considered unethical, such as seeking unauthorized access to Internet resources, disrupting intended Internet use, wasting resources, destroying the integrity of computer-based information, and compromising user privacy. These guidelines serve as a foundation for many ethical codes, providing a clear distinction between acceptable and unacceptable online behavior.

Understanding and Promoting Professional Ethics

Information security professionals are often guided by established codes of ethics, such as the ISC2 Code of Professional Ethics. These codes serve as a framework for ethical behavior, emphasizing the importance of acting honorably, honestly, justly, responsibly, and legally. Professionals are encouraged to protect society, the commonwealth, and the infrastructure; act honorably, honestly, justly, responsibly, and legally; provide diligent and competent service to principals; and advance and protect the profession.

Ethical Dilemmas and Decision-Making

Security professionals frequently encounter ethical dilemmas that require careful consideration and decision-making. These situations often involve balancing the need to protect organizational assets with the rights and privacy of individuals. Professionals must weigh the potential impact of their actions on various stakeholders and consider the long-term implications of their decisions.

The Role of Ethics in Investigations

Ethics plays a critical role in the conduct of investigations into security incidents. Investigators must ensure that their actions are guided by ethical principles, particularly when collecting and handling evidence. They must respect the rights of individuals involved in investigations and ensure that their actions do not infringe upon civil liberties. Ethical conduct in investigations helps maintain the integrity of the process and ensures that evidence is admissible in legal proceedings.

Promoting an Ethical Culture

Organizations can foster an ethical culture by promoting awareness and understanding of ethical principles among employees. This can be achieved through training programs, workshops, and open discussions about ethical issues in information security. Encouraging employees to speak up about ethical concerns and providing mechanisms for reporting unethical behavior without fear of retaliation are also important steps in promoting an ethical culture.

Ethical considerations are integral to the practice of information security. By adhering to professional and organizational codes of ethics, making informed decisions in the face of ethical dilemmas, and promoting an ethical culture, security professionals can uphold the highest standards of integrity and trust in their work.

CHAPTER 14

Threat Intelligence and Cyber Defense

Understanding the intricate web of cybersecurity threats is crucial for professionals tasked with safeguarding sensitive information. This chapter explores the multifaceted world of cyber threats, providing you with a comprehensive overview of the actors, vectors, and intelligence that shape the modern threat landscape. As a security and privacy professional, it is imperative to grasp these concepts to effectively anticipate, identify, and mitigate potential threats to your organization's digital assets.

This chapter equips you with the knowledge to navigate the complex realm of threat intelligence, offering insights into the various sources and methodologies that can enhance your organization's defensive posture. By understanding the motivations and tactics of different threat actors, as well as the channels through which they operate, you will be better prepared to implement robust defense strategies. Additionally, the chapter explores advanced threat detection and response techniques, empowering you to proactively hunt for threats and assess the effectiveness of your threat intelligence efforts. Ultimately, this chapter aims to bolster your ability to protect your organization's digital infrastructure, ensuring the confidentiality, integrity, and availability of critical information.

Threat Actors

In today's rapidly evolving digital landscape, understanding the various types of threat actors and their methodologies is crucial for cybersecurity professionals. This knowledge forms the backbone of effective threat intelligence and cyber defense strategies. By identifying and classifying threat actors, organizations can tailor their security measures to better protect against potential breaches. This section delves into the different types of threat actors, their motivations, and the sources of malicious code that they might use, providing a comprehensive overview for security professionals.

Types of Threat Actors

Threat actors are individuals or groups that pose a risk to an organization's information systems. They differ significantly in their skills, capabilities, resources, and motivations. Recognizing these differences is essential for developing effective security controls.

- **Script kiddies:** These are typically inexperienced individuals who use prewritten scripts or tools to launch attacks. Their primary motivation is often curiosity or the thrill of causing disruption. Although they lack the sophistication of more advanced threat actors, they can still cause significant damage, especially if they stumble upon vulnerabilities in poorly secured systems.
- **Hacktivists:** Motivated by political or social causes, hacktivists use their skills to promote their agenda. They often target organizations or governments they perceive as adversaries. Their attacks can range from website defacements to more sophisticated operations aimed at disrupting services or stealing sensitive information to further their cause.
- **Cybercriminals:** These actors are primarily motivated by financial gain. They engage in activities such as identity theft, credit card fraud, and ransomware attacks. Cybercriminals are often part of organized crime syndicates, providing them with significant resources and capabilities.
- **Competitors:** In some cases, businesses may engage in corporate espionage to gain a competitive edge. These actors seek to steal proprietary information, trade secrets, or intellectual property. While less common than other threat actors, the impact of such activities can be devastating to the targeted organization.
- **Nation-state actors:** These are highly skilled and well-funded groups that operate on behalf of a government. Their objectives can include espionage, sabotage, or gaining a strategic advantage over other nations. Nation-state actors are often responsible for advanced persistent threats (APTs), which involve prolonged and targeted attacks designed to infiltrate and maintain access to critical systems.
- **Insiders:** One of the most dangerous types of threat actors, insiders are individuals within an organization who misuse their access to cause harm. They may be motivated by financial gain, revenge, or coercion. Insiders have the advantage of knowing the organization's systems and processes, making their attacks particularly challenging to detect and prevent.

Detecting Advanced Persistent Threats

APTs are a sophisticated form of cyberattack typically associated with nation-state actors and other highly skilled groups. These attacks are characterized by their stealth and persistence, often going undetected for extended periods. Detecting APTs requires a multifaceted approach:

- **Threat intelligence:** Organizations must leverage both open-source and proprietary threat intelligence to stay informed about emerging threats. By understanding the tactics, techniques, and procedures (TTPs) used by APT actors, security teams can better anticipate and respond to potential threats.
- **User and entity behavior analytics (UEBA):** UEBA tools help identify unusual patterns of behavior that may indicate an APT. By establishing baselines for normal activity, these tools can detect anomalies that suggest malicious activity, such as unauthorized access attempts or data exfiltration.
- **Intrusion detection and prevention systems (IDPSs):** These systems monitor network traffic for signs of malicious activity. They can alert security teams to potential threats and, in some cases, automatically block suspicious activity. IDPSs are essential for detecting the initial stages of an APT, such as phishing attempts or the exploitation of vulnerabilities.
- **Endpoint detection and response (EDR):** EDR solutions focus on monitoring endpoints for signs of compromise. They provide visibility into endpoint activities, enabling security teams to quickly identify and contain threats before they spread throughout the network.

Sources of Malicious Code

Malicious code, or malware, is a common tool used by threat actors to compromise systems. Understanding the sources and types of malware is crucial for developing effective defenses.

- **Viruses and worms:** These types of malware are designed to spread rapidly across systems and networks. While viruses require user interaction to propagate, worms can spread autonomously. Both can cause widespread disruption and data loss if not promptly addressed.
- **Trojan horses:** Disguised as legitimate software, Trojans deceive users into installing them, granting attackers access to the system. Once installed, they can perform various malicious activities, such as stealing data or creating backdoors for future access.

- **Ransomware:** This type of malware encrypts a victim's data, demanding payment for the decryption key. Ransomware attacks have become increasingly common and sophisticated, often targeting critical infrastructure and large organizations.
- **Spyware and adware:** These programs collect information about a user's activities without their consent. While adware is primarily used for targeted advertising, spyware can be used for more malicious purposes, such as stealing sensitive information.
- **Rootkits:** Designed to gain unauthorized root or administrative access, rootkits enable attackers to control and manipulate systems without detection. They often modify system files and processes to hide their presence, making them difficult to detect and remove.

By understanding the various threat actors and their tools, organizations can better prepare for and defend against cyberattacks. A robust threat intelligence and cyber defense strategy is essential for maintaining the security and integrity of information systems in an increasingly hostile digital environment.

Threat Vectors

Understanding threat vectors is crucial for professionals tasked with safeguarding organizational assets. Threat vectors are the pathways or methods that adversaries use to infiltrate and compromise systems. Identifying and mitigating these vectors are essential components of a comprehensive cybersecurity strategy.

Cybersecurity professionals must be vigilant in recognizing the diverse array of threat vectors that can be exploited by malicious actors. These vectors can range from traditional methods, such as email phishing and social engineering, to more sophisticated techniques like supply chain attacks and zero-day exploits. Each vector presents unique challenges and requires tailored defensive measures to effectively counteract them.

Email and Social Media

One of the most common threat vectors is email, which is often used to deliver phishing attacks and malicious attachments. Attackers exploit human vulnerabilities, tricking users into divulging sensitive information or executing harmful software. Social media platforms also serve as a vector, where attackers can gather intelligence on targets or spread malware through seemingly benign interactions.

Physical Access

Physical access remains a significant threat vector, as unauthorized individuals can gain direct access to systems and data. This vector underscores the importance of robust physical security measures and access controls to prevent unauthorized entry and data breaches.

Network-Based Attacks

Network-based attacks, such as distributed denial-of-service (DDoS) and man-in-the-middle (MitM) attacks, exploit vulnerabilities in network infrastructure. These attacks can disrupt services, intercept communications, and compromise data integrity. Implementing strong network security protocols and continuous monitoring can help mitigate these risks.

Removable Media

Attackers frequently use removable media, such as USB drives, to introduce malware into an organization's systems. By distributing infected devices in public areas, attackers rely on curiosity or negligence to gain access when someone plugs the device into their computer. To counteract this threat vector, organizations should implement strict policies regarding the use of removable media and educate employees on the associated risks.

Cloud

Cloud services present unique security challenges as an attack vector. Attackers may exploit misconfigured cloud settings, improperly secured data, or exposed APIs to gain unauthorized access to sensitive information. Organizations must ensure that their cloud environments are configured securely and that data is protected through encryption and robust access controls. Regular audits and monitoring are essential to maintaining cloud security.

Third Parties and Supply Chain

Supply chain attacks have gained prominence as attackers target third-party vendors and service providers to infiltrate organizations. These attacks exploit the trust relationships between organizations and their suppliers, emphasizing the need for rigorous supply chain risk management and due diligence. Establishing strong vendor management practices and conducting thorough security assessments of third-party partners can help mitigate these risks.

Defending Against Threat Vectors

To effectively defend against these threat vectors, organizations should build robust threat intelligence programs. These programs involve collecting, analyzing, and disseminating information about potential threats and attack methods. By staying informed about emerging threats and adapting security controls accordingly, organizations can enhance their resilience against cyberattacks.

Understanding and addressing threat vectors is a fundamental aspect of cybersecurity defense. By recognizing the various pathways that attackers may use, organizations can implement targeted security measures to protect their assets and maintain the confidentiality, integrity, and availability of their information systems.

Threat Intelligence

Cybersecurity professionals must stay informed about the latest threats to safeguard their organization's assets effectively. Threat intelligence involves the collection and analysis of information about potential or existing threats to an organization's security. This section delves into various aspects of threat intelligence, including the assessment and management of threat indicators. For information about threat feeds, such as open-source intelligence and close-source intelligence, see the section "Threat Feeds."

Assessing Threat Intelligence

Assessing the quality of threat intelligence is critical to its effective use. Organizations must evaluate the timeliness, accuracy, and relevance of the information they receive. Timely intelligence allows for proactive threat mitigation, while accuracy ensures the reliability of the data. Relevance is crucial, as even accurate and timely information may be useless if it does not pertain to the organization's specific context. By assessing these factors, organizations can prioritize threats and allocate resources efficiently.

Threat Indicator Management and Exchange

Managing and exchanging threat indicators is a vital part of threat intelligence. Indicators of compromise (IoCs) such as IP addresses, file hashes, and URLs are used to detect and respond to threats. Organizations often share threat indicators through standardized protocols and platforms to enhance collective security efforts. This exchange of information allows for a more comprehensive understanding of the threat landscape and fosters collaboration among cybersecurity professionals.

Public and Private Information

Threat intelligence encompasses both public and private information sources. Public sources include government alerts and community-driven platforms, while private sources may involve proprietary data from commercial vendors. Organizations must balance the use of public and private information to build a comprehensive threat intelligence program. Leveraging both types of information can provide a more complete picture of potential threats and enhance an organization's ability to respond effectively.

Conducting Your Own Research

Organizations are encouraged to conduct their own research to supplement external threat intelligence sources. By analyzing internal data and monitoring their own networks, organizations can identify unique threats and vulnerabilities specific to their environment. Conducting independent research allows organizations to tailor their threat intelligence efforts to their specific needs and enhances their ability to anticipate and mitigate risks.

Building a robust threat intelligence program is a fundamental component of an organization's cybersecurity strategy. It involves gathering information from diverse sources, assessing its quality, managing threat indicators, and conducting independent research. By staying informed about the current threat landscape, organizations can better protect themselves against cyber threats and ensure the security of their information systems.

Threat Feeds

Threat intelligence plays a pivotal role in safeguarding organizations against potential threats. Threat feeds, a crucial component of threat intelligence, provide continuous streams of data that help organizations detect, analyze, and respond to cyber threats. These feeds can be derived from various sources, including open-source intelligence and proprietary closed-source intelligence. Understanding and effectively leveraging these feeds is essential for building a robust cyber defense strategy.

Understanding Threat Feeds

Threat feeds are streams of raw data related to current and potential cybersecurity threats. They provide information such as suspicious domains, known malware hashes, malicious IP addresses, and code shared on Internet sites. These feeds are essential for cybersecurity professionals as they offer insights into the threat landscape, enabling organizations to anticipate and mitigate potential attacks. However, in their raw form, threat feeds can be overwhelming and challenging to interpret. Therefore, threat intelligence feeds aim to extract actionable intelligence from this data, making it more useful for security operations.

Open-Source Intelligence

Open-source intelligence (OSINT) refers to threat intelligence gathered from publicly available sources. The open sharing of threat information has become increasingly common, with numerous organizations recognizing its value. OSINT is accessible through various platforms that provide lists of open-source threat information. For instance, **Senki.org**, the Open Threat Exchange by AT&T, and the MISP Threat Sharing project are popular sources that offer standardized threat feeds. These platforms allow security professionals to access a wealth of information, helping them stay informed about emerging threats.

Government and public sources also contribute significantly to open-source intelligence. Agencies like the Cybersecurity and Infrastructure Security Agency (CISA) provide alerts and threat intelligence through their websites. Other countries have similar cybersecurity sites, such as the Australian Signals Directorate's Cyber Security Centre. These sources offer valuable insights into the global threat landscape, helping organizations understand and respond to threats in real time.

Proprietary and Closed-Source Intelligence

In addition to open-source intelligence, many organizations rely on proprietary or closed-source intelligence. This type of intelligence is typically gathered and curated by commercial security vendors, government organizations, and other security-centric entities. These organizations use proprietary tools, analysis models, and methods to create threat feeds that are often part of a service offering. Closed-source intelligence is particularly valuable for organizations that require specialized or highly sensitive threat data.

One of the primary advantages of proprietary intelligence is its exclusivity. Organizations may choose to keep their threat data confidential to maintain a competitive edge or to prevent threat actors from accessing their methods and sources. Additionally, these services often provide curated and validated data, reducing the burden on organizations to sift through vast amounts of raw information. This can be particularly beneficial for organizations with limited resources or expertise in threat analysis.

Challenges and Considerations

Despite the benefits of threat feeds, there are challenges associated with their use. The sheer volume of data can be overwhelming, and organizations must ensure that the feeds they rely on are timely, accurate, and relevant. A delay in receiving threat information can leave an organization vulnerable to attacks, while inaccurate or irrelevant data can lead to wasted resources and ineffective defenses. Therefore, it is crucial for organizations to assess the quality of their threat feeds and consider using multiple sources to cross-verify information.

Moreover, threat intelligence is a dynamic field, with threat actors constantly evolving their tactics, techniques, and procedures. As a result, threat feeds must be continuously updated and refined to remain effective. Organizations should also be aware of the limitations of threat maps, which provide geographic views of threat intelligence. Geographic attribution can be unreliable, as attackers often mask their true locations through cloud services and compromised networks.

Building a Robust Threat Intelligence Program

To effectively leverage threat feeds, organizations should integrate them into a comprehensive threat intelligence program. This involves selecting reliable sources, both open and proprietary, and ensuring that the data is actionable and relevant to the organization's specific needs. Security professionals should also stay informed about emerging threats and continuously update their threat intelligence capabilities. By doing so, organizations can enhance their cyber defense strategies and better protect themselves against the ever-changing threat landscape.

In conclusion, threat feeds are an essential component of threat intelligence, providing valuable insights into the cybersecurity threat landscape. By understanding and effectively utilizing both open-source and proprietary intelligence, organizations can build a robust defense against potential threats. However, it is crucial to assess the quality and relevance of threat feeds and to continuously update threat intelligence programs to stay ahead of evolving cyber threats.

Threat Hunting

Threat hunting has emerged as a proactive approach to identifying and mitigating potential security threats before they can inflict damage. Unlike traditional security measures that rely on automated systems to detect known threats, threat hunting involves a more hands-on and investigative approach. This process is conducted by skilled cybersecurity professionals who actively seek out hidden threats that may have bypassed existing security measures.

The Need for Threat Hunting

Unfortunately, not all threats can be predicted during the design phase, so a reactive approach to threat management is still needed to address unforeseen issues. This concept is often called *threat hunting* or may be referred to as an *adversarial approach*. Threat hunting is the activity of looking for existing evidence of a compromise once symptoms or an indicator of compromise (loC) of an exploit become known. Threat modeling looks for zero-day exploits before harm is experienced, whereas threat hunting uses loC information to find harm that has already occurred. An adversarial approach to threat modeling takes place after a product has been created and deployed. This deployment could be in a test or laboratory environment or in the general marketplace. This technique of threat hunting is the core concept behind ethical hacking, penetration testing, and source code review.

Threat Hunting Process

The threat hunting process involves several key steps. It begins with the development of a hypothesis about potential threats based on intelligence, past incidents, or anomalies detected in the environment. Hunters then conduct a thorough investigation using advanced tools and techniques to analyze data and identify indicators of compromise. The goal is to uncover patterns or behaviors that suggest malicious activity.

Data Collection and Analysis

Collecting and analyzing data is a crucial component of threat hunting. Threat hunters gather data from various sources, including network traffic, endpoint logs, and threat intelligence feeds. They use this data to identify anomalies and investigate suspicious activities. Advanced analytical tools, such as machine learning and behavioral analysis, are often employed to assist in this process.

Collaboration and Communication

Collaborating and communicating are essential in threat hunting. Threat hunters work closely with other cybersecurity teams, sharing findings and insights to bolster the organization's overall security posture. This collaborative approach ensures that any identified threats are addressed promptly and effectively.

Continuous Improvement

Continually improving is a hallmark of successful threat hunting programs. As new threats emerge and evolve, threat hunters must adapt their techniques and strategies. Regular reviews and updates to threat hunting methodologies help ensure that organizations remain resilient against the ever-changing threat landscape.

Incorporating threat hunting into an organization's cybersecurity strategy enhances its ability to detect and respond to threats in real time. By proactively seeking out potential threats, organizations can strengthen their defenses, minimize the impact of security incidents, and protect their critical assets from harm.

Assessing Threat Intelligence

Understanding and anticipating cybersecurity threats is crucial for organizations aiming to safeguard their information assets. Threat intelligence involves the collection and analysis of data regarding potential or current threats to an organization. It serves as a foundational element in developing effective cyber defense strategies, allowing organizations to proactively identify and mitigate risks before they manifest as actual incidents. This section delves into the process of assessing threat intelligence, emphasizing the importance of a structured approach to understanding the threat landscape.

Understanding the Threat Landscape

The cybersecurity threat landscape is diverse and constantly changing, characterized by a wide array of threat actors with varying levels of sophistication and resources. These actors range from lone hackers to organized cybercriminals and state-sponsored groups, each with distinct motivations, such as financial gain, political objectives, or corporate espionage. To effectively assess threat intelligence, organizations must first understand these actors and the specific threats they pose. This involves classifying threats based on characteristics such as their origin (internal or external), level of sophistication, available resources, and intent.

Building a Threat Intelligence Capability

Developing a robust threat intelligence capability involves several key steps. First, organizations must gather data from various sources, including open-source intelligence, commercial threat intelligence feeds, and information shared by industry peers or government agencies. This data needs to be analyzed to identify patterns and trends that could indicate potential threats. Analytical tools and techniques, such as machine learning and artificial intelligence, can enhance the ability to process large volumes of data and extract actionable insights.

Vulnerability Assessment and Threat Analysis

Once potential threats are identified, organizations must conduct comprehensive vulnerability assessments to determine how these threats could exploit weaknesses in their systems. This involves evaluating the organization's existing security controls and identifying any deficiencies that could be leveraged by threat actors. Regular vulnerability scans and penetration testing are essential components of this process, helping to uncover potential entry points for attackers and assess the effectiveness of current defenses.

Prioritizing Threats and Vulnerabilities

Not all threats and vulnerabilities pose the same level of risk to an organization. Therefore, it is crucial to prioritize them based on factors such as the potential impact on the organization, the likelihood of occurrence, and the organization's risk tolerance. By focusing on the most critical threats and vulnerabilities, organizations can allocate resources more effectively and ensure that their defenses are aligned with their overall risk management strategy.

Integrating Threat Intelligence into Cyber Defense

The ultimate goal of threat intelligence is to inform and enhance an organization's cyber defense mechanisms. This requires integrating threat intelligence into the organization's security operations center (SOC) and incident response processes. By doing so, organizations can improve their ability to detect, respond to, and recover from cyber incidents. Additionally, threat intelligence can guide the development of security policies and procedures, ensuring that they are based on the latest information about emerging threats.

Continuous Monitoring and Adaptation

The dynamic nature of the threat landscape necessitates continuous monitoring and adaptation of threat intelligence processes. Organizations must regularly update their threat intelligence capabilities to keep pace with new developments and ensure that their defenses remain effective. This involves not only staying informed about the latest threats but also evaluating the performance of existing security controls and making necessary adjustments to address any identified gaps.

Assessing threat intelligence is a critical component of an organization's cybersecurity strategy. By understanding the threat landscape, conducting thorough vulnerability assessments, prioritizing risks, and integrating intelligence into cyber defense efforts, organizations can better protect themselves against the ever-evolving array of cyber threats. Continuous monitoring and adaptation are essential to maintaining an effective defense posture in the face of new and emerging challenges.

Cyber Kill Chain and the MITRE ATT&CK

Understanding the methodologies that attackers use is crucial for developing effective defense strategies. This section delves into two prominent frameworks: the Cyber Kill Chain and the MITRE ATT&CK Matrix. Both models provide insights into the tTTPs employed by malicious actors, enabling organizations to enhance their threat intelligence and fortify their cyber defenses.

Understanding the Cyber Kill Chain

The Cyber Kill Chain is a framework initially developed by Lockheed Martin, adapted from military strategies to identify and prevent cyber intrusions. It outlines a series of steps that attackers typically follow to achieve their objectives. By understanding these stages, organizations can disrupt the attack process at various points.

The Cyber Kill Chain consists of seven phases:

1. **Reconnaissance:** In this initial phase, attackers gather information about the target, identifying potential vulnerabilities and entry points. This may involve scanning networks, researching employee profiles, or analyzing the organization's infrastructure.
2. **Weaponization:** Attackers create a payload, often by pairing malware with an exploit, to take advantage of the identified vulnerabilities. This step involves crafting a method to deliver the malicious payload to the target.
3. **Delivery:** The weaponized payload is transmitted to the target using various methods such as phishing emails, compromised websites, or malicious attachments. This phase is critical as it marks the transition from planning to execution.
4. **Exploitation:** Upon delivery, the payload exploits a vulnerability in the target system, allowing the attacker to gain unauthorized access. This is often where the initial breach occurs.
5. **Installation:** After exploitation, attackers install malware on the compromised system to maintain persistent access. This may include backdoors or remote access tools that facilitate ongoing control over the system.
6. **Command and control (C2):** Attackers establish communication channels with the compromised system, allowing them to issue commands and control the target remotely. This phase is crucial for coordinating further actions on the target.
7. **Actions on objectives:** Finally, attackers execute their ultimate goals, which may include data theft, system disruption, or further propagation of malware. The objectives vary based on the attacker's intent, such as financial gain, espionage, or sabotage.

Understanding the MITRE ATT&CK Matrix

While the Cyber Kill Chain provides a linear view of the attack process, the MITRE ATT&CK Matrix offers a more comprehensive and dynamic perspective. Developed by MITRE, the ATT&CK Matrix is a living document that catalogs the TTPs used by adversaries in various attack scenarios. Unlike the sequential nature of the Cyber Kill Chain, the ATT&CK Matrix presents tactics and techniques in a matrix format, allowing for a more flexible understanding of attack strategies.

The ATT&CK Matrix includes the following tactics:

- **Reconnaissance:** Similar to the Cyber Kill Chain, this involves gathering information about the target to identify potential vulnerabilities.

- **Resource development:** Attackers develop or acquire resources necessary to carry out the attack, such as infrastructure, tools, and accounts.
- **Initial access:** Techniques used to gain an initial foothold within the target network including phishing, exploitation of public-facing applications, and supply chain compromises.
- **Execution:** Methods employed to run malicious code on the target system, such as scripting, command–line interfaces, or exploitation of software vulnerabilities.
- **Persistence:** Techniques that ensure the attacker maintains access to the target system, even after restarts or credential changes.
- **Privilege escalation:** Methods to gain higher-level permissions on the target system, allowing broader access and control.
- **Defense evasion:** Techniques used to avoid detection and bypass security measures, such as obfuscation, disabling security tools, or modifying system artifacts.
- **Credential access:** Methods to obtain credentials, such as password dumping or keylogging, enabling further access and lateral movement within the network.
- **Discovery:** Techniques to gather information about the internal network, systems, and security posture of the target environment.
- **Lateral movement:** Methods to move through the network, accessing additional systems and resources beyond the initial foothold.
- **Collection:** Techniques to gather and consolidate data of interest from the target for exfiltration.
- **Command and control:** Establishing communication channels with compromised systems to issue commands and control operations.
- **Exfiltration:** Methods to transfer data out of the target network, often to external locations controlled by the attacker.
- **Impact:** Actions taken to disrupt, destroy, or manipulate the target's systems and data, achieving the attacker's ultimate objectives.

Both the Cyber Kill Chain and MITRE ATT&CK frameworks are invaluable tools for cybersecurity professionals. By leveraging these models, organizations can better understand the attack life cycle, identify vulnerabilities in their defenses, and implement strategies to detect and mitigate threats. Integrating these frameworks into cybersecurity operations enhances threat intelligence capabilities and strengthens the overall security posture, ultimately reducing the risk of successful cyberattacks.

CHAPTER 15

Business Continuity and Disaster Recovery

In today's business environment, the resilience of an organization is not just a competitive advantage but a necessity. As a security and privacy professional, your role in safeguarding your organization extends beyond the implementation of security measures to ensuring that business operations can withstand and quickly recover from unforeseen disruptions. This chapter examines the critical components of business continuity and disaster recovery, equipping you with the knowledge to prepare your organization for a wide range of potential threats from natural disasters to cyberattacks.

Understanding the intricacies of business continuity and disaster recovery planning is essential for developing a robust strategy that minimizes downtime and protects critical assets. This chapter provides you with a comprehensive guide to establishing a well-defined scope for your continuity projects, analyzing potential impacts through a business impact analysis (BIA), and implementing effective recovery strategies. By exploring these concepts, you will gain insights into creating a resilient framework that ensures your organization can maintain operations and recover swiftly in the face of adversity.

By the end of this chapter, you will be equipped with the tools and strategies necessary to design and implement a comprehensive business continuity and disaster recovery plan. This knowledge will empower you to not only protect your organization's assets but also to ensure its longevity and success in an unpredictable world.

Project Scope and Planning

In the realm of information security and privacy, the ability to maintain business operations during and after a disaster is crucial. Business continuity planning (BCP) and disaster recovery planning (DRP) are essential processes that ensure an organization can continue to function and recover swiftly from unforeseen events. This section explores the initial phase of developing a robust business continuity plan, focusing on setting clear objectives, identifying necessary resources, and understanding the organizational structure and dependencies.

Project scope and planning is the foundational phase of business continuity planning. It involves establishing a structured approach to ensure that the organization is well-prepared to handle crises. The primary objectives during this phase include conducting an organizational review, selecting the BCP team, assessing resource requirements, and understanding external dependencies.

Organizational Review

Organizational review is a critical initial step in the project scope and planning phase. It involves a detailed analysis of the organization's structure to identify departments and individuals with a vested interest in the BCP process. This review should encompass the following:

- Operational departments responsible for delivering the core services that the business provides to its clients.
- Critical support services such as IT, facilities management, and maintenance personnel, who ensure the smooth functioning of systems that support these operations.
- Corporate security teams, responsible for physical security and often the first responders during incidents, play a vital role in safeguarding both the primary and alternate processing facilities.
- Senior executives and key individuals essential for the organization's ongoing viability must be considered, as their involvement is crucial for strategic decision-making during a crisis.

BCP Team Selection

BCP team selection is pivotal to the success of the business continuity plan. The team should be composed of representatives from each operational and support department, ensuring that all critical functions are covered. Technical experts from the IT department are necessary to address technological challenges, while physical and IT security personnel bring expertise in safeguarding assets. Legal representatives familiar with corporate legal, regulatory, and contractual responsibilities ensure compliance and risk mitigation. Including senior management is essential, as they set the vision, define priorities, and allocate resources. A well-rounded team ensures diverse perspectives and comprehensive coverage of all potential risks and recovery strategies. Such a team should include at least the following members:

- Representatives from each of the organization's departments responsible for the core services performed by the business
- Business unit team members from the functional areas identified by the organizational analysis
- IT subject-matter experts with technical expertise in areas covered by the BCP
- Cybersecurity team members with knowledge of the BCP process
- Physical security and facility management teams responsible for the physical plant
- Attorneys familiar with corporate legal, regulatory, and contractual responsibilities
- Human resources team members who can address staffing issues and the impact on individual employees
- Public relations team members who need to conduct similar planning for how they will communicate with stakeholders and the public in the event of a disruption
- Senior management representatives with the ability to set the vision, define priorities, and allocate resources

Resource Requirements

Resource requirements assessment is vital to understanding the scope of resources needed for BCP activities. This includes evaluating human resources, technological assets, and financial investments necessary for executing continuity strategies. Human resources encompass the effort and time required from BCP team members and support staff. Technological resources may involve hardware and software commitments essential for testing, training, and maintenance phases. Financial investments are necessary for implementing the plan, especially during a full-scale activation in response to a disaster.

Assessing the resources required by the BCP effort involves understanding the resources needed by three distinct BCP phases:

1. **BCP development:** The initial phase where the foundation of the business continuity plan is laid. During this phase, the BCP team engages in project scope and planning, BIA, continuity planning, and plan approval. The major resource consumed in this phase is the effort and time expended by the BCP team members and the support staff assisting in plan development. This phase requires a comprehensive understanding of the organization's structure, critical functions, and potential risks. Resources such as personnel time, analytical tools, and documentation systems are essential to ensure a thorough and effective plan is created.
2. **BCP testing, training, and maintenance:** The next phase that focuses on validating the effectiveness of the BCP and ensuring that all personnel are well-prepared to execute the plan. This phase requires some hardware and software commitments to simulate disaster scenarios and test the plan's robustness. However, the major commitment in this phase is the effort of employees involved in these activities. Training sessions are conducted to educate staff on their roles and responsibilities, while maintenance activities ensure the plan remains current and responsive to evolving business needs. Regular testing and exercises are crucial to identify gaps and areas for improvement, necessitating ongoing resource allocation.
3. **BCP implementation:** The final phase, activated when a disaster strikes, necessitating the full-scale execution of the business continuity plan. This phase requires significant resources, including a large amount of effort from the organization, as BCP becomes a primary focus. Direct financial expenses may also be incurred to support the implementation of continuity strategies. The BCP team must act decisively and judiciously to ensure the plan's success. Resources such as emergency supplies, communication systems, and backup facilities are critical during this phase to maintain operations and minimize disruptions.

By thoroughly assessing resource requirements, organizations can plan effectively and ensure that the necessary support is available when needed.

External Dependencies

External dependencies are a significant consideration in business continuity planning. These dependencies include technology vendors supplying critical hardware, software, and cloud services, as well as legal and regulatory frameworks that shape operational landscapes. Each external factor carries potential risks that could disrupt business operations if left unaddressed. A comprehensive BCP must look beyond internal processes and consider the roles and responsibilities of external parties. This involves understanding the legal and regulatory landscape to ensure compliance with industry standards and government regulations. Business leaders must exercise due diligence to protect shareholders' interests and meet contractual obligations to clients before, during, and after a disaster.

Overall, the project scope and planning phase is integral to developing a resilient business continuity plan. By conducting a thorough organizational review, selecting a diverse and capable BCP team, assessing resource requirements, and understanding external dependencies, organizations can establish a strong foundation for their business continuity and disaster recovery efforts. This phase ensures that the organization is well-prepared to handle emergencies, safeguarding its operations and minimizing the impact of disruptions.

Conducting Business Impact Analysis

Conducting a BIA is a critical step that organizations must undertake to ensure their resilience in the face of disruptions. The BIA process is designed to identify and evaluate the potential effects of interruptions to business operations and processes. By understanding these impacts, organizations can prioritize their resources and efforts to mitigate risks effectively and maintain operational continuity. Here is a detailed breakdown of each phase involved in conducting a BIA.

Identifying Priorities

The BIA process begins with identifying priorities, which involves determining the essential business processes and tasks that are crucial for the organization's ongoing viability. This step is foundational, as it sets the stage for assessing which functions require the most protection and swift recovery in the event of a disruption. To effectively identify priorities, organizations often conduct interviews and workshops with department heads and key stakeholders to gain insights into their operational dependencies. This collaborative approach ensures that all critical functions are considered, including those that may not be immediately obvious. Additionally, organizations may use tools like process flowcharts and dependency matrices to visualize and document interdependencies among various business units.

Risk Identification

Following the identification of priorities, the next step is risk identification. This involves recognizing the various threats and vulnerabilities that could potentially disrupt critical business functions. These threats can range from natural disasters, such as earthquakes and hurricanes, to cyberattacks, human errors, and technological failures.

Hazards come in two forms: natural and person-made. The following list includes some events that pose natural threats:

- Violent storms, hurricanes, tornadoes, and blizzards
- Lightning strikes
- Natural wildfire
- Earthquakes
- Mudslides and avalanches
- Volcanic eruptions
- Pandemics

Person-made threats may include the following events:

- Terrorist acts, wars, and civil unrest
- Workplace violence
- Theft and vandalism
- Fires, arson, and explosions
- Prolonged power outages
- Building collapses
- Transportation failures
- Internet disruptions
- Service provider outages
- Economic crises

The risk identification phase is purely qualitative, aiming to compile a comprehensive list of potential risks without yet considering their likelihood or impact. Organizations often conduct brainstorming sessions and risk workshops involving cross-functional teams to ensure a wide range of perspectives are considered. This phase may also involve reviewing historical incident data and industry reports, and conducting environmental scans to uncover potential threats.

Likelihood Assessment

Once risks are identified, the BIA process moves to the likelihood assessment phase. Here, the organization evaluates how likely each identified risk is to occur. This assessment helps in understanding the probability of different scenarios, allowing for more informed decision-making when it comes to risk management and resource allocation. The likelihood of each threat is often expressed using the annualized rate of occurrence (ARO), which reflects the expected frequency of each risk materializing over a year. To accurately assess likelihood, organizations may consult historical data, industry benchmarks, and expert opinions. Additionally, tools like probability matrices and risk heat maps can be used to visualize the likelihood and potential impact of each risk, aiding in prioritization efforts.

Impact Analysis

The impact analysis phase is crucial for determining the potential consequences of each identified risk. This analysis considers both quantitative and qualitative factors to provide a comprehensive view of the potential impacts on the organization. *Quantitative impact assessment* involves using specific metrics to estimate the financial implications of disruptions.

On the other hand, *qualitative impact assessment* takes into account non-numerical factors such as reputation, customer confidence, and workforce stability, categorizing risks into levels of prioritization like high, medium, and low. Organizations may use scenario analysis and impact workshops to explore the broader implications of disruptions, ensuring a comprehensive understanding of potential impacts.

On the quantitative side, metrics such as the exposure factor, single loss expectancy, and annualized loss expectancy are commonly used. The next three sections provide a detailed look at these metrics, along with a real-world example to illustrate each.

Exposure Factor

The *exposure factor* (EF) represents the percentage of loss that an organization would experience if a specific asset were violated by a realized risk. It indicates the expected overall asset value loss due to a single realized risk and is expressed as a percentage. For example, if a risk is expected to cause 70 percent damage to a building, the EF would be 70 percent.

Real-world example: Consider a company that owns a building valued at $1 million. After consulting with fire safety experts, it is determined that a fire would destroy 60 percent of the building. In this case, the EF for the building in the event of a fire is 60 percent.

Single Loss Expectancy

The *single loss expectancy* (SLE) is the potential monetary loss associated with a single realized threat against a specific asset. It is calculated by multiplying the asset value (AV) by the exposure factor (EF). The SLE provides an estimate of the financial impact of a single incident.

Real-world example: Using the previous example, if the building is valued at $1 million and the EF is 60 percent, the SLE for a fire would be calculated as follows:

$$SLE = AV \times EF = \$1{,}000{,}000 \times 0.60 = \$600{,}000$$

This means that a single fire incident is expected to result in a $600,000 loss.

Annualized Loss Expectancy

The *annualized loss expectancy* (ALE) is the expected monetary loss from a risk occurring over the course of a year. It is calculated by multiplying the SLE by the annualized rate of occurrence (ARO), which reflects how often the risk is expected to occur annually.

Real-world example: Continuing with the building fire scenario, suppose fire experts estimate that a fire is likely to occur once every 20 years. This gives an ARO of 0.05 (1/20). The ALE would be calculated as follows:

$$ALE = SLE \times ARO = \$600{,}000 \times 0.05 = \$30{,}000$$

This means the organization can expect an average annual loss of $30,000 due to the risk of fire.

By using these metrics—EF, SLE, and ALE—organizations can quantitatively assess the financial impact of potential risks. This information is invaluable for prioritizing risks and making informed decisions about resource allocation and risk mitigation strategies. Additionally, organizations can use these metrics to conduct cost/benefit analyses when considering investments in risk mitigation measures, ensuring that resources are allocated efficiently to address the most significant risks.

Resource Prioritization

The final phase of the BIA process is resource prioritization. This step involves allocating business continuity resources based on the prioritized list of risks developed during the impact analysis. Organizations must balance their available resources to address both quantitative and qualitative concerns effectively. This often requires collaboration between the BCP team and senior management to merge quantitative data with qualitative insights, ensuring that the most critical risks receive the necessary attention and mitigation efforts. During this phase, organizations may develop detailed action plans, allocate budgets, and assign responsibilities to ensure preparedness and resilience. The goal is to develop a prioritized list of actions that align with the organization's strategic objectives and risk appetite, ensuring resilience in the face of potential disruptions.

Conducting a BIA is a comprehensive process that involves identifying critical business functions, assessing risks, evaluating their likelihood and impact, and prioritizing resources accordingly. By systematically analyzing these factors, organizations can develop robust business continuity and disaster recovery plans that enhance their ability to withstand and recover from disruptive events.

Business Continuity Planning Essentials

Business continuity planning is a critical process that ensures an organization can continue its operations during and after a disaster. Business continuity planning is distinct from disaster recovery planning, although they are closely related. While BCP focuses on maintaining business operations with reduced resources, DRP deals more with technical recovery post-disruption. This section delves into the essentials of business continuity planning, highlighting the key aspects of strategy development and the provisions and processes necessary to protect an organization's people, buildings, and infrastructure.

Strategy Development

The strategy development phase in business continuity planning serves as a bridge between the BIA and continuity planning. This phase involves evaluating the prioritized list of potential risks identified during the BIA and determining which ones require mitigation. The goal is to identify and prepare for risks that could significantly disrupt business operations. It's crucial to balance the cost of implementing continuity measures against the potential impact of the risks. For example, while the risk of a monsoon in New Delhi may necessitate mitigation measures due to its high likelihood and potential impact, a blizzard in Egypt might be considered an acceptable risk due to its improbability.

In this phase, the BCP team must decide which risks are acceptable and which require mitigation through continuity provisions. The team assesses the maximum tolerable downtime (MTD) for critical business functions to guide these decisions. The strategy should be comprehensive yet cost-effective, focusing on maintaining essential operations without incurring excessive costs. Once the team determines the necessary resources and mitigation strategies, they can proceed to the provisions and processes phase.

Provisions and Processes

The provisions and processes phase is the core of the business continuity plan. It involves designing specific procedures and mechanisms to mitigate the risks identified during strategy development. This phase covers three main categories: people, buildings and facilities, and infrastructure.

People The safety and well-being of employees are paramount in any business continuity plan. The organization must ensure that all personnel are safe before, during, and after an emergency. This involves creating emergency response plans, conducting regular training and drills, and ensuring clear communication channels are in place. Employees should be equipped with the necessary resources to perform their roles under adverse conditions. In situations where employees must remain on-site for extended periods, provisions for shelter and food should be made. Stockpiles of essential supplies should be maintained and rotated regularly to prevent spoilage.

Buildings and Facilities Many organizations rely on specialized facilities to conduct their operations. These facilities must be protected to ensure business continuity. The continuity plan should address two key areas for each critical facility: hardening provisions and alternate sites. Hardening provisions involve implementing measures to protect facilities from identified risks, such as reinforcing structures against natural disasters or enhancing security measures. If hardening is not feasible, alternate sites should be identified where operations can resume with minimal disruption. These sites should be equipped to handle the critical functions of the organization and be ready for activation in case of an emergency.

Infrastructure Infrastructure, particularly IT systems, is vital to the continuity of business operations. The BCP must outline how the organization will protect its IT infrastructure from identified risks. This includes ensuring data backups, maintaining redundant systems, and establishing secure communication links. The plan should detail procedures for maintaining and restoring critical systems to minimize downtime. Additionally, the organization should invest in technologies that enhance system resilience, such as high availability solutions and fault-tolerant systems, to ensure continuous operation even in the face of disruptions.

A robust business continuity plan is essential for any organization to withstand and recover from disruptions. By focusing on strategy development and implementing comprehensive provisions and processes, organizations can safeguard their people, facilities, and infrastructure, ensuring continued operations and minimizing the impact of unforeseen events.

Recovery Planning Essentials

Recovery planning is a critical component of business continuity and disaster recovery efforts, ensuring that organizations can swiftly and effectively respond to and recover from disruptive events. A comprehensive recovery plan outlines the necessary steps and resources required to restore operations, protect assets, and minimize downtime. In this section, you will examine the essential elements of recovery planning, including emergency response, personnel and communications, assessment, backups and offsite storage, utilities, and logistics and supplies.

The following sections explore some important items to include in your disaster recovery plan. Depending on the size of your organization and the number of people involved in the DRP effort, it may be a good idea to maintain multiple types of plan documents intended for different audiences. The following list includes various types of documents worth considering:

- Executive summary providing a high-level overview of the plan
- Department-specific plans
- Technical guides for IT personnel responsible for implementing and maintaining critical backup systems
- Checklists for individuals on the disaster recovery team
- Full copies of the plan for critical disaster recovery team members

Using custom-tailored documents becomes especially important when a disaster occurs or is imminent. Personnel who need to refresh themselves on the disaster recovery procedures that affect various parts of the organization will be able to refer to their department-specific plans. Critical disaster recovery team members will have checklists to help guide their actions amid the chaotic atmosphere of a disaster. IT personnel will have technical guides helping them get the alternate sites up and running. Finally, managers and public relations personnel will have a simple document that provides them a high-level view of the coordinated symphony that is an active disaster recovery effort without requiring interpretation from team members busy with tasks directly related to that effort.

Emergency Response

A disaster recovery plan must include clear and concise instructions for essential personnel to follow immediately upon recognizing that a disaster is in progress or imminent. These instructions will vary depending on the nature of the disaster, the type of personnel responding, and the available time before evacuation or equipment shutdown is necessary. Emergency response plans are often structured as checklists, prioritizing tasks to ensure the most critical actions are taken first. For example, in the event of a fire, the checklist might include activating the building alarm, ensuring an orderly evacuation, and contacting emergency services. The formal declaration of a disaster is also a key task, with the plan specifying criteria for activation, who has the authority to declare a disaster, and the notification procedures to follow.

Personnel and Communications

A disaster recovery plan should include a comprehensive list of personnel to contact in the event of a disaster. This list typically includes key members of the disaster recovery team and individuals responsible for executing critical recovery tasks across the organization. It is important to provide alternate means of contact, such as mobile phone numbers and pager numbers, as well as backup contacts for each role in case the primary contact is unavailable. Effective communication is vital to coordinating the recovery efforts and ensuring that all team members are informed and aligned with the recovery objectives.

Assessment

Once the disaster recovery team is on-site, one of their first tasks is to assess the situation. This initial assessment is crucial for triaging activities and initiating the disaster response. As the incident progresses, more detailed assessments are conducted to evaluate the effectiveness of recovery efforts and prioritize resource allocation. The assessment process helps identify the extent of damage, the operational status of critical systems, and any additional resources or actions needed to facilitate recovery.

Backups and Offsite Storage

Backups are a fundamental component of any recovery plan, ensuring that critical data and systems can be restored in the event of a disaster. Organizations should implement a robust backup strategy that includes regular data backups, secure storage of backup media, and periodic testing of backup restoration procedures. Offsite storage of backups is essential to protect against localized disasters that could compromise on-site data. Utilizing cloud-based storage solutions or geographically dispersed data centers can enhance the resilience of backup systems and ensure data availability during recovery efforts.

Software Escrow Arrangements

Software escrow arrangements are a valuable tool for organizations that rely on custom-developed software or products from small firms. These arrangements protect the organization against the failure of a software developer to provide adequate support or the possibility of the developer going out of business. Under a software escrow agreement, the developer provides copies of the application source code to an independent third-party organization. The agreement specifies trigger events, such as the developer failing to meet service-level agreements or liquidating their firm. When a trigger event occurs, the third party releases the source code to the end user, allowing them to resolve application issues or implement updates.

Utilities

Utilities, such as power, water, and telecommunications, are essential for the operation of critical systems and facilities. A recovery plan should include strategies for ensuring the availability of these utilities during a disaster. This may involve establishing agreements with utility providers for priority service restoration, implementing backup power solutions such as generators or uninterruptible power supplies, and identifying alternative communication methods if primary systems are disrupted. Ensuring the continuity of utility services is vital to maintaining operational capabilities and supporting recovery efforts.

Logistics and Supplies

Logistics and supplies play a crucial role in supporting recovery operations. A recovery plan should outline the logistics of transporting personnel, equipment, and materials to recovery sites, as well as the procurement and distribution of necessary supplies. This may include establishing agreements with vendors for emergency supplies, maintaining an inventory of essential materials, and identifying alternative transportation routes in case of infrastructure damage. Effective logistics planning ensures that recovery teams have the resources they need to carry out their tasks efficiently and effectively.

Recovery Versus Restoration

It is useful to differentiate between recovery and restoration tasks in disaster planning. Recovery focuses on quickly establishing operations at an alternate site to maintain critical functions, while restoration involves returning the primary site to full operational capacity. Recovery tasks may be assigned to a disaster recovery team, while a separate salvage team handles restoration. This separation is particularly important when recovery efforts are expected to be prolonged. Allocating tasks according to organizational needs and disaster types ensures a more efficient and effective response, ultimately leading to a successful return to normal operations.

Recovery planning is a multifaceted process that requires careful consideration of various elements to ensure a swift and effective response to disasters. By addressing emergency response, personnel and communications, assessment, backups and offsite storage, utilities, and logistics and supplies, organizations can enhance their resilience and ability to recover from disruptive events. A well-developed recovery plan not only protects assets and minimizes downtime but also supports the long-term viability and success of the organization.

Disaster Recovery Strategies and Solutions

Disaster recovery strategies and solutions are paramount for ensuring that an organization can swiftly recover from disruptions and maintain its critical operations. These strategies encompass a range of activities and considerations, including prioritizing business functions, managing crises, establishing effective communication channels, and implementing robust recovery solutions for workgroups, processing sites, and databases. This section will delve into these critical components, providing a comprehensive overview of effective disaster recovery strategies and solutions.

Business Unit and Functional Priorities

The foundation of any disaster recovery strategy lies in identifying and prioritizing business units and functions critical to the organization's mission. This prioritization ensures that recovery efforts focus on restoring the most vital operations first. A BIA plays a crucial role in this process by assessing the potential risks and impacts of disruptions on various business functions. The BIA helps organizations understand the financial, operational, and reputational implications of potential failures, guiding the prioritization of recovery efforts. The result is a prioritized list of business units and functions, each with defined recovery objectives and timelines, such as *maximum tolerable downtime* (the maximum amount of time that a business process or system can be unavailable before the organization experiences irreversible damage or severe consequences) and *recovery time objective* (RTO: the target duration within which a business process or system must be restored after a disruption to avoid unacceptable consequences).

Crisis Management

Effective crisis management is essential for minimizing the impact of disasters on an organization. This involves a coordinated response to emergencies, ensuring that the organization can maintain or quickly resume critical operations. Crisis management plans should include predefined roles and responsibilities, decision-making processes, and communication protocols. The goal is to provide a structured approach to handling crises, enabling the organization to respond swiftly and effectively. Regular training and awareness programs ensure that personnel are prepared to execute the crisis management plan, while lessons learned from past incidents are used to continuously improve the plan.

Emergency Communications

Communication is a critical component of disaster recovery, as it ensures that all stakeholders are informed and coordinated during a crisis. Emergency communication plans should outline the methods and channels for disseminating information to employees, customers, partners, and regulators. These plans should include contact lists, message templates, and escalation procedures to ensure that communication is timely, accurate, and consistent. Testing and updating communication plans regularly is vital to ensure their effectiveness in a real-world scenario.

Workgroup Recovery

Workgroup recovery focuses on restoring the operational capabilities of specific teams or departments within an organization. This involves ensuring that workgroups have access to the necessary resources, such as equipment, data, and communication tools, to continue their functions during and after a disaster. Strategies for workgroup recovery may include establishing remote work capabilities, providing alternative workspaces, and ensuring access to critical applications and data. The goal is to minimize downtime and disruption for workgroups, enabling them to maintain productivity and support the organization's overall recovery efforts.

Alternate Processing Sites

Alternate processing sites are essential for ensuring the continuity of operations when primary facilities are unavailable. These sites can be classified into cold, warm, and hot sites, each offering different levels of readiness and cost. Cold sites provide basic infrastructure and require significant setup time, while warm sites offer partially configured environments that can be activated more quickly. Hot sites are fully operational facilities that can take over operations almost immediately. Organizations should select alternate processing sites based on their recovery objectives, budget, and risk tolerance. Additionally, multiple processing sites can provide redundancy and resilience, further enhancing the organization's ability to withstand disruptions.

Database Recovery

Databases are critical assets that store essential information for business operations. As such, database recovery is a vital component of disaster recovery strategies. Organizations can employ various technologies to ensure database availability and integrity during and after a disaster. Electronic vaulting involves transferring database backups to a remote site as part of a bulk transfer, ensuring data is preserved offsite. Remote journaling provides more frequent data transfers, capturing changes to the database at regular intervals. Remote mirroring offers real-time replication of database transactions at a backup site, providing the highest level of data protection and availability. Selecting the appropriate database recovery solution depends on the organization's recovery objectives, data criticality, and budget.

Effective disaster recovery strategies and solutions are essential for ensuring that an organization can quickly recover from disruptions and maintain its critical operations. By prioritizing business units and functions, managing crises, establishing robust communication channels, and implementing comprehensive recovery solutions, organizations can enhance their resilience and ability to withstand disasters. Regular testing, training, and continuous improvement of these strategies are crucial for maintaining their effectiveness and ensuring organizational preparedness.

Testing and Simulation Exercises

Testing and simulation exercises are critical components that ensure the effectiveness and reliability of recovery plans. These exercises help organizations prepare for unforeseen events by evaluating the readiness of their disaster recovery plans and identifying areas for improvement. By conducting various types of tests, organizations can ensure that they are well-prepared to respond quickly and efficiently to any disruptions, minimizing their impact on business operations.

Read-Through

The *read-through test* is a foundational exercise in DRP. It involves distributing copies of the disaster recovery plan to all relevant team members for review. The read-through lets you accomplish three goals simultaneously:

- It ensures that key personnel are aware of their responsibilities and have that knowledge refreshed periodically.
- It provides individuals with an opportunity to review the plans for obsolete information and update any items that require modification because of changes within the organization.
- In large organizations, it helps identify situations in which key personnel have left the company and nobody bothered to reassign their disaster recovery responsibilities. This is also a good reason why disaster recovery responsibilities should be included in job descriptions.

Tabletop

Tabletop exercises bring disaster recovery team members together in a conference room setting to role-play a hypothetical disaster scenario. Typically, the scenario is known only to the test moderator, who presents the details to the team during the meeting. Team members then refer to their copies of the disaster recovery plan to discuss and strategize appropriate responses. This type of exercise fosters collaboration and critical thinking, allowing team members to explore different response strategies and identify potential gaps in the plan.

Walk-Through

Walk-through exercises take testing a step further by involving physical actions or considering their impact on the scenario. These exercises may require participants to leave the building and return home to simulate a real-world response. By engaging in these activities, team members gain a deeper understanding of the logistical challenges they may face during an actual disaster. Walk-throughs help ensure that all aspects of the plan are practical and executable, from evacuation procedures to remote work arrangements.

Simulation Test

In *simulation tests*, team members are presented with a scenario and asked to develop an appropriate response. Unlike tabletop exercises, simulation tests involve testing some of the response measures, such as interrupting noncritical business activities and utilizing operational personnel. This hands-on approach allows organizations to evaluate the effectiveness of their response strategies and make necessary adjustments. Simulation tests provide valuable insights into the plan's strengths and weaknesses, helping organizations enhance their overall resilience.

Parallel Test

Parallel tests involve relocating personnel to an alternate recovery site and implementing site activation procedures. During these tests, employees perform their disaster recovery responsibilities as they would in an actual disaster without interrupting operations at the main facility. This exercise allows organizations to validate their recovery site capabilities and ensure that personnel are familiar with their roles and responsibilities. By simulating a real-world recovery scenario, parallel tests help identify potential issues and improve the organization's overall readiness.

Full-Interruption Test

Full-interruption tests are the most comprehensive and high-risk exercises, as they involve shutting down operations at the primary site and shifting them to the recovery site. These tests require the complete operational shutdown of the primary site and the subsequent transfer back. Due to the significant risks and challenges involved, full-interruption tests are often met with resistance from management. However, when executed successfully, they provide the most accurate assessment of an organization's disaster recovery capabilities.

Lessons Learned

After conducting any test or exercise, it is crucial to analyze the outcomes and identify lessons learned. This process involves reviewing the test results, documenting any issues or gaps, and developing action plans to address them. By capturing and implementing lessons learned, organizations can continuously improve their disaster recovery plans and enhance their preparedness for future disruptions. This iterative process ensures that the organization remains agile and adaptable in the face of evolving threats and challenges.

In SP 800-61, NIST offers a series of questions to use in the lessons learned process. They include the following:

- Exactly what happened and at what times?
- How well did staff and management perform in dealing with the incident?
- Were documented procedures followed?
- Were the procedures adequate?
- What information was needed sooner?
- Were any steps or actions taken that might have inhibited the recovery?
- What would the staff and management do differently the next time a similar incident occurs?
- How could information sharing with other organizations have been improved?
- What corrective actions can prevent similar incidents in the future?
- What precursors or indicators should be watched for in the future to detect similar incidents?
- What additional tools or resources are needed to detect, analyze, and mitigate future incidents?

The responses to these questions, if given honestly, will provide valuable insight into the state of the organization's incident response program. They can help provide a road map of future improvements designed to bolster disaster recovery. The facilitator should work with the team leader to document the lessons learned in a report that includes suggested process improvement actions.

Maintenance

Regular maintenance of the disaster recovery plan is essential to ensure its continued effectiveness. This involves updating the plan to reflect changes in the organization's structure, processes, and technology. Regular reviews and updates help ensure that the plan remains aligned with the organization's current needs and objectives. Maintenance activities also include verifying the accuracy of contact information, ensuring the availability of necessary resources, and updating documentation as needed.

Test Communications

Effective communication is a critical component of any disaster recovery test. During testing, it is important to keep all stakeholders informed of the test status, objectives, and results. Clear communication ensures that everyone involved understands their roles and responsibilities, reducing confusion and enhancing collaboration. Additionally, communicating test results to stakeholders, including regulators and management, demonstrates the organization's commitment to preparedness and resilience.

Testing and simulation exercises are vital for ensuring the effectiveness of business continuity and disaster recovery plans. By conducting a variety of tests and continuously refining the plan based on lessons learned, organizations can enhance their ability to respond to disruptions and maintain operational continuity.

Index

3DES (Triple DES), 209

A

AAA (authentication, authorization, accounting), 5–6, 60–62
ABAC (attribute-based access control), 58, 63–65
access abuses, 231
access control, 44
  data centers, 232–233
  physical access, 229–232
  server rooms, 232–233
access control attacks, 74–76
access controls, 44
access review, 60, 73
account provisioning and deprovisioning, 71–72
accounting, 6
administrative law, 30
adware, 174, 256
AES (Advanced Encryption Standard), 81, 207, 209
AI (artificial intelligence), 94
AICPA (American Institute of Certified Public Accountants), 9
alteration, 4–5
antimalware, 132
application attacks, 191–198
application security
  code security, 200–201
  controls, 198–201
  databases, 199
  DevOps, 187–189
  DevSecOps, 189–191
  injection vulnerabilities, 192–194

APTs (advanced persistent threats), 255
assessment and testing, 145–147
asymmetric key management, 221–222
auditing, 6, 60
  compliance, 31
authentication, 6, 58, 62
  VPNs, 133–134
authorization, 6, 58, 194–196
automated decision-making, 94
availability (CIA triad), 4, 45–46, 56
awareness programs, 20

B

backdoors, 192
backups, 45
BAS (breach and attack simulation) platforms, 155
BCP (business continuity planning), 270–278
BCRs (binding corporate rules), 91
Bell-LaPadula security model, 46, 47
BIA (business impact analysis), 274–277
Biba security model, 46, 47
birthday attacks, 223–224
black-box penetration test, 153
botnets, 174
Brandeis, Louis D., 7
Brewer-Nash security model, 48
brute force attacks, 222
buffer overflows, 150, 191
Burp Suite, 154
business plan. *See* BCP (business continuity planning)

C

cameras, 230–231
captive portals, 138
CAs (certificate authorities), 208
CC (Common Criteria) security model, 49
CCTV (closed-circuit television), 230–231
change management, 44
CI/CD (continuous integration/continuous deployment), 201
CIA (confidentiality, integrity, availability) triad, 3–4, 24, 44–46
ciphertext, 206, 223
Clark-Wilson security model, 46, 47–48
cloud security, 139–141
COBIT (Control Objectives for Information and Related Technology), 12
code injection attacks, 193–194
code review, 156–157
code security, 200–201
coding best practices, 201–203
command injection attacks, 194
competitors as threat actors, 254
compliance, 20, 25–26, 29–32
   conflict, multinational, 92
   legal issues, 249–250
compliance risk, 31
computer crimes, 238–240
confidentiality (CIA triad), 3, 44–45
configuration vulnerabilities, 151–152
corporate governance, risk management and, 34
CPO (chief privacy officer), 88
credential management, 59–60
criminal law, 30
cryptographic attacks, 222–225
cryptography, 205–206
   algorithms, 207
   asymmetric, 210–212
   decryption, 206
   digital signatures, 208, 216–217
   encryption, 206
   hash functions, 208, 213–216
   hybrid, 212
   key management, 220–222
   keys, 207
   PKIs, 208
   protocols, 207
   quantum, 212–213
   symmetric, 208–210
CSIRT (computer security incident response team), 101, 102
CSRF (cross-site request forgery), 197
Cyber Kill Chain, 265–266
cybercrime, 30
cybercriminals, 254

D

DAC (discretionary access control), 58
DAD (disclosure, alteration, destruction) triad, 4–5
DAST (dynamic application security testing), 156, 200
data, third-party sharing, 95
data archiving, 97–98
data breaches, 30
data center security, 232–233
data classification, 25, 44, 77–80
data destruction, 95
data disposal, 98–99
data exfiltration, 4
data governance, 25
data integrity, 3

data inventory, 25
data labeling, 77–78
data management life cycle, 25
data masking, 80
data protection methods, 83–84
data remanence, 99
data retention, 95, 96–97
data security requirements, 95
data subject rights, 93–94
data transfer, international, 90–91
degaussing, 98
DES (Data Encryption Standard), 207, 209
design, 39–41
   facility design, 227–229
   PbD (privacy by design), 85–87
device security, 124–125, 166–169
DevOps, 187–189
DevSecOps, 189–191
dictionary attacks, 74
differential privacy, 82
Diffie-Hellman, 212
digital signatures, 45, 208, 216–217
directory traversal vulnerabilities, 195–196
disaster recovery, 45. *See also* DRP (disaster recovery planning)
DLP (data loss prevention), 83–85
documentation
   compliance, 31
   IRP (incident response plan), 104
DoS (denial of service) attacks, 138
DPIAs (data protection impact assessments), 28
DPO (data protection officer), 28
DRM (digital rights management), 84
DRP (disaster recovery planning), 270, 278–284
dumpster diving, 52

E

ECC (Elliptic Curve Cryptography), 212
EDR (endpoint detection and response), 163–166
ElGamal, 212
email as threat vector, 256
encryption, 44, 81–82
   device security, 167
   malware, 176
   private keys, 207
   public keys, 207
   VPNs, 133
endpoints, 123, 127, 163–166
engineering processes, 41
environmental controls, 233–235
EOL (end of life), 83
ERM (enterprise risk management), 36
error handling, 202
error-detection, 45
ethics, 250–252
evil twin attacks, 138
exception handling, 158

F

facility design, 228–229
failover, 4, 125
fault injection attacks, 225
fault tolerance, 55
FedRAMP (Federal Risk and Authorization Management Program), 12
FERPA (Family Educational Rights and Privacy Act), 29
fileless malware, 175
FIM (federated identity management), 59
fire detection and suppression, 233–235
firewalls, 123, 130–131, 199

G

gap analysis, security frameworks, 12
GAPP (generally accepted privacy principles), 9–10
GDPR (General Data Protection Regulation), 26, 27–28, 248–249
GLBA (Gramm-Leach-Bliley Act), 28
governance, 20
  CEOs, 24
  CIA triad, 24
  CISOs, 24
  compliance, 25–26, 31–32
  data governance, 25
  DPO, 28
  due diligence, 24
  information governance, 25
  organizational processes, 24
  regulatory requirements, 25–26
  risk management integration, 34
  roles and responsibilities, 24
  SCRM, 25
  security control frameworks, 24
  third-party, 35
  threat modeling, 24
Graham-Denning security model, 48
gray-box penetration test, 153

H

hacktivists, 254
hard-coded credentials, 202
hardware vulnerabilities, 151
hash functions, 208, 213–216
hashing, 45
HIDS (host-based IDS), 131
high availability, 55
HIPAA (Health Insurance Portability and Accountability Act), 26–27
hoaxes, 51
homomorphic encryption, 82
honeypots/honeynets, 132
HRU (Harrison-Ruzzo-Ullman) security model, 48

I

IAM (identity and access management), 57
  AAA model, 60–62
  ABAC (attribute-based access control), 62–65
  access control attacks, 73–76
  access review, 60
  auditing, 60
  authentication, 58, 62
  credential management, 59–60
  FIM (federated identity management), 59
  identification, 58, 62
  identity federation, 65–68
  identity governance life cycle, 71–73
  identity life cycle, 59
  RBAC, 62–65
  SSO, 59, 66–68
  ZTA, 68–70
IAST (interactive application security testing), 156, 200
identity federation, 65–68
identity governance life cycle, 71–73
identity life cycle, 59
IDOR (insecure direct object references), 195
IDPS (intrusion detection and prevention systems), 130–131
IDS (intrusion detection systems), 123–124, 130–131, 230
impersonation and masquerading attacks, 51

implementation attacks, 224
import/export controls, 30
import/export laws, 244–246
incident management, networks, 143–144
incident response, 20. *See also* IRP (incident response plan)
   automating, 112
   communication plans, 110–111
   containment, 109
   detection and triage, 106
   device security, 167
   eradication, 109
   escalation, 112
   impact assessment, 115
   incident types, 105–106
   investigation process, 108
   investigation types, 107–108
   notification procedures, 112
   phases, 104–105
   planning, 150
   post-incident communication, 113–117
   recovery, 110
information governance, 25
information security, 20–21
injection vulnerabilities, 192–194
input validation, 198–199
integrity (CIA triad), 3–4, 45
intellectual property, 30, 241–242
international data transfer, 90–91
inventory building, 89
invoice scams, 51
IPS (intrusion prevention systems), 123–124, 131
IPSec (Internet Protocol Security), 124, 207
IRP (incident response plan), 103–104. *See also* CSIRT (computer security incident response team)

IS (information systems), 1
ISO (International Organization for Standardization) Standards, 11
IT (information technology), 1

K
Kerberos exploitation, 74
key management, 220–222
keyloggers, 174–175
know plaintext attacks, 223
KRACK (key reinstallation attacks), 138

L
lattice-based security model, 49
LDAP (Lightweight Directory Access Protocol), 193
least privilege, 6, 42
legal issues, 12, 30
   compliance, 249–250
   computer crimes, 238–241
   import/export laws, 244–246
   intellectual property, 241–243
   privacy laws, 246–249
   software licensing, 243–244
licensing requirements, 30
load balancing, 4
logging
   device security, 167
   networks, 142–143
logic bombs, 174
logical segmentation, 124, 126

M
MAC (mandatory access control), 58
maintenance, 4, 45
malicious code sources, 255–256
malvertising, 175
malware, 173–178
MD5 (Message Digest), 214
media management, 43
media storage facilities, 231

memory management, 203
Metasploit framework, 154
MFA (multifactor authentication), 58, 60–62
microsegmentation, 126
MitM attacks, 75
MITRE ATT&CK Matrix, 266–267
mobile device management, 169–173
monitoring
  compliance, 31
  device security, 167
  networks, 142–143
  physical security, 229–232
  risk assessment and, 36–37

N

NAC (network access control), 122–123, 127
nation-state actors, 254
need-to-know, 42
networks
  device security, 124–125, 166–169
  endpoints, 123
  failover, 125
  firewalls, 123, 130–131
  IDPS, 131–133
  IDS, 123–124
  incident managements, 143–144
  logging, 142–143
  monitoring, 142–143
  NAC, 122–123
  operation of infrastructure, 122
  redundancy, 125
  secure protocols, 124
  segmentation, 124–127
  system hardening, 128–129
  tools, 132–133
  transmission media, 122
  virtual, 126
  VPNs, 133–134
  vulnerability scans, 149
  wireless, 136–139
NIDS (network-based IDS), 131
NIST (National Institute of Standards and Technology), 11–12
Nmap, 154

O

on-path attacks, 223
OSINT (open source intelligence), 260
OWASP (Open Worldwide Application Security Project), 155

P

pass-the-hash attacks, 74
passlisting/blocklisting, 132, 144
passwords
  attacks, 74
  OTPs (one-time passwords), 62
patch management, 43–44, 150, 178–180
path traversal vulnerabilities, 195–196
PbD (privacy by design), 85–87
PCI DSS (Payment Card Industry Data Security Standard), 12, 28
penetration testing, 2, 149, 200
  tools, 154
  types, 153
personnel safety, 44
personnel security, 49–52
PETs (privacy-enhancing technologies), 82
PGP (Pretty Good Privacy), 207
PHI (protected health information), 26–27, 78
phishing, 51, 74
physical security
  access controls, 229–232
  data centers, 232–233

facility design, 227–229
fire detection, 233
internal, 236
KPIs, 236
monitoring, 229–232
perimeter controls, 235
server rooms, 232–233
physical segmentation, 124, 125
PIAs (privacy impact assessments), 86
piggybacking, 52
PII (personally identifiable information), 78
PKI (public key infrastructure), 208, 218–220
plaintext, 206
policies and procedures
  compliance, 31
  PDP, 69
  PEP, 70
  security frameworks, 13
port security, 168
privacy, 6
  accountability, 8
  assessments, 89
  breaches, 117–119
  by design, 41
  control implementation, 89–90
  cross-border enforcement, 91–92
  differential privacy, 82
  documentation, 15
  GAPP, 9–10
  guidelines, 14
  legal requirements, 30
  Olmstead v. United States, 7
  policy creation, 14
  policy documents, 14
  policy enforcement, 15–16
  policy types, 14
  privacy notices, 7
  procedures, 14
  program development, 8, 87–90
  standards, 14
  user preference management, 7–8
privacy frameworks, benefits, 13
privacy laws, 246–249
privacy notices, 95
privacy requests, 95–96
privilege escalation, 75, 192
privileged account management, 42–43
process integrity, 4
process vulnerabilities, 152
protection mechanisms, 52–54

Q

QKD (quantum key distribution), 212
quantum cryptography, 212–213

R

ransomware, 174, 256
RAs (registration authorities), 208
RBAC (role-based access control), 58, 62–65
redundancy, 4, 45, 125
regulatory compliance. *See* compliance
regulatory requirements, 25–29
replay attacks, 75, 224
reporting, compliance, 31
request forgery attacks, 197
resource allocation, security frameworks, 12
RIPEMD (RACE Integrity Primitives Evaluation Message Digest), 215
risk assessment, 2, 31
  monitoring and, 36–37
risk management, 20, 32–36
risk mitigation, 31

risk-based access control, 58
Rivest-Shamir-Adleman, 212
role management, 72–73
rootkits, 174, 192, 256

S

SABSA (Sherwood Applied Business Security Architecture), 12
sandboxing, 132
SASE (Secure Access Service Edge), 41, 134–135
SAST (static application security testing), 156, 200
SCA (software composition analysis), 156, 200
SCCs (standard contractual clauses), 91
script kiddies, 254
SCRM (supply chain risk management), 25
SDLC (Secure Software Development Life Cycle), 183–187
security
  awareness programs, 16–20
  compliance, 20
  cost-effectiveness, 2
  governance, 20
  incident response, 20
  IT/IS, 1
  legal issues, 2
  management, 20
  operations, 42–44
  penetration testing, 2
  policy creation, 14
  policy development, 20
  policy enforcement, 15–16
  risk assessment, 2
  vulnerability assessments, 2
security audits, 146

security control frameworks, 11–13, 24
security models, 46
  Bell-LaPadula model, 46, 47
  Biba model, 46, 47
  Brewer-Nash model, 48
  CC model, 49
  Clark-Wilson model, 46, 47–48
  Graham-Denning model, 48
  HRU model, 48
  lattice-based, 49
  take-grant model, 48–49
security training, 159
segmentation, 124–127
server room security, 232–233
session hijacking, 75, 197–198
SHA (Secure Hash Algorithm), 214
shared responsibility, 41
shoulder surfing, 51
side-channel attacks, 151, 224
SLAs (service-level agreements), 35–36, 43
social engineering attacks, 51–52
SoD (segregation of duties), 42
software licensing, 243–244
software testing, 155–157
software vulnerabilities, 150–151
SOX (Sarbanes-Oxley Act), 28
spam, 51
spear phishing, 51
SPOF (single point of failure), 56
spyware, 174, 256
SQL injection, 150, 192–193
SSH (Secure Shell), 124
SSL/TLS (Secure Sockets Layer/Transport Layer Security), 124, 207
SSO (single sign-on), 59, 66–68
SSRF (server-side request forgery), 197

statistical attacks, 225
switches, security, 168
symmetric cryptography, 208–210
symmetric key management, 220–221
system hardening, 128–129
system integrity, 4
system resilience, 55–56

T

tailgating, 51
take-grant security model, 48–49
testing, penetration testing, 2
testing exercises
   communications, 287–288
   full-interruption tests, 286
   parallel tests, 286
   read-through tests, 285
   simulation tests, 286
   tabletop exercises, 285
   walk-through exercises, 285–286
third-party disclosure, 10
third-party governance, 35
third-party risks, 35–36
threat actors, 253–254
threat detection, 255
threat feeds, 259–261
threat hunting, 262–263
threat intelligence, 258–259
   assessment, 263–265
   cyber defense and, 264–265
threat modeling, 24, 200
threat vectors, 256–258
timing attacks, 224
TOCTTOU (time of check to time of use), 191–192
tokenization, 81
training and awareness, 44
   compliance, 31
   security training, 159
transborder data flow, 30

Trojan horses, 174, 255
typosquatting, 52

U–V

updates, 45
vendors, third-party risks and, 35–36
version control, 45
virtual networks, 126
viruses, 173, 255
VPNs (virtual private networks), 133–134
VRRP (Virtual Router Redundancy Protocol), 125
vulnerabilities
   authorization vulnerabilities, 194–196
   configuration, 151–152
   firmware vulnerabilities, 151
   hardware, 151
   process, 152
   reducing, 180
   remediation workflow, 180
   software, 150–151
vulnerability assessments, 2
   techniques, 149
   threat analysis and, 264
vulnerability management, 43–44, 147–150

W

WAFs (web application firewalls), 199
WANs (wide-area networks)
   SASE, 134–135
   SD-WAN, 134–135
war driving, 138
web application attacks, 196–198
whaling, 51
white-box penetration test, 153

wire closets, 230
wireless attacks, 138–139
wireless networks, 136–139
Wireshark, 154
work area security, 231
worms, 173, 255
WPA (Wi-Fi Protect Access), 137

X–Z

XSS (cross-site scripting), 151
   attacks, 196–197
zero-day exploits, 176
zero-knowledge proofs, 82
zero-trust model, design, 40–41
ZTA (zero trust architecture), 68–70